War Stuff

In this path-breaking work on the American Civil War, Joan E. Cashin explores the struggle between armies and civilians over the human and material resources necessary to wage war. This war "stuff" included the skills of white Southern civilians, as well as such material resources as food, timber, and housing. At first, civilians were willing to help Confederate or Union forces, but the war took such a toll that all civilians, regardless of politics, began focusing on their own survival. Both armies took whatever they needed from human beings and the material world, which eventually destroyed the region's ability to wage war. In this fierce contest between civilians and armies, the civilian population lost. Cashin draws on a wide range of documents, as well as the perspectives of environmental history and material culture studies. This book provides an entirely new perspective on the war era.

Joan E. Cashin is a Professor of History at Ohio State University. An award-winning scholar of nineteenth-century American history, she is the author or editor of five books, including *First Lady of the Confederacy: Varina Davis's Civil War*.

CAMBRIDGE STUDIES ON THE AMERICAN SOUTH

Series Editors

Mark M. Smith, *University of South Carolina, Columbia*
Peter Coclanis, *University of North Carolina at Chapel Hill*

Editor Emeritus
David Moltke-Hansen

Interdisciplinary in its scope and intent, this series builds upon and extends Cambridge University Press's long-standing commitment to studies on the American South. The series offers the best new work on the South's distinctive institutional, social, economic, and cultural history and also features works in a national, comparative, and transnational perspective.

Titles in the Series

War Stuff

The Struggle for Human and Environmental Resources in the American Civil War

JOAN E. CASHIN

Ohio State University

CAMBRIDGE
UNIVERSITY PRESS

CAMBRIDGE
UNIVERSITY PRESS

University Printing House, Cambridge CB2 8BS, United Kingdom

One Liberty Plaza, 20th Floor, New York, NY 10006, USA

477 Williamstown Road, Port Melbourne, VIC 3207, Australia

314–321, 3rd Floor, Plot 3, Splendor Forum, Jasola District Centre,
New Delhi – 110025, India

79 Anson Road, #06–04/06, Singapore 079906

Cambridge University Press is part of the University of Cambridge.

It furthers the University's mission by disseminating knowledge in the pursuit of
education, learning, and research at the highest international levels of excellence.

www.cambridge.org
Information on this title: www.cambridge.org/9781108420167
DOI: 10.1017/9781108332750

First published 2018

Printed in the United States of America by Sheridan Books, Inc.

A catalogue record for this publication is available from the British Library.

ISBN 978-1-108-42016-7 Hardback
ISBN 978-1-108-41318-3 Paperback

For my sister Beverly

Contents

Illustrations

Acknowledgments

When a book is finished, it is always a great pleasure to thank the many people who have helped along the way.

Research funding from two institutions paid for highly productive trips to different archives: a Faculty Research Grant from the Mershon Center for International Security Studies at Ohio State University, and a Filson Research Fellowship from the Filson Historical Society in Louisville, Kentucky.

These archivists gave prompt, cordial assistance during my research at various institutions: DeAnne Blanton of the National Archives; John Coski of the American Civil War Museum; Jeff Flannery, Patrick Kerwin, and Bruno Kirby of the Library of Congress; Katherine Hall of the Moritz Law Library at Ohio State University; Noel Harrison of the Fredericksburg Area Museum and Cultural Center; Elizabeth Holland, then of the Chicago Public Library; James Holmberg of the Filson Historical Society; Ronald Lee and Darla Brock of the Tennessee State Library and Archives; James Lewis of the Stones River National Battlefield; Kathy Niedergeses of the Lawrence County, Tennessee, Archives; and Liz Novara of the Hornbake Library at the University of Maryland.

For their kind help with the illustrations, I wish to thank Germain Bienvenu of Louisiana State University; Bill Dorman of the Tangipahoa Parish Library in Louisiana; Laura Seeger of the Department of History at Ohio State University; David Wooldridge of the National Park Service office at Appomattox Court House; and Cathy Wright of the American Civil War Museum. My research assistants John Knight, Megan Real, and Laura Smith were diligent and thorough in their pursuit of books, articles, and documents.

Specialists in other fields graciously shared their expertise: Colonel (retired) Fred L. Borch, the Regimental Historian and Archivist of the Army Judge Advocate General's Corps, regarding military history and the law, and Thomas Waldrop, the fire researcher with the United States Forest Service at Clemson University, regarding forestry.

These august friends and colleagues suggested leads, listened carefully as I talked about the book, and offered warm encouragement during the research and writing: Terry Alford, Jean Baker, Mark Baldwin, Steve Berry, Sidney Blumenthal, John Brooke, Michael Burlingame, John Burnham, Anya Jabour, Stephanie Kermes, Daniel Kornstein, Michael Martoccio, Steve Mintz, David Moltke-Hansen, Randy Roth, Lesley Rowland, Ed Rugemer, Jonathan White, and LeeAnn Whites. I deeply appreciate their generosity.

At Cambridge University Press, the series editors Mark M. Smith and Pete Coclanis were enthusiastic about the manuscript, and Deborah Gershenowitz, my book editor, was wise and judicious.

My colleagues Mark Grimsley and Brooks Simpson each read a chapter and gave useful feedback. Over the past twenty-plus years, I have had many productive conversations with Mark about aspects of the Civil War era.

Three colleagues gave a close, meticulous reading of the entire manuscript: William Harris, Earl Hess, and George Rable. I am indebted to them for their astute criticisms on style and argument, which they offered in a true spirit of comradeship. They caught some murky phrases and factual slips, but any remaining shortcomings are of course my responsibility.

I am grateful to Christopher Wood for his companionship and his delightful perspective on all things past and present. This book is dedicated to my sister Beverly, an artist, an inspiration, and a citizen of the world.

Abbreviations

ALA	Alabama Department of Archives and History
ASI	Arkansas Studies Institute, Center for Arkansas History and Culture
BU	Bradley University, Peoria, Illinois
CHMRC	Chicago History Museum Research Center
CHSL	Cincinnati Historical Society Library
CMLS-VHS	Confederate Memorial Literary Society, under the management of the Virginia Historical Society
CPL	Chattanooga Public Library
DHS	Dallas Historical Society
DML	Dayton, Ohio, Metro Library
DU	Duke University, David M. Rubenstein Rare Book and Manuscript Library
ETHS	East Tennessee Historical Society
FHS	Filson Historical Society, Louisville
GC	Gettysburg College, Special Collections and College Archives
HSWP	Historical Society of Western Pennsylvania
ISL	Indiana State Library
KHS	Kentucky Historical Society, Frankfort
LC	Library of Congress, Manuscript Division
LCTA	Lawrence County, Tennessee, Archives
LMRL	Lincoln Museum Research Library, Fort Wayne, Indiana
LSU	Louisiana State University, Hill Memorial Library
NARA	National Archives and Records Administration, Washington, DC

NARA-II	National Archives and Records Administration – II, College Park, Maryland
NYPL	New York Public Library
OCM	Old Courthouse Museum, Vicksburg
OHC	Ohio History Connection
OR	*The War of the Rebellion: A Compilation of the Official Records of the Union and Confederate Armies*, 128 vols. (Washington, DC: U.S. Government Printing Office, 1880–1901)
OSU	Ohio State University, Department of History, eHistory
RG	Record Group
SCC	Southern Claims Commission
SCHS	South Carolina Historical Society, Charleston
TSLA	Tennessee State Library and Archives
UGA	University of Georgia, Hargrett Rare Book and Manuscript Library
UKL	University of Kentucky – Lexington
UM	University of Michigan, William L. Clements Library
UMCP	University of Maryland–College Park, Hornbake Library
UMIS	University of Mississippi, Special Collections
UMS	University of Memphis, Special Collections
UNC-SHC	University of North Carolina, Southern Historical Collection
USC	University of South Carolina, South Caroliniana Library
UTA	University of Texas at Austin, Dolph Briscoe Center for American History
UTK	University of Tennessee at Knoxville
UVA	University of Virginia, Albert and Shirley Small Special Collections Library
VHS	Virginia Historical Society
VMI	Virginia Military Institute
VSP	Valley of the Shadow Project, University of Virginia
WIU	Western Illinois University
WRHS	Western Reserve Historical Society

Introduction

In September 1861, Confederate troops camped in the yard of David Waters, a forty-year-old overseer residing in Amite, Louisiana. Waters had labored in the area before the Civil War, and he moved to Amite, a village in Livingston Parish north of Lake Pontchartrain, in the winter of 1860–1861. He welcomed the soldiers camping outside his house, at least at first, and he freely shared his food with them. But the relationship soured quickly. After the soldiers stole his fruit and damaged the trees, Waters threatened to fire on the plundering troops. One day he did shoot at them, killing a man. The soldiers, convulsed with fury, razed his home to the ground as the officers and a few comrades in the ranks tried and failed to stop them. The men, still "greatly enraged," then tore down Waters' trees and fences, set fire to his barn and other buildings, and obliterated his food supply while his female relatives watched, terrified. Waters escaped with his life, but he was ruined financially. The residence and the yard property were his only assets, his neighbor Sarah Lois Wadley said, and he had not been able to find work since the war broke out in April.[1]

Sarah Wadley might be expected to excuse the actions of these rampaging Confederate troops. The teenaged daughter of a slaveowning railroad executive, she lived a comfortable life, passing her time visiting, sewing, going to church, and reading. She had an introspective turn of mind, admonishing herself to trust God, be a better person, and count her blessings. She had kinfolk all over the region, and she was fond of Amite, which featured the intricate social life of many small towns. The Wadleys

FIGURE I.I Courthouse in Amite, Louisiana, late nineteenth century.
Courtesy of Tangipahoa Parish Library.

had many friends, including David Waters, whom they visited during the holidays in 1860 as custom dictated. When the political crisis unfolded that winter, some of the Wadleys supported the Union, but Sarah firmly believed in secession, and when the war broke out, she supported the Confederacy. Her father served in a noncombat capacity as a railroad superintendent, and she and her mother volunteered for a Confederate sewing society. She cheered the news of the rebel victory at the Battle of First Bull Run in July 1861.[2]

But the attack on Mr. Waters and his property horrified Sarah Wadley. She was stunned to hear about this onslaught on a friend and neighbor, calling it "dreadful" that "our own soldiers" could behave that way. The villagers feared that the rebel troops might set fire to the town, expanding their attack from a single family to the entire community, so a local guard patrolled the area for several days afterwards. Amite did not burn, much to the relief of the town-dwellers. Wadley blamed the debacle on Polish-American troops from New Orleans, yet the incident troubled her, particularly because Waters had been generous to the troops just before they demolished his property. What happened to him was wrong, she thought. Worst of all, Confederate officers could not stop it. This occurred when the Civil War was only six months old, and, although Wadley did not say so, all of it violated the Confederate Articles of War.[3]

Readers may find it astonishing that such a thing could transpire so early in the war, and even more shocking that rebel troops could act in such a way inside the Confederacy. But such things did happen. In my research, I have frequently come upon similar accounts of harm visited on civilians and their property. Other rebel soldiers took food and timber and destroyed private homes, as did Union troops. Soon I began to wonder about military policy, which was supposed to provide some constraints on soldier behavior. As I did further research, I did not expect to find a simon-pure fidelity to policy; I have taught for too long at big state universities to expect people to follow bureaucratic regulations with perfect efficiency. But I was increasingly surprised at the indifference toward or defiance of policy among officers and privates in both armies. Then I began to wonder about prevailing attitudes among all soldiers toward resources, both human resources, such as the goodwill of someone like David Waters, and material resources, such as his food, his fences, and his house. The result is this book.

THE ARGUMENT OF THIS BOOK

The book focuses on attitudes toward resources, both human and material, and the wartime struggle for resources between soldiers and civilians. One of the major themes is that official policy had little impact on restraining armies in that struggle. The armies were composed largely of ordinary citizens, North and South, who were the products of a rural, small-town culture, and before the war, white people in both regions adhered to similar values of communalism and stewardship. Most of them accepted the notion that human beings had some obligations to each other and the corollary that they should be good stewards of valuable material resources, although some people mistreated each other, of course, and they sometimes wasted their resources. Neither region was an agrarian utopia, but the values of communalism toward other whites and stewardship of resources prevailed among most people in the South and North.

Then the war came. Both armies exploited fully the South's human resources – the knowledge and skill of the white population – and both armies destroyed, misused, and wasted material resources as they foraged, well beyond anything that occurred before 1861. Both armies always contained some men who tried to protect civilians and conserve physical resources, yet military needs triumphed over civilian society and the prevalent values of antebellum culture. Both armies made the maximum use of what Yankee Private Edgar Ely called the "stuff" of war – the materials necessary for the contest – wherever they went in the Confederacy, the Border States, and the North. This was true regardless of their ethnic backgrounds, religious faith, political views, or when they joined the service. Most of the warriors in both armies – blue and gray – privileged their own needs over everything else.[4]

This was not the work of a few delinquents, random deserters, or occasional stragglers, but routine conduct among men in both armies. This was true for the infantry and the cavalry, officers of different ranks, in the eastern and western theaters. Historians have disagreed on the efficiency, professionalism, and organizational ability of the antebellum US Army, but very few career officers served in the Civil War armies, and West Point graduates who did serve did not always abide by procedure. The "laws" of war as they evolved over the centuries had little impact on actual behavior, nor did the small literature on military theory. The US Supreme Court did not give clear guidance, and the Confederacy never created its own Supreme Court; neither Abraham Lincoln nor Jefferson Davis was closely involved in setting policy on civilians and their resources. American troops were supposed to rely on the Articles of War, which dated from 1806, and Henry Lee Scott's *Military Dictionary*, published in 1861, a kind of almanac on military topics. The federal army's pronouncements by John Pope in 1862 and Francis Lieber in 1863 were designed to give soldiers more latitude in the field, but, just as important, they were supposed to give some protections to noncombatants and the material environment. Those protections did not work well in practice. Policy made a thin patch on the voracious needs of the two armies, which had their own momentum independent of military directives.[5]

Wars encourage transgressions of all kinds, and they typically consume an immense amount of resources. Throughout the modern era, armies have injured civilians and destroyed their property despite the prohibitions of official policy, and the American Civil War was no different. What is surprising is the scale of violation, and what is revealing is the impact on civilians. Too often, scholars have assumed that wartime policies automatically clicked into place, but military regulations were not self-enforcing; human beings had to enforce them. Officers and soldiers conformed to policy intermittently, or sometimes not at all. This book is about, among other things, the inability of policy to constrain human misconduct as the juggernaut of war hurtled forward. This was indeed a "total" war, in that it involved the complete exploitation of human and material resources. There was no "rosewater" period, as it is sometimes called, when the armies refrained from exploitation. From the beginning, both armies practiced "hard" war because of failures of supply and discipline.[6]

The military bureaucracies in charge of supply worked about as well as systems created quickly to function across vast geographic distances might work – that is, not very well. Both armies had difficulties with command structures, transportation, technology, and funding, since such large-scale operations had never been attempted before, but scholars have dissected these problems at the "wholesale" side of the supply process.[7] We need to scrutinize the "retail" story, that is, the interactions between soldiers and civilians on the ground. Historians have generally assumed that the Yankee army, after a bumpy start, figured out how to supply its men, while the Confederate army never figured it out. The evidence at ground level indicates that neither army functioned very efficiently when it came to supplying the troops. Even the Union army was not a well-oiled machine.[8]

Both armies practiced the "learn by doing" approach to training key officers in the military bureaucracy. Volunteer quartermasters and commissary officers underwent little or no instruction, and after they arrived on the front, some of them did not even know which powers could be wielded by their fellow officers, such as provost marshals. Whatever Yankee Captain Charles Francis Adams learned about the army, he recalled, he taught himself. He depicted the army as a machine in which no one knew what the machine was doing, and this was not just a federal problem. In November 1862, Confederate Adjutant General Samuel Cooper admonished a rebel major general to read the Articles of War, since the man did not seem to know the contents. George Cary Eggleston, like many other Confederate soldiers, blasted the incompetent rebel bureaucracy and said that its efficiency, whether it concerned passports or commissary supplies, did not improve during the war.[9]

What is more, neither army had reliable mechanisms to discipline soldiers who violated procedure. The courts-martial, which happened quickly with no set procedures, rarely convened to address mistreatment of civilians or their property. In the entire war, the Northern military commissions tried only thirteen Union soldiers for crimes against civilians or their property; scholar Robert Alotta estimates that ten federal soldiers, total, were executed for plunder, pillage, or theft of civilian property. The establishment of the US Judge Advocate General's Department in 1862, intended to bolster the court-martial system, had little influence on the men in the field. No records survive for rebel courts-martial or executions, and the Confederacy never created a judge advocate office, but the historical evidence suggests that the outcome was much the same. The many soldiers in both armies who admitted violating regulations in their wartime or postwar writings correctly assumed that there would be no punishment. Nor did the compensation systems designed to reimburse civilians work very smoothly. The military, whether it was Northern or Southern, had no safeguards to ensure that operations took place within accepted parameters, something every functioning organization needs.[10]

The principal reason the bureaucracies did not work was the mentality that prevailed among many soldiers in both armies. The men in the ranks from both regions constituted an unruly populace, hard to control, as historians have noted; many of the troops voiced the same opinion. The Confederacy's size made it impossible for officers to monitor each other and men in the ranks, as federal officer Charles Wills remarked. The chain of command did not necessarily sway men in the field. Officers issued jeremiads about the abuse of civilians and their property, but they had a mixed impact on men in uniform, partly because other officers tolerated bad behavior or indulged in it themselves. Many soldiers perceived regulations as an annoyance that they would get around. Privates defied their conscientious officers and did as they wished, from the war's first months until the very end.[11]

Charles Perrow, the specialist in organizational studies, argues that bureaucracies can fail because their members bring with them preexisting attitudes from the rest of their lives, and, moreover, that bureaucracies do not always create new sets of values that everyone finds acceptable. Civil War troops did not have the business-like habits, the organizational skills, or the values to be good bureaucrats, and they were often indifferent toward process and procedure. To the contrary, they were the creatures of a political culture that harbored a strong distrust of government bureaucracies. Many of them did not want to fill out forms for civilians or give them paperwork while confiscating food, timber, or housing, so they did not. Many of them did not want to follow orders, so they did not. The military bureaucracy was not rigid and unyielding – the typical complaint about bureaucracies – but overextended and lax. And soldiers in both armies were driven by primal needs for sustenance, warmth, and shelter, and they were willing to do almost anything to meet their needs. The result was a "total" war in terms of destructiveness, without modern execution or efficiency.[12]

During the war, there were many points of contact between soldiers and civilians, some of which conformed to regulations. Historian Paul

Escott wisely observes that there was much "interpenetration" between the white civilian world and the Southern army, and the same was true for white Southern civilians and the Northern army. The military and civilian populations were in some respects fascinated with each other. Many civilians were not *hors de combat* but deeply involved in war-making. Military interests and civilian interests did not always coincide, however, and those interests diverged more as time passed. When military necessity clashed with civilian necessity, noncombatants thought their needs should take priority, especially if their own survival was at stake. Alongside the fight between the armies, a parallel contest broke out between armies and civilians, an intense mutual endeavor more complicated than mere victimization. A few civilians benefited from relationships with the military, but a much greater number relinquished people, food, timber, and housing to the war. Many of them did not even understand the specifics of military policy, for either army. In this terrible struggle, the civilian population lost.[13]

When American men put on the uniform, many of them experienced an abrupt shift in outlook about human conduct and material things. Scholars disagree about their ideological commitments, their racial views, their styles of self-expression, their enthusiasm for their respective causes, their support for emancipation, and other issues,[14] but all troops sometimes needed help from civilians, and they all had to have food, warmth, and shelter. Many soldiers came to assume that they could take whatever resources they needed, freed from antebellum values of stewardship and community, and some of them relished defying authority. They enjoyed the freedom from restraint, according to Yankee Quartermaster Aldis Brainerd, as if they had "no fear of man or God." Neuroscientists argue that individuals removed from their usual social constraints will take liberties that would be otherwise unimaginable, even more so if they are part of a crowd, and many wartime civilians made similar comments. Esther H. Hawks, the Union doctor working in South Carolina, stated that federal troops delighted in destroying things because they were away from the "refining influences of home" and coping badly with the war's privations.[15]

Soldiers in both armies nonetheless maintained a vigorous moral debate about the damage inflicted on civilians and the physical world, with some men advocating limits on military actions. They found the mistreatment of civilians and abuse of resources shocking, and they could not be persuaded to accept such conduct. One Union soldier, appalled by the looting in Virginia in 1862, remarked that "the genius of destruction is let

loose in war" and "Soldiers acquire a passion for destruction." Some of
the troops framed it as a religious issue or a violation of moral standards,
while others felt appalled by the sheer waste of so many resources. But
these men were frequently overruled, ignored, or shouted down. When
Confederate soldier J. M. Waddill argued that stealing while in the army
was not the same as in civilian life, he expressed the views of many troops
from the South and North.[16]

This work also explores the political divisions within the white
Southern population and how they affected the war's outcome. Many
people ardently supported the Confederacy, of course, believing that
slavery should expand into the far West, the chief issue in the Election
of 1860, and that secession should be attempted if slavery's expansion
was blocked. But Confederate nationalism never took hold for many
whites, and a substantial percentage opposed the war. Some 40 percent
of white men in the slave states voted against immediate secession in the
Election of 1860, and that number does not include white women who
felt the same way but could not vote. Pro-Union politicians in the South
failed to organize these people during the secession winter, yet the federal army quickly reached out to them when the war commenced, asking
Unionists of both genders for help. In the early stages, they usually got
it, just as the rebel army received help from its supporters. The incessant
demands of both armies wreaked damage on all civilians, however, and
many of them pulled back as their material resources disappeared. Yet
being anti-Confederate did not necessarily mean supporting the Union,
and the white South contained apolitical civilians who just wanted to
stay out of the way.[17]

HISTORIOGRAPHY

This book builds on a dynamic historiography of excellent scholarship in several fields, although it departs from current scholarship in
some important respects, beginning with relations between soldiers
and civilians. Other scholars emphasize the inconsistency in how both
armies treated civilians, and the inherent tension in those relationships,[18]
without addressing the material consequences, as I do here. Historians
have queried the role of gender during the war, since most soldiers
were male and many civilians were female. They note that antebellum
assumptions about the unchanging, inherent nature of the sexes proved
to be malleable in time of war,[19] but, again, without treating how men
and women used material resources. Military historians have noted the

difficulty officers had in controlling their soldiers but have not followed through on what that meant for the material basis of civilian survival. In terms of the greater political implications, these unwieldy, undersupplied armies suggest that neither the Southern government nor the Northern government had matured into a fully modern nation-state.[20]

This volume is part of the material turn in the Civil War field, in which scholars have begun to focus on the war's material dimension. Historians Joan E. Cashin and Michael DeGruccio have described monuments and relic-hunting, although they left much of the physical world untouched, as it were.[21] In addition, the book relies on the new environmental history by such scholars as Lisa Brady, Mark Fiege, and Brian Drake, which has alerted us to the significance of natural forces during the war, although we need more work on the interplay between armies, civilians, and the natural world.[22] The few historians who discuss wartime foraging tend to concentrate on food, and they neglect the civilian perspective; the best work on that subject remains Bell Wiley's work from years ago. He notes that rebel soldiers who took food from civilians contrary to procedure were either "blamable" or "innocent" and leaves it at that; Yankee foragers sometimes followed procedure, but he admits that expeditions could get out of hand, again without pursuing the implications.[23] A few pioneering historians have addressed the military's impact on timber and the built habitat. Megan Kate Nelson emphasizes the Northern army's actions, however, and she concentrates on urban life, while Mark Grimsley portrays Union General John Pope's Orders of July 1862 as a dramatic turning point in policy and behavior.[24] No one has investigated prewar attitudes toward material resources in both the North and South and connected them to wartime events. This book is the first monograph to take such an approach.

WHAT THIS BOOK DOES AND DOES NOT COVER

The opening chapter surveys the antebellum South and North, and the wartime chapters present case studies on people, food, timber, and habitat in the South, because these resources were essential to waging war. These chapters cover the years 1861 through 1863, in order to examine conduct before and after the policy landmarks of John Pope in 1862 and Francis Lieber in 1863. The last two chapters cover 1864 and 1865, when the war's cumulative impact on the South's resources became overwhelming. In all the chapters, I draw on the perspectives of other disciplines, such as material culture studies, culinary studies, forestry, architecture, and disaster studies. The focus is on soldiers in the regular armies, and the book is about events on land. Since the wartime South consisted mostly of farms, plantations, villages, and modest towns, it concentrates on these places rather than the big cities. Black Southerners appear occasionally in the narrative as witnesses and participants, but slaves had fewer material resources than most whites, and both armies had separate policies for black Americans. Furthermore, important scholarship has already been done on many aspects of African-American life during the war. This work does not address court seizures of cotton or land, measures initiated by the governments, such as the First and Second Confiscation Acts in the United States in 1861 and 1862, or the Confederate tax-in-kind bill from 1863.[25]

Like most works of scholarship, this book is based on the surviving manuscripts. Many papers of the Confederate bureaucracies burned or disappeared at the war's end, but numerous other manuscripts are available, permitting a scholar to close many of the gaps. The written evidence for both sides is tremendous, including correspondence, diaries, memoirs, newspapers, the WPA Narratives, the US Southern Claims Commission, court-martial records, quartermaster records, and other collections in the National Archives. There is much more evidence on the topics discussed in this volume beyond what I have included here. The *Official Records of the War* is an exceptionally rich source in which thorny issues about armies, civilians, and resources surface from the beginning of the conflict to the end.

A few terms need to be defined: a "planter" is the owner of at least twenty slaves, and the "round forty," a common nineteenth-century phrase, refers to the practice of squatters who claimed 40 acres of public land, took all the wood, and then moved on. Out in the field, troops in both armies defined the noun "forage" as food and timber for both animal and human use, and they defined the verb "to forage" as the quest for those resources. Last of all, some famous names from the military and civilian worlds appear, but most of the book is concerned with ordinary people. Whenever possible, I have provided biographical information, including wealth-holdings and military ranks, but sometimes the details could not be recovered or confirmed. In other cases, soldiers changed ranks as they were promoted during the war.

I

Old South

In the generation before the Civil War, white Southerners of both genders had a wealth of useful knowledge about the places where they lived. They knew the landscape, the geography, the complicated social relations among its people, and the nuances of local history. In addition, many residents had a set of highly developed skills which were necessary for the functioning of individual households and entire communities. These skills provided human beings with status among their peers, as well as personal satisfaction in the exercise of their talents. In their daily lives, Southerners relied on each other for companionship, fellowship, and assistance in times of trouble. They had their share of conflicts based on class and other issues, but most people from different social backgrounds fostered an ethic of communalism, the notion that they had obligations to one another.[1]

In the antebellum years, white Southerners also lived in a world of abundant material resources. They knew how to manage these resources – food, timber, and habitat – each of them valuable in a distinctive way, each of them necessary for human survival. This was true throughout the South, despite subregional differences in diet, landscape, and architecture. Most white people valued their material resources, using them for their own well-being and the benefit of their relatives, friends, and neighbors, whether they were planters, yeomen, attorneys, doctors, editors, ministers, or craftsmen in the rural and small-town South. They were willing to share their resources with each other, too, in the spirit of both obligation and cooperation. This universe of "rude plenty" seemed to provide enough for everybody, according to Letitita Dabney Miller, a judge's daughter. Some white people wasted, abandoned, or misused resources, although most of them practiced stewardship, trying to avoid the needless destruction of resources whenever possible.[2]

PEOPLE

We should begin with the people themselves. Most white Southerners shared an interlocking set of values on family duty, gender, religious faith, and honor, all of which could be subsumed under the rubric of communalism. The foundation of communalism was the family, the central institution in the lives of most people. Kinfolk mattered well beyond the nuclear core of parents and children, embracing a wide network of relatives. Many people knew the detailed histories of their families back to their great-grandparents and beyond, and many of them lived surrounded by their kin. Within the boundaries of Anderson County, South Carolina, Micajah A. Clark had relatives in sixteen households, embracing cousins, aunts, and uncles with seven different surnames. Multiple generations sometimes lived in the same household, for months or even years at a time.[3]

Kinfolk, male and female, were expected to help each other in daily life, a concept they absorbed early in life. They practiced the idea as adults, creating a dense web of favors and obligations. James Deaderick, an attorney in Tennessee, borrowed money from a cousin to purchase land, and he knew he could rely on the man's generosity. Kentuckian Sarah Thompson, a plantation mistress, asked her kinfolk about household tasks such as how to weave a carpet properly and how much cloth was required. Relatives male and female congregated at the local church to worship together and visit after the service, and they attended court day once a month at the county seat to hear the news, do business, and talk some more. They readily gave lodging to kindred passing through the area. Plantation mistress Ann Archer sheltered her cousin's son as he traveled through Mississippi, even though he drank too much and was "very disagreeable to us."[4]

Friends and neighbors engaged in similar habits of mutuality, creating another layer of obligation between community members. White people swapped many favors large and small in their daily lives. In Walnut Hill, South Carolina, one Mrs. Pledger visited her neighbors, the McLeods, to ask them to write some letters for her. Young Kate McLeod did not especially enjoy writing these "rigamaroles" for her elderly neighbor, but she did it, as expected. When some drunken white men serenaded the Carney household in Tennessee before the local elections in 1859, one of the songsters dozed off on the porch, so Mr. Carney, a merchant, asked him to come into the house and sleep it off. Neighbors sometimes collected mail for each other at the county seat and distributed it to the different households. Being a good neighbor was something that other people in this social world noticed and remembered.⁵

Hospitality was a time-honored, highly effective way to forge these social bonds. Relatives, friends, and neighbors visited each other's houses regularly, sometimes on the spur of the moment, while other visits, lasting several days or longer, were planned in advance. Southerners enjoyed formal social gatherings, as well. Every comfortable home had a room for receptions and parties, Texan Mary Maverick recalled, and the celebrations increased at the holidays, when people gathered to talk, listen to music, and eat. During the rest of the year, many whites felt obliged to give shelter to white people passing through. John Franklin Smith's father, who owned a plantation in Bates County, Missouri, never turned travelers away and gave them free lodging in his house. Not everyone measured up to such generosity, but that was the ideal.⁶

The communalism of the Old South included white Yankees who moved into the region, as well as European immigrants, so long as they accepted the institution of slavery. Jason Niles, a Vermont native, moved to Mississippi in the 1840s to practice law, and by 1861 he had a thriving legal practice in Attala County, where he was a respected neighbor with many friends. The same process happened with the region's population of European immigrants. Germans and Irishmen settled in towns such as Staunton, Virginia, not just in the big cities, and, despite some bursts of nativism and anti-Catholic prejudice – since many of these newcomers were Catholics – they lived for the most part peacefully with their Anglo-Saxon Protestant neighbors. The same was the case for the small numbers of Jews who settled in the South's towns and villages.⁷

Class relations between whites in this society was a delicate matter. Slaveowners, who held most of the property, had to ensure the loyalty or at least the acquiescence of other whites. Many of them tried to keep these relations in good repair, out of enlightened self-interest, religious obligation, and what seems like a genuine desire to help other people. In Manchester, Virginia, Rebecca Harris was much sought after by her neighbors for her nursing skills. White people of every background asked her to care for them, and she usually responded. In low-country South Carolina, plantation owners realized that yeomen farmers needed money when they would offer to sell baskets or yarn to their affluent neighbors. One planter's daughter said that parties on both sides understood these wordless transactions. Family connections to prominent people could mediate the snobbery of elite whites. Anne Broome, an ex-slave living near Winnsboro, South Carolina, noted that local planters were "good" to a working-class white man named Marshall because he was related to the Chief Justice of the United States, John Marshall.[8]

Gender influenced how white Southerners learned to manage certain material resources. Beginning in childhood, they absorbed the idea that the sexes had to play distinct roles in the world. Boys learned how to hunt, fish, ride, and handle a gun, while girls learned how to cook, sew, and run a household. In adult life, this clear differentiation continued in the use of material resources, as was true for many cultures. The sexes had diverging areas of expertise, although both men and women had knowledge that was necessary to keep households running. Men made most of the important decisions in the family, and women were expected to resign themselves to their subordination; in return they would be protected. Women who could not accept these strictures, such as the South Carolinians Sarah and Angelina Grimké, left the region for the North, where they embarked on careers as reformers.[9]

Southern communities were brimming with all kinds of personal information, acquired by the residents over years of observation. Most white people cared a great deal about the good opinion of their neighbors, and both sexes could communicate their disapproval with sharp talk. Hardy Wooten, a doctor, called the young men who collected in the grog-shop in Lowndesboro, Alabama, drinking and talking, "gossips in the strongest sense of the term." Women queried each other about rumors of misconduct, and the consequences could be serious. Texan Elizabeth Clary and her sister speculated that a neighbor in Grimes County had committed adultery, and, when that item of gossip spread through the community, the local Methodist church opened an investigation into the matter. Women and men did not want to be subjected to social disapproval. Ann Gale, a plantation mistress, advised her son not to repeat her candid opinions about some difficult relatives because she had "a dread of being talked about" herself.[10]

When a disaster occurred, such as a fire, white Southerners expected everyone to help out. Many communities had volunteer fire departments, but when a fire broke out, everyone, adults and children, rushed to the scene. Neighbors sometimes called for assistance by sounding a horn. After a carpenter's shop went up in flames in Alexandria, Virginia, firemen and local citizens worked together to prevent the fire from spreading. The Great Dismal Swamp, which covered over 100,000 acres on the Virginia–North Carolina border, sometimes caught fire, and the conflagration spread into both states, consuming homes, trees, and fences as citizens tried to fight the flames. They had a justifiable fear of fire, which often started with a lightning strike and could spread rapidly in the countryside.[11]

For good or for ill, local institutions shaped the existence of most whites in the rural and small-town South. The national government had a negligible presence in their lives. The postmaster was probably the most visible federal employee, and, even then, local people sometimes took over that function and delivered mail to their neighbors. The federal census-taker, who came around once every decade, was a local resident, as warranted by law. The court system, staffed by magistrates almost everyone knew, met in taverns, mills, and private dwellings, and they resolved the cases – disorderly conduct, drunkenness, theft, assault, and murder – that caused shame and heartbreak in the community.[12]

Ordinary breaches in communalism happened, of course, in every county, village, and town. Every community saw its share of rivalry, pettiness, and meanness, as white people criticized, reproached, or snubbed their contemporaries. Class tensions could never be completely suppressed, breaking the surface of daily life. In Mississippi, yeomen were known to insult white women riding in fancy carriages and white men who wore fine clothes. Not all members of the planter class tried to conceal their disdain for working-class people. Robert Williams, a former slave, said that his master Clinton Clay made poor whites go to the back door if they wanted to speak to him. The worst penalties were inflicted on those who breached customs about race. In North Carolina, planters who caught working-class whites bartering with slaves "banded together" to force them to sell their farms and leave the area, threatening them with death if they did not comply. Renegades such as Sarah Grimké, Angelina Grimké, William H. Brisbane, and James G. Birney who openly criticized slavery chose to leave the region or were forced to leave.[13]

SUSTENANCE

White Southerners expressed their communalism in tangible ways, among them the consumption of food. The region was an agrarian wonder, replete with fertile farms and plantations where cattle and hogs grazed in the fields, poultry pecked in the yards, fish teemed in the rivers, and wild game roamed in the woods. Most planters ate a better diet than middling slaveowners, who in turn ate better than most yeoman farmers, but the region had enough provisions for most of its people. Many Southerners consumed a diet that was high in protein, salt, and sugar, and most of them perceived food as an essential resource that should not be wasted. Willis Lea, a physician who lived in a log cabin, proudly told his brother that he lived well, he ate well, and his family was healthy. Having a healthy appetite and plentiful food were important components of the good life, Alabaman Matilda Finley remarked.[14]

Women were responsible for most of the food preparation, which has been true for many societies. In the Old South, this was the case for white women of all social classes, from yeomen farmer's wives to plantation mistresses. Eliza Robertson of Louisiana, a planter's wife, could make head cheese, mincemeat, citron preserves, and sausage, although most wealthy families made slaves do the hardest work in the kitchen. White women tried to preserve their culinary knowledge. Martha Dinsmore, a Kentuckian whose husband owned eleven slaves, kept recipe books for almost thirty years, collecting plant cuttings, newspaper articles, and recipes from family members. Inside the household, women performed ceremonial duties, as well. The oldest woman present, either the mother or the eldest daughter, sat at the head of the table during meals.[15]

White men, too, contributed to the household fare. Yeomen farmers and small-scale slaveholders worked hard in the fields, planting in the spring, tending crops in the summer, and harvesting crops in the fall. Some planters made agricultural experiments on their farms, breeding and raising different varieties of legumes. Most men learned to hunt and fish as boys, and adult men from all backgrounds practiced those skills. Yeomen farmers went hunting to supplement their diets, and attorney Maxcy Gregg, a sportsman, passed many hours hunting with his friends in coastal South Carolina. Another South Carolinian, planter Thomas Chaplin, loved the outdoors and plumbed the waterways for drum fish, sheepshead, and bass for his family's table.[16]

Most white Southerners gladly shared their food with relatives and friends. Kinfolk gave each other gifts of fish, figs, and other comestibles, which they in turn shared with other family members, and some of them went to a lot of trouble. S. R. Eggleston sent a barrel of flour, a barrel of herring, and a bundle of fruit trees from his home in Richmond to his cousins in Claiborne County, Virginia. Female relatives exchanged gifts of food, proffering coffee for eggs, and women could be generous with their friends, as well. One South Carolinian, plantation mistress Keziah

Brevard, made a steeple cake (a kind of sponge cake) for her neighbor's wedding, even though she did not really approve of the match.[17]

The South's cuisine included regional specialties such as grits and cornbread, Native American in origin, which dated back to colonial times. White Southerners employed some ancient implements in their preparation of meals. In Mississippi, plantation mistress Martha Maney kept a hominy mortar, used to separate corn kernels, in her kitchen. European influences survived in parts of the region. In Louisiana, local folk consumed jerked beef served in the so-called "French style," the meat dried in strips and cooked over a smoky fire. White people also borrowed foodways from the black Americans in their midst, including methods of preparing rice that came from Africa to the Carolina low country by way of the Caribbean.[18]

White Southerners were enthusiastic carnivores, enjoying meat of all types. They consumed other kinds of protein, including seafood and freshwater fish, but they loved meat. The prosperous customarily ate more meat, and more than one type of meat, as Frances Kemble, an English-born plantation mistress, noted. She recorded helpings of duck, geese, turkey, and venison at the table. Other class differences appeared in the diet. Beef has long been the most prestigious meat, partly because beef cattle require a lot of acreage for grazing, so it was more common on a planter's table. Yeoman farmers favored pork, which was a staple of the working-class diet, partly because pigs are easier and cheaper to raise.[19]

Bread was the staff of life, and the grain mills in the Old South both reflected and reinforced the ethos of communalism. In the fall, most residents took their corn or wheat to be processed at a local mill powered by animals – a mule treading in an endless circle – or water from nearby streams or bayous. So-called "combination mills" processed corn and lumber by turns, the wheels cleaned between rounds. The miller was an important figure in the community, essential to the food supply. William S. Blunt, the miller in Maumelle, Arkansas, charged a toll of one-eighth of the corn crops his customers brought in, and he sold cornmeal directly to the public. He developed a regular clientele and thanked them in the local newspaper for their patronage.[20]

On festive occasions, whites supped together to celebrate good fortune while simultaneously confirming their social ties. This, too, has been the case for many societies over the centuries. When relatives called on each other, lavish feasts were served as a gesture of welcome, and when longtime friends met, they marked the occasion, as Texan Branch T. Archer did, by

FIGURE 1.1 Mill in Spartanburg, South Carolina, founded 1785.
Courtesy of Spartanburg County Historical Association.

bringing out Virginia fowl, Smithfield ham, and whiskey. The emphasis was on volume, heaps of food spread out on tables, and, during holidays, the elaborate presentation of food and drink. On New Year's Day, one planter family in Florida set up in their parlor a table covered with decorative little cakes, a large punch bowl with a silver ladle, and patterned glasses for the guests as they streamed through the house.[21]

To be sure, some hungry white people lived in the South. Near Murfreesboro, Tennessee, beggars sometimes appeared at the door of wealthy households asking for something to eat, and when the winter was bad, neighbors occasionally stole food from each other. Conversely, some affluent people would not share their bounty with working-class whites, and they could be vicious in punishing thefts. When planter John Devereaux caught the young Andrew Johnson trying to steal some fruit from his property, he had the boy whipped. Families who were perpetually short on food could be charged with vagrancy, but relatives and neighbors were expected to share their provender with the less fortunate, and most of them did so.[22]

TIMBER

The same assumptions prevailed about the South's forests, that there was plenty of timber for everyone, and that the woodlands should be shared. Evergreens, deciduous trees, hardwoods, and softwoods grew all over the region, the different species flourishing in different geographic zones: mixed hardwoods such as live oaks grew in the coastal sandy soil, while conifers appeared in the red clay of the Piedmont. The South was heavily forested when the first Anglo-Americans arrived in the 1600s, and the intervening centuries of settlement had cleared only a portion of the woodlands. The region included vast tranquil forests, tidy little groves, and ancient giants; the Oglethorpe Oak, planted by the Georgia colony's founder in the eighteenth century, was still alive in the 1830s. Most white people saw the woodlands as an endlessly renewable resource, generating enough fuel for everybody. Planter James Avirett depicted the forest as inexhaustible.[23]

Most people believed that corridors of forests constituted an essential part of a pleasing landscape, and they engaged in a complex silviculture, drawing on their knowledge of forestry and their personal preferences. Boys began learning about timber when they were young. Robert Jones, the twelve-year-old son of a Virginia planter, impressed his tutor with his extensive knowledge of trees, their characteristics, and their financial value. In adulthood, men advised each other on which trees to plant and where to plant them, and they could develop fondness for a particular species on their own land. One yeoman farmer in South Carolina planted cedars on his property, and he would not cut them down even if they sprouted in his cotton fields. Women also acquired an extensive knowledge of trees, plants, shrubs, and flowers, as they devised their gardens and yards.[24]

Wood was an extremely valuable resource since it could be put to so many uses on a farm, to make homes, barns, stables, gin-houses, storehouses, plows, churns, and furniture. Timber was an essential fuel for the fireplace, in every household. Many white men assumed as John C. Cook did that forested acres were necessary to support a farm, so most planters and farmers purchased land that was at least partially wooded. They cleared some acreage every year for their own use, even as they planted more trees for future use. John J. Frobel planted hickory on his Virginia plantation as an investment, in case his descendants had to harvest it one day during hard times.[25]

Much of the wood went into building fences, which were necessary for the functioning of a farm economy. Fences marked property boundaries and kept livestock out of the fields, so crops could flourish. The zigzag fence – also known as the worm fence or the Virginia fence – was common in the antebellum South. To build a zigzag fence, a man had to cut rails and stack them, six to ten rails in a panel (or section), fit the panels together, and secure the panels by crossed poles. Water-resistant and rot-resistant wood, such as longleaf pine, cypress, cedar, or white oak, made the best fences, and winter was the right time of year to make rails, when the sap was down. The zigzag fence required as many as 26,000 rails for 4 miles of fence, but it was easy to fix and easy to move. Such a fence could be expected to last over thirty years. In the Old South, keeping fences in good repair was considered part of being a good neighbor.[26]

When men cut down trees, which was very hard work, they used a pole axe with a single sharp edge. They cut trees at waist-high height from the ground, notching trunks on the side where they wanted the trees to fall, and then chopping hard on the other side. Farmers chose smaller trees with trunks less than 2 feet in diameter, avoiding trees with knotted, twisty trunks. Clearing the woods off one acre of land usually took one man about thirty days of labor. Yeomen farmers did this work themselves, as did other white men, such as minister Francis McFarland and editor Joseph Waddell, both Virginians. Some slaveowners did woodwork themselves, trimming trees in their yards, although they spared themselves the hardest labor. That work was performed by slaves or white men employed by the master.[27]

The forest offered a host of medicinal and pharmacological benefits, as well. White Southerners drew on a large body of folk knowledge about trees and shrubs accumulated by both races. White people saved the roots from certain trees, including may apple and black haw, for their healing powers, and they published books such as *The Planter's Guide and Family Book of Medicine* (1848), which suggested an infusion with leaves of the mountain ash as a treatment for typhus. Some whites shared the ancient folk belief that trees could by their very presence ensure good health. Planter Thomas Dabney of Mississippi put a wide belt of trees around his residence to protect his family from illness, and most people agreed that pine forests were particularly healthy.[28]

The appreciation of the forest's medicinal benefits coexisted with a pragmatic knowledge of how to make money from the woodlands. The timber business across the South could be very profitable. Cypress shingles cut from forests in North Carolina sold well in the North, and the turpentine and naval stores business thrived in the state for most of the antebellum era. All over the region, timber growing near a river was deemed especially valuable because it could be transported easily on the water or sold to steamboat companies. White Southerners with an entrepreneurial bent perceived the forest as a way to get rich. One attorney purchased 750 acres of white oak in Kentucky and reckoned he could earn 10,000 dollars a year by making staves from the wood.[29]

Because the region's woodlands seemed inexhaustible, white Southerners could be careless with timber. Some planters were known to let diseased trees decay on their land, "defacing" the countryside, in the view of one Alabaman, while turpentine workers left the gouged trunks of pine to rot and collapse. Citizens from all backgrounds cut down too many trees, which caused eyesores of unsightly stumps and contributed to soil erosion and soil exhaustion. Some white Southerners decried the recklessness of their fellows. In Covington County, Mississippi, Duncan McKenzie criticized the poor management of land and everything that grew on it by his neighbors, who wasted everything "precious."[30]

Many white Southerners nonetheless cherished trees, which have always provided emotional comfort to human beings beyond their practical benefits. They often engaged in their own landscape design. Samuel W. Leland, a doctor in Richland County, South Carolina, planted fifteen elms on the avenue in front of his house, and he did not want them to ever be cut down. Sally Jane Hibberd, a yeoman farmer's daughter, derived pleasure from the honeysuckle and woodbine entwined around the porch at her aunt's Virginia home. Because of the ancient custom of carving names on their trunks – what are called arborglyphs – trees could also serve as historical documents of a sort. In northwest Georgia, local people carved their names by the hundreds in some old trees on the Bitting property.[31]

White people did not have to be rich to love the forest, in any part of the region. Kate Plake, who hailed from a modest family in Bath County, Kentucky, loved to wander through the woods near her house, and Lizzie Jackson Mann, a minister's daughter, delighted in strolling with her relatives through the forest in Gloucester County, Virginia. Citizens of all backgrounds who grew up in the piney woods of antebellum Mississippi felt nostalgic for the forests of their childhoods. Some people held to an older mentality, a fear of the wild woods, but the more romantic nineteenth-century view of the forest as a bower of repose and beauty seems to have prevailed.[32]

Most white Southerners assumed that there was plenty of wood for everyone. They followed the custom of lifting the occasional fence rail in their neighborhoods for their own use, and travelers cut trees from

FIGURE 1.2 Smith's Old Fort Plantation, Port Royal Island, South Carolina.
Courtesy of the US Army Heritage and Education Center.

the roadside without asking anyone's permission if they had to repair a
wagon; steamboat crews routinely took wood from river banks, paying
on the honor system by slipping money into boxes nailed on trees. The
national government tried to halt the "round forty," when squatters took
wood from public land, and some private landowners prosecuted individuals for cutting wood on their property, but many white people took it
for granted that there was enough timber and that everyone should have
access to the woodlands.[33]

HABITAT

The most important building in the landscape was the private dwelling,
laden with cultural meaning as a refuge and a sanctuary. In this enclosed

domestic space, a place set apart, they were supposed to be protected from all hazards. Here the landmarks of private life registered, as kith and kin witnessed weddings, celebrated childbirths, and grieved for the dead. Here they entertained guests, enjoying a robust social life with neighbors and friends. For many white Southerners, including yeomen farmers, their childhood homes had what Albert Blue called "sacred" associations. In adulthood, they loved the homes where they resided with the same fervor. Sarah H. Brown, a slaveholder's wife, said that when she returned from a trip, her house in Wilkesboro, North Carolina, looked more beautiful than ever.[34]

The home's placement in the countryside mattered, too, for the purposes of good health and visual effect. In the countryside, most white Southerners perceived hilltops as healthier than lowlands, so that is where the affluent put their houses. Yeomen tended to live on less desirable lots on sandy soil that did not produce the best crops. Trees around an edifice served as windbreakers, although the home should not be built too close to a body of water, which could breed mosquitoes, as one South Carolinian discovered. The structure, known afterwards as "Mr. B.'s Folly," had to be abandoned after three months because he chose an unhealthy location for his house. Most people had specific ideas about spatial organization outside the house, too, expecting that the yard should be filled with trees, shrubs, and flowers.[35]

When most white Southerners constructed their homes, they used local woods of different types and vernacular designs, building homes that were one room deep, two rooms long, and two stories high, or two cabins connected by a walkway or dogtrot. The affluent employed professional architects in tune with national trends who produced larger buildings in the Federal or Italianate style, while yet others made their own idiosyncratic variations. E. M. Perine, a merchant, added a vestibule with a turret to the front of his brick mansion in Cahaba, Alabama. Some whites designed their houses themselves, putting a lot of time, thought, and energy into the plan. Mary and William Starnes planned a six-room structure with four fireplaces and a piazza for their residence in Limestone County, Texas.[36]

In the construction of their houses, slaveowning men frequently used their bondsmen, while others hired white men or free black men. Mead Carr paid white men to put up his residence, an ordinary frame building 18 by 20 feet, in rural Missouri. Yet other slaveholders did some of their own work, building the chimneys themselves. Yeomen farmers, artisans, and schoolteachers constructed log cabins of one or two rooms, and they stood ready to help their relatives and neighbors build their homes. About eighty logs were necessary to build a log cabin, and, depending on the number of workers, it could be completed in one to three days. Other white men were expected to assist in some way, and anyone, regardless of wealth, who failed to pitch in could be perceived as arrogant.[37]

The oldest homes dated from the eighteenth century, some of them built in the Georgian style, such as Berkeley, a three-story brick residence constructed on the James River in 1726. Other planters lived in domiciles that originated in the early nineteenth century as log cabins, which they expanded to include porches and second stories and later covered with clapboard. Some whites were very proud of their aged homes. John Wyeth's birthplace in Marshall County, Alabama, stood for forty years before 1861, and he hoped the building would last another hundred years. Houses could stay in the same family for multiple generations, which was one way to conserve a material resource. Duncan Blue, a turpentine farmer in Cumberland County, North Carolina, lived in the building that once belonged to his grandfather.[38]

Planter mansions, although few in number, dominated the landscape. Set back from the road on hilltops, constructed of brick or wood, they had to be approached via long lanes bordered with trees. These estates were intended to do more than provide a haven for the owners: they reflected their wealth and advertised their elite status. In Bledsoe County, Tennessee, Lee Billingsley recalled, his father built a brick mansion of twelve rooms. White-pillared mansions constructed in the Greek Revival style were popular for their formality, symmetry, and visual splendor, and for practical reasons, since the colonnades kept the buildings cool in hot weather. Plantation homes had many rooms constructed with the "best materials," one owner asserted, and mansions could cost several thousand dollars, far beyond what the average white Southerner could afford.[39]

Inside their houses, white Southerners of all backgrounds kept a mélange of objects, some of them necessary, others merely decorative, some of them handmade, and others store-bought. Many of these objects were utilitarian, necessary for daily life, such as the fishing tackle and medicine chest displayed in an overseer's house in South Carolina. People of all social classes had belongings that had no function other than pure pleasure. Harriet Vann, a yeomen farmer's wife in Chesterfield County, South Carolina, counted among her possessions a violin. Yet other objects, not necessarily expensive, gave solace to the occupants. Mary Ann Cobb, a congressman's wife, relished the "warm looking" cotton carpet, calico curtains, and bookshelves in her home in Athens, Georgia. The mansions of the wealthy included such luxury objects as mahogany bedsteads and other markers of a consumer culture that elites had joined in the late eighteenth century.[40]

The home was a memory hoard, replete with beloved objects that represented the family history. Many whites saved their Bibles, and men typically left them, with other "family books," to their wives and daughters in their wills. In fact, women frequently served as curators of the family's material history. They collected daguerreotypes of their relatives, preserved in elaborate frames, and they saved correspondence from previous generations, irreplaceable documents of their own history. The sentimental value of these material objects, even the most mundane, could be enhanced over time. As the decades went by, something useful like a spinning wheel could be transformed into an heirloom. Some women felt a powerful connection to the objects displayed inside the house. Ellen Wallace, a Kentuckian, visited her parent's home after they died, and the inanimate objects "shout aloud as I pass," she wrote.[41]

Whites of all social backgrounds felt love for their homes and the objects within the house. Georgian A. E. Harris, whose husband owned a few slaves, thought their log cabin was quite "pretty," and other whites drew their own conclusions about neighborhood buildings. In Mississippi, Letitia Dabney Miller admired her rich uncle's house with its ornate furnishings, but she did not think it very comfortable, and she preferred her own more modest abode. The loss of a house, regardless of its status, size, or age, could be deeply unsettling. Physician Hardy Wooten felt depressed when he stopped by his childhood home in Burke County, Georgia, to find the building deserted and the yard turned into a cornfield. The vacant dwelling and furrowed ground made him feel severed from his past.[42]

Not every white Southerner cared so deeply for their homes, however, as John Graydon observed. Some of his neighbors in Alachua County, Florida, simply threw their houses together and took no pride in the buildings. Other people neglected the condition of the home. Farmer Hugh McLaurin acknowledged that the "Old House" where he lived with his wife had fallen into "a State of Decay," so he left money in his will for his sons to fix it if they wished. Most communities had a few abandoned houses. In Hardeman County, Tennessee, several empty houses stood, the buildings left empty in 1860 for reasons we cannot discern. But the owners probably departed under duress, since a house of any kind was a valuable material asset.[43]

FIGURE 1.3 A member of the Hunt-Morgan family of Kentucky.
Courtesy of University of Kentucky Archives.

POLITICS AND WAR

Politics had always been a vital part of community life, a manifestation of both neighborly bonds and energetic competition. Candidates from the mainstream parties, the Democrats and the Whigs, campaigned with zeal, hosting parades, dinners, and serenades. Throughout the South, neighbors came to barbeques to hear speeches from candidates for county offices, as rivals made mostly good-natured jibes at each other. Local races could be very personal. William Kinney of Staunton, Virginia, knew a lot about the candidates for his district's state senate seat in 1857, their strengths, their shortcomings, and the names of their friends and foes. Politics was reserved for white men, since white women did not vote anywhere in the United States, and most people considered it unseemly for white females to show much interest in political matters. Some white men, too, were apolitical, although they of course could vote.[44]

In the mid-1850s, after the Whig Party disintegrated and the Republican Party formed, questions related to slavery moved front and center in the national discourse. Many white Southerners began to assume that all white Northerners were different from themselves, not just on issues pertaining to slavery or race but on every issue, as if they were an alien people. Robert H. Armstrong, traveling by boat from Memphis to New Orleans in the 1850s, evoked what he saw as a distinctly Southern communalism as he complained about the Yankee families on board. They were unsociable, with none of the "warm gushing of feeling and sympathy" that Southerners exhibited; instead, "all was cold, hard, real." Despite Armstrong's complaints, the two regions actually had much in common. Most of the white Northern population lived in rural, small-town communities that featured a rich social life, and like the South, that included both cooperation and conflict. They approached material resources in much the same way, with the same mix of stewardship and carelessness. They ate a somewhat different diet, with more helpings of clam chowder than people consumed in Dixie, but they too savored lots of meat, and they agreed that food should not be wasted. They found trees in a rural landscape pleasing to the eye, and they harvested the forests for the same diversity of purposes, sometimes leaving behind eroded, damaged soil. They loved their homes, whether they lived in log cabins, frame houses, or spacious mansions, and their dwellings contained a range of purchased and handmade objects that brought enjoyment to the owners.[45]

The presidential election of 1860 opened unbridgeable political differences not only between North and South but also within the white Southern population. Four candidates ran, posing different answers to the overriding question: Should slavery expand into the trans-Mississippi West? In the South, the race mostly came down to a contest between the Southern Democrat John Breckinridge, who argued that the slave states should consider secession if anyone tried to stop slavery's expansion, and the Constitutional Unionist John Bell of Tennessee, who stated that all political issues should be decided within the existing government. (The Republican Abraham Lincoln, who opposed the expansion of slavery, and the Northern Democrat Stephen Douglas, who believed that the decision should be made at the territorial stage, did not attract many votes in the region.) Most people understood the election's significance, with secessionists threatening to leave the country if Lincoln won. Breckinridge took the Deep South, while Bell carried three states in the Upper South – Virginia, Kentucky, and Tennessee – and won impressive support in states taken by Breckinridge, such as Alabama, where Bell garnered a third of the vote, and North Carolina, which Bell lost by fewer than 4,000 votes; he lost Missouri to Douglas by fewer than 500 votes. Bell, whom many historians have dismissed or forgotten, took about 40 percent of the vote in the slave states (the Border States and the future Confederacy). As South Carolina launched itself out of the Union in December 1860, the white population in the slave states was deeply divided on the wisdom of secession.[46]

The turbulent political debate continued into the spring, as secessionists went on the offensive. Local firebrands created vigilance committees to examine their neighbors on their political views, and they monitored the behavior of anyone who might be opposed to secession. Every Southern state contained whites loyal to the Union, and they in turn held public meetings and signed petitions. Historians still do not know how civilians chose sides. Many working-class people felt ambivalent or hostile toward secession because they resented the planter elite, while others had kinfolk in the North. Some citizens of all backgrounds, including slaveholders, opposed secession because they too had Yankee relatives; others thought secession was illegal, unreasonable, an appeal by demagogues, or a betrayal of the Revolution; yet others still loved the Union, adhered to the old Whig Party, or opposed war itself. Maybe the choice came down to attitudes toward risk, for secession was if nothing else an enormous risk. But regardless of how they made their choices, neighbors started to turn against each other, and longtime friendships ended. The communalism of the past, carefully nurtured by so many people, began to fall apart. By April 1861, seven states had formed a new country, the Confederacy.[47]

Secession might bring war, as many Americans realized, and as white Southerners weighed that prospect, most of them had little understanding of how destructive a war could be. The generation that served in the Revolution had passed away, and public memory focused on the glorious victory over the British rather than the war's damage to civilians or their resources. The Mexican War, which lasted only two years, was fought mostly outside the South. The War of 1812 did take place in the region, and some inhabitants did remember the harm it inflicted on the material world. William Chamberlaine's grandmother, who lived through that war, told her family that civilians should remain in their houses until the shingles flew off so they could protect them from the armies. A few other voices warned of trouble ahead. David Strother's father, a Virginian who served in the War of 1812, predicted that it would take several years to turn volunteers into responsible soldiers. But most young men knew about war only from reading books, rebel soldier William L. Sheppard later admitted, and most white Southerners were dangerously naive about a war's impact on civilians and the material framework they needed to survive.[48]

When war was officially declared after the shelling at Fort Sumter, the acrid political climate inside the South deteriorated even further. Confederates interrogated neighbors whom they feared might be pro-Union, opened their mail, threatened them, and forced them out of their homes. Soon they resorted to violence, burning down houses and shops belonging to Unionists. Anyone who seemed opposed to the Confederacy or even reluctant in their support now became suspect. The political crisis reached into the family, turning relatives against each other. Some Unionists – but not all – fell silent. Other people, indifferent to politics or afraid of antagonizing their neighbors, tried to avoid taking sides.[49]

The growing turmoil prompted hundreds of white people to leave the South. After April 1861, pro-Union citizens departed because of friendly warnings from neighbors who believed they might be hurt, while others fled because their property was seized by the newly created rebel government, or because they refused to take loyalty oaths to the Confederacy. Not until August 1861 did the Confederate Secretary of War begin to require passports, and then only in some locations, so people could travel out of the South for months after Fort Sumter. Where pro-Union sentiment was tenacious, the reverse happened: pro-Confederate residents fled such Unionist strongholds as eastern Tennessee.[50]

The white people who remained behind were about to live through a series of quick transformations in attitudes toward people and things. The imperatives of war took over, *war*, that deadly business that would exploit almost all of society's human resources and material resources. Troops in both armies developed new assumptions about the resources they needed to survive, a rapid shift in outlook by white men from the South and North who had practiced communalism and stewardship at home. This seems to have taken place immediately, in the first weeks of the conflict. The population was sorted into new two categories, civilian and military, with new identities, new roles, and diverging ideas about resources. Civilians with strong political loyalties proved to be willing to take action to help the respective causes, while others were more interested in self-preservation. In the spring of 1861, a terrific struggle broke out over the region's resources, starting with the people themselves.

2

People

When the fighting started in 1861, the civilian population and the military faced off against each other, just as the two armies squared off. Many soldiers, whether they were Yankees or Confederates, wanted the attention of white civilians, whom they perceived in some respects as an audience. Civilians did indeed watch the armies closely, and soldiers, in turn, paid close attention to civilians as they went about their daily lives. Troops in the two armies wanted understanding from the civilians they met, expounding their views, although they realized that civilians who began as onlookers or debate partners might turn into antagonists. Noncombatants could either help the armies or hurt them, building on the knowledge they already possessed and the proficiencies they had developed before 1861. During the war, they could lift morale, smuggle goods, deliver letters, provide information, engage in espionage, and work for the armies. They could even serve as hostages, which turned civilians themselves into a kind of resource. As the two armies vied with each other for every advantage, civilians became embroiled in that struggle, as they have in many other wars.[1]

The two armies had their own resources and their own specialists, of course, but they did not have endless resources and infinite skill, and soldiers could not always depend on their comrades, some of whom were unreliable, maladroit, or unavailable. The decision to ask civilians to do what the armies could not do, a decision often made on the fly, happened throughout the war. All this made for complex interactions between armies and civilians, with shifting combinations of sympathy, good will, bargaining, haggling, threats, and outright hatred. Some civilians were deeply ideological, true believers in one cause or the other, while others were not especially political, although they did take sides when forced to choose. Still others felt no interest in the conflict and tried to avoid the trouble it brought. Unionists, defined as people who were willing to help the federal cause in any way, constituted a numerical minority, probably 30 to 40 percent of the white population in the Confederacy and the Border States, but both armies were fully aware of their existence.[2]

In theory, at least, military policy governed relationships between civilians and the military. Both armies adopted the Articles of War, written in 1806, and both armies immediately applied them to civilians in the Confederacy and the United States, including the Border States. The Articles were chiefly concerned with how soldiers should treat each other, but they also made it clear that civilians were subordinate to the military. The two armies believed that they took the Articles with them wherever they went, and the respective war departments endorsed this view early in the conflict; troops in both armies arrested civilians whether or not the local court system was still operating. Article 56 prohibited anyone "whosoever" from assisting the enemy with money, victuals, or ammunition, and Article 57 prohibited anyone "whosoever" from corresponding with or giving intelligence to the enemy, while Article 60 declared that civilians who worked for the army could be subjected to military discipline. The United States Army published the Articles in their *Regulations* in 1861; the Confederate States also published the Articles that year, and in January 1863, when they formally published their own *Regulations*, they included the 1806 Articles verbatim.[3]

Yet both armies proved willing to exploit civilians for their own purposes, regardless of what policy might say. They permitted, encouraged, and rewarded certain actions by friendly civilians while punishing civilians who did the same to abet their foes. Rebel troops saw pro-Confederate whites as allies and pro-Union whites as enemies, while federal soldiers had the opposite perspective, of course. But men in both armies realized that civilians possessed extensive knowledge and many skills, and they cultivated civilians precisely because of the resources they had to offer. To complicate matters further, Northern commander John Pope issued several General Orders in July 1862, which were intended to shape military–civilian relations. Then Francis Lieber composed his eponymous Code in April 1863, which addressed in more general terms how armies could treat civilians. But, as events would prove, official policy had little impact on the behavior of soldiers on the ground.

PUBLIC OPINION

Troops in both armies knew that white Southern opinion was divided over secession and war, and they were acutely sensitive to manifestations of civilian support. Even though policy did not regulate these public dialogues, they constituted a significant psychological resource. Yankee troops arriving in Dixie in 1861 and early 1862 noticed any sign of pro-Union sentiment, and they rejoiced to see it. Private Oscar Ladley saw hundreds of local people waving the US flag as he and his comrades entered Grafton, Virginia, in June 1861. He knew it took courage to do so in front of their secessionist neighbors, whom he expected to retaliate against Unionists when they had the chance. Such brave, enthusiastic welcomes uplifted Northern troops wherever they traveled.[4]

Many rebel troops knew full well that the South included white Unionists, as well as whites who reluctantly went along with secession, so evidence of pro-Confederate feeling naturally reassured them. As men left home to join the army, the community organized farewell ceremonies replete with flag presentations, speeches, and loud cheers. When Corporal James E. Hall and his comrades marched through Beverly, Virginia, he was thrilled to see the inhabitants throw bouquets at their feet. While troops were in camp in the spring of 1861, civilians showed their loyalties with some elaborate political theater. At an army camp in Georgia, a group of civilians appeared toting a portrait of Edward Everett, the vice-presidential candidate on Unionist John Bell's ticket in 1860. After a rebel officer stabbed it with a bayonet, two women set fire to it with a torch.[5]

Conversely, men in both armies were acutely sensitive to signs of hostility from noncombatants. Yankee troops noticed who was amicable and who was not. In Culpeper, Virginia, Private Austin Stearns watched dumbfounded as a white woman prayed at a window for God to punish his army, which sent a chill through him. Lieutenant Colonel Charles Denby groused in Huntsville, Alabama, that "Nobody is friendly to us," and he felt so bad dealing with the "suppressed hate" of local civilians that he wished the war was over. Such antagonism could take an emotional toll among other officers. Colonel Joseph Revere proclaimed that "even the non-combatants conspire to destroy us by every means in their power." To defeat such a people, he believed the North needed a bigger, better-disciplined army.[6]

Southern troops wanted to be welcomed, too, and they could be just as closely attuned to civilian views. Colonel Patrick Cleburne reported that his troops did not meet a single "friend" as they marched through

HON. CHARLES DENBY,
Of Indiana.
Photograph by Hatton.

FIGURE 2.1 Federal Colonel Charles Denby.
Courtesy of the Library of Congress.

Kentucky in the fall of 1861, even though the state had officially declared its neutrality. Residents closed up their houses as women and children sprinted away, except for an elderly white lady who held up her Bible and told Cleburne she was ready to die. He obviously felt rattled. The same was true inside the Confederacy. In parts of Tennessee and Virginia, both states that had favored John Bell in 1860, Union supporters jeered as rebel troops marched through in 1861. Other whites simply did not respond to waving Confederate troops going by, which could be unnerving for soldiers in gray. One rebel soldier saw a family watching him from a porch in stone-cold silence, something he remembered for years afterwards.[7]

Indifference from civilians could disturb the troops just as much as signs of antagonism. Most soldiers in both armies seem to have assumed

FIGURE 2.2 Confederate Colonel Patrick Cleburne.
Courtesy of Duke University.

that everyone cared about the war, but some people did not care. Rebel
Private Edward Moore, who was strongly pro-Confederate, felt shocked
to hear a civilian say he had not lost an hour's sleep over the conflict,
just as Yankee General Jacob Cox, who was thoroughly pro-Union, was
stunned to meet people who had no interest in the world beyond their
own neighborhoods. Soldiers found neutral civilians almost as appalling.
J. M. Godown, an engineer with the US Army, believed that some white
Southerners had fluctuating loyalties, with both Union and Confederate
flags at the ready to display when different armies came through. Such
behavior raised the unsettling possibility that the armies could never win
some civilians to their side.[8]

After the fighting started, civilians and soldiers continued to
debate vigorously the war's politics. As troops marched through the
Confederacy, they sometimes paused to argue the issues with civilians,

although officers tried to silence these exchanges. In 1861 and 1862, in Charlestown, Virginia, Aquia Creek, Virginia, and Memphis, Tennessee, pro-Confederate men and women rushed into public places to dispute the war's causes with Yankee troops. In other places, such as Knoxville, Tennessee, rebel soldiers arriving in town taunted Unionists, who complained in return about how they were treated. But the troops could not always discern the opinions of civilians, some of whom maintained a prudent silence. Federal soldier James Graham talked to some small-scale slaveholders in Virginia, "nice people," he wrote, but he could not tell what they really thought about the war.[9]

SMUGGLING

In this uncertain political environment, white civilians expressed their loyalties, or the lack of them, in concrete fashion by smuggling goods. Even though Article 56 of the Articles of War prohibited anyone from giving money, victuals, or ammunition to the enemy, thousands of civilians became involved in smuggling, an important if unmeasured segment of the wartime economy, and they smuggled many items, not just money, victuals, or ammunition. After Fort Sumter, the illicit traffic of goods between the North and the South exploded. The North had many supplies that the rebel military needed, and, as time passed, the civilian population in the South also needed increasingly scarce household goods. A brisk, high-volume illegal trade began as soon as the war broke out. In May 1861, civilians were already smuggling military stores from Baltimore into Virginia, and soon the most mundane items, such as matches, would become valuable. Plenty of Northerners were willing to sell goods to people on the other side, and pro-Confederate Southerners were eager to pay for them.[10]

The motives of civilian smugglers ran the gamut – financial, familial, and political. Alive to the possibility of making a quick profit, a common motive in wartime, many people became involved for that simple reason. In the autumn of 1861, the *Richmond Examiner* estimated that smugglers working between Virginia and the Union states had already made several million dollars in gold. Individuals who were not particularly interested in lucre smuggled to aid their kinfolk, leaving their surnames off their letters as the Northerner "Dick" did when he wrote to "Ned." Southerners who believed in the Confederacy acted out of political conviction, such as the disabled rebel soldier who embarked on a career as a smuggler, moving goods between Virginia,

Pennsylvania, and Maryland. Conversely, Southerners who wanted to assist the Union smuggled cotton, sugar, and rice into the North through Kentucky and sold it. But since most of the fighting took place in Dixie, and the Southern economy was never as productive as its Northern counterpart, most of the smugglers were importing goods from the North to the South.[11]

Smugglers relied on the time-honored methods of subterfuge, as civilians have done in other wars. Some of them used aliases, and many showed considerable entrepreneurial skill. One gang shipped goods hundreds of miles, sending goods overland through Kentucky and then by boat up the Tennessee River to railroad stations, where the materials were reshipped to other destinations. Others hid their cargo inside trunks with false bottoms, or, for the even more creative, inside the carcasses of dead horses. One especially clever fellow, William T. Wilson of Saint Mary's County, Maryland, put liquid quinine in an animal bladder and concealed it in his hat before he was caught.[12]

White Southern women, too, smuggled goods into the Confederacy and within the Confederacy. Newly politicized and eager to serve the rebel cause, they were willing to deploy traditional assumptions about gender – that women were purely domestic beings – as a cover. Mrs. Wood, her full name unknown, ran a smugglers' gang based in Hopkinsville, Kentucky, shipping goods to regular partners in Nashville and Richmond in 1861 and 1862. Female smugglers took advantage of similar notions that women were physically weak and would not use firearms. Nannie Webster pulled a gun and forced a man to row her across the Potomac River from Maryland to Virginia, bringing with her quinine, thread, and needles. The fashions of the day, such as the hoop skirt, allowed the wearer to hide goods such as boots and newspapers inside its wide circumference.[13]

Smugglers trafficked in a wide array of material goods, including but not restricted to those prohibited by the Articles of War. They brought in salt, guns, luxury items such as lace, and lots of drugs, including morphine. People from many backgrounds participated, including a doctor from Memphis and a minister from Baltimore. The stereotype developed that Jewish Americans dominated the smuggling business, and US Brigadier General Ulysses S. Grant acted on that belief when he expelled Jews from his department in Kentucky, Tennessee, and Mississippi with General Orders No. 11 in December 1862; President Lincoln quickly revoked the order in the face of protests. Most smugglers, like the vast majority of white civilians in the North and South, were in fact Gentiles.[14]

Civilian smugglers tended to favor certain routes, which are revealed in the footprints of those who were caught. From the Border State of Maryland, individuals crossed the Potomac River into the Confederacy, taking advantage of that river's coves, islands, and tributaries, and southern Maryland had a number of rebel sympathizers willing to traverse the Potomac with verboten goods for the Confederacy. Smugglers frequently traveled through Kentucky, a slave state that remained in the Union, albeit as a neutral party, in 1861. The Bluegrass State was a perfect crossroads, hugging the Ohio River, facing a major inland port in the United States, Cincinnati, and bordering two Confederate states, Virginia and Tennessee, with a deeply divided civilian population within its borders. Kentucky reached an informal, temporary agreement with Tennessee in 1861 to let trains move between the two states without Yankee officers examining the luggage, but even after Kentucky allied with the United States in 1862, smugglers continued to work through the state.[15]

Smugglers did get caught, and sometimes they were punished. Civilians such as John Fowler, a teamster in Union-occupied Virginia, eagerly turned them over to authorities. He identified an Englishman, or a man claiming to be English, who carried illegal goods between northern Virginia and southern Maryland. When smugglers were captured in Union territory, they were typically hauled before military commissions or courts-martial, rather than the local courts. They could receive severe punishments from the military, such as Myer Lusky, a tavern-keeper in Nashville, who faced a year at hard labor for smuggling drugs, while others escaped with light sentences. Sely Lewis, who was convicted in Tennessee of smuggling and spying for the Confederacy, had his death sentence commuted to six months in prison by Abraham Lincoln.[16]

Efforts to stop smuggling could fall short because of corruption and ineptitude in the Yankee military. In every war, soldiers have violated the rules to make money, and enforcement mechanisms in the military have failed to prevent wrongdoing. In 1862, smugglers working between Memphis and Hernando, Mississippi, put on federal army uniforms and posed as commissary clerks and quartermaster clerks, and they got away with it, trafficking in quinine and morphine. The Northern army used detectives to sniff out smuggling in US-occupied territories with some success, but they never could completely halt the illicit activity. Major General William T. Sherman bemoaned the way that goods were smuggled over the Mississippi River into Memphis and the Confederate interior, despite the Union military's presence.[17]

For obvious reasons, the Confederate War Department did not try to interrupt smuggling into the region. Colonel Dorsey Pender, in camp near Manassas, Virginia, in August 1861, conversed with some white women who had smuggled trunks of soldier uniforms into the state from Maryland. He seemed to admire their dedication, and he did not have them arrested. In fact, the Confederate military participated directly in such activities. Officers contracted to smuggle arms over the Rio Grande from Mexico, a frequent resort to avoid the Union naval blockade, while other officers, such as General Samuel G. French, discovered smuggling rings and urged rebel quartermasters to join them to benefit the Southern military.[18]

Blockade-runners possessed of even more daring, or maybe more powerful greed, could make a great deal of money. The Union blockade terminated much but not all of the naval traffic in and out of the Confederacy, and those men who slipped through could reap large profits. Southern newspapers informed readers that blockade-runners could sell cargo for ten times the cost. The vessels sold cotton overseas and returned laden with arms, munitions, and gunpowder. The identities of blockade-runners are hard to trace, but we can flesh out the biographies of those who were captured. Stephen Barton, the brother of Union army nurse Clara Barton, smuggled out of greed. In the 1850s, he left Massachusetts after being charged with bank robbery; although he was acquitted, his reputation never recovered. He moved to North Carolina, where he prospered as a miller until 1861, but he wanted to make yet more money, so he started running the Union blockade. He was caught, court-martialed, and eventually released. Just before the war ended, he died.[19]

CORRESPONDENCE

White civilians managed to evade another Article of War, Article 57, which prohibited anyone from corresponding with or conveying information to the enemy; it further stipulated that any person doing so could be court-martialed, with a possible death sentence. The war prompted a huge outpouring of personal correspondence by soldiers and civilians, as people wrote for practical reasons to convey information and for personal reasons, among them to document the fact that the author was still alive. Whatever the purpose of the letter, mail delivery between the United States and the Confederacy was supposed to end in June 1861, but some postmasters delivered mail between the regions for several months afterwards. Kentucky's declaration of neutrality in 1861 allowed its residents to send letters to both sides, and in other places in the South, the mail was exchanged by agreement between officers or bureaucrats on both sides so long as the letters were apolitical.[20]

White Southern civilians soon figured out how to transmit letters outside these channels. Some of them turned to civilian mail runners who delivered packets of letters between the North and South, but most of them seem to have acted on their own. They smuggled letters out of the Confederacy on heavily traveled routes from northern Virginia to southern Maryland and within the Confederacy. There were "*many ways*" to transmit letters despite the Yankee army's presence, Sallie McDowell of Tennessee remarked. Just as they had before the war, civilians turned to friends, kinfolk, and neighbors who slipped through federal lines to hand-deliver letters, a few missives at a time, running what one Unionist angrily called their own "Rebel Post office."[21]

Both armies attempted to stem this flood of illicit correspondence whenever it hurt their own interests. The US War Department intercepted personal letters sent outside approved channels and examined them for political content. The army court-martialed a few civilians for carrying "rebel mail," and some of them received tough sentences, such as Thomas Dibboe of Tennessee, who was sentenced to hard labor at Johnson's Island for the war's duration. Confederate officers in turn arrested civilians for sending letters to the North containing information beneficial to the enemy. In these cases, too, the punishments could be serious. John H. Larhhorne went to prison for taking a family epistle – a single letter by his sister to her husband – from Virginia to Maryland. There were apparently no executions of civilians who carried mail, but the high volume of mail overwhelmed both armies. Joseph Ives, a colonel on Jefferson Davis's staff, observed in 1862 that no one had the "endurance" to check dozens of personal letters for military information.[22]

Yet soldiers in the two armies wanted to benefit from the contents of the mail, harvesting the letters while preventing the adversary from doing the same. When pro-Confederate civilians spontaneously took over mail delivery in parts of the region during the secession winter, the Southern government compensated them for their services, but in the summer of 1861, Confederate officers arrested civilians for trying to send letters northward that allegedly gave information to the enemy. Soldiers in both armies opened letters that came into their hands by chance, scouring for reliable knowledge of army size, travel routes, and the health of the men. In July 1862, Yankee Brigadier General Philip

Sheridan discovered a package of thirty-two private letters in Ripley, Mississippi, which gave him useful information on the movements of Braxton Bragg's army.[23]

ESPIONAGE

White civilians did more than smuggle letters: they gathered information themselves for the military, although this too violated Article 57 of the Articles of War. Both armies hoped to obtain intelligence from their civilian allies, while preventing the enemy from doing the same. The history of wartime espionage is underdocumented because of its very nature, but information gathered by human beings has always been considered the most reliable form of intelligence. During the Civil War, many civilians spied for the armies, although we will never know all of their names. Military figures often referred to their sources only as "citizens," probably to conceal their identities. Southern communities buzzed with rumor, gossip, and speculation, just as they had before 1861. In Bowling Green, Kentucky, Unionist Josie Underwood saw "people in groups, earnestly talking" about the latest news, clustered together according to their political loyalties, as women drove by in carriages paying social calls. Now citizens assiduously collected information about each other. When Thirza Finch visited neighbors in Virginia, they pressed her for details about her brother's service in the federal army, but she hardly dared speak for fear that what she called "the secesh" would give information to other Confederates.[24]

Many civilians demonstrated their fealty by giving the armies information about the South's geography, particularly the transportation routes. The Confederacy was a big place, and much of the landscape was unfamiliar to the soldiers. Both armies encountered a byzantine network of plank roads, aging turnpikes, and winding footpaths dating from Native American times, not to mention fast-moving rivers and rushing creeks without bridges or discernible fords. Rebel soldiers serving far from home did not always know the terrain, so knowledgeable civilians could assist a great deal. These civilians acted spontaneously, stepping forward when the armies appeared. In the summer of 1861, Mr. Skeen, a local white man, offered to make a map of the countryside near Huntersville, Virginia, for Confederate General Stephen Lee, who happily accepted. The same was true, of course, for Unionists. White residents who knew "every hog-path in the country" guided Union troops through Virginia, much to the chagrin of Southern officers.[25]

Pro-Confederate civilians also helped their army by gathering information about enemy troop movements. They eagerly shared what they knew with the rebel army, sometimes because they received payments, other times out of Confederate patriotism. They could deliver useful information in the very midst of combat. During the Battle of First Bull Run, a young woman galloped up to tell rebel officers about the position of Northern troops, and a witness noted she seemed indifferent to physical danger. Soldiers could be saved by a quick tip-off from civilians. Whites living near Corinth, Mississippi, warned rebel officers that they were about to be ambushed by federal troops, so they escaped.[26]

Pro-Union civilians did what they could to assist the Northern army, giving similar insights about enemy troops to their allies. Yankee troops received information from slaves, but many of them seemed more likely to rely on white people. These civilians, too, spied out of political conviction, and other did it to fill their pockets. Whatever their motives, they did what they could. In rural Virginia, a white man, unidentified, warned troops of the enemy cavalry's presence in an orchard half a mile away. From Tennessee, William Blount Carter wrote directly to a federal general in October 1861, giving the number of Confederate soldiers in Knoxville and other concrete details about the foe. He added that he was risking his life by sending the letter.[27]

Troops in both armies realized that white Southern civilians could deliberately provide misinformation, what we would call counterintelligence, to put them in jeopardy. One Mr. Rodan, a farmer near Bird's Point, Missouri, assured a federal captain that there were no rebel soldiers in the area, but moments later Confederate troops ambushed the captain and his men. Union sympathizers purposely gave false information in order to "cripple our movements," according to Felix Zollicoffer, the Southern brigadier general. Some officers understandably came to distrust many noncombatants, as have other soldiers in other wars. Union General Jacob Cox concluded that civilians could provide useful intelligence, with some qualifications: he thought that well-meaning, friendly civilians overdid the information, while hostile civilians found it hard to remain silent.[28]

Neither side had an organized spy service, so the two armies improvised, allowing officers to set up their own espionage networks. In June 1861, Yankee Colonel Harvey Brown, serving at Fort Pickens, Florida, asked the commanding officer for "secret-service money" to be spent at his own discretion, while Confederate General Robert E. Lee gave a subordinate officer several hundred dollars for his own "secret service." Flashy civilian personalities such as Rose Greenhow, Belle Boyd, and James J. Andrews engaged in espionage, but spying was more often conducted by people who avoided the limelight. The numbers were probably small, since today's professional spies assert that very few people are capable of doing effective espionage.[29]

The specter of professional, full-time spies nevertheless seemed to frighten people more than civilians who spontaneously gave information to soldiers. Any person out of place, anyone who seemed to ask too many questions could arouse suspicion. In May 1861, two citizens persuaded Confederate Brigadier General Joseph E. Johnston that R. W. Latham, a banker from Washington, DC, was traveling the South to spy for the Union. Johnston communicated this to Robert E. Lee, exclaiming that Latham, who had not even been interviewed, deserved to be hanged. In a similar vein, local whites suspected a man working as a sutler near Fort Monroe, Virginia, was a Yankee spy, but they could not prove it. The authorities sometimes made mistakes when they released suspects. Federal authorities arrested Meredith Gilmore of Maryland as a rebel spy in 1861, then released him, whereupon he joined the Southern army.[30]

Civilians who worked full-time as spies had strong ideological commitments, daring, and guile. Early in the war, one affluent white family moved to Virginia for the purpose of espionage. The wife, name unknown, declaimed about her Confederate loyalties, but she was actually spying for the Union, something a white man in her employ disclosed after the family abruptly disappeared with the federal army. Civilians from all social backgrounds committed espionage, as rebels came to understand. In New Orleans, Confederate authorities kept two carpenters under surveillance for months before arresting them in January 1862 for espionage. Yankee soldiers suspected that neighborhood people spied on them, as well. They forced one Mrs. Tompkins, a Confederate officer's wife, to leave her Virginia mansion in the winter of 1861–1862 because they feared that she was signaling the enemy about troop movements.[31]

Female spies proved willing to defy traditional gender conventions even as they simultaneously turned them to their advantage. In 1862, a US provost marshal in Wheeling, West Virginia, arrested a female spy dressed in a Yankee cavalryman's uniform. Calling herself Marian McKenzie, she led a life full of melodrama and what seems to be a high level of spycraft. She professed to be a Scottish immigrant and an orphan who worked as an actress, a prostitute, and at other occupations before the war, and she joined the military out of "love of excitement." Disguising herself as a man, she managed to serve in both armies and was a good soldier by one account. When she was arrested for spying for the Confederacy, she insisted she had done nothing wrong except perhaps donning men's attire. She had multiple identities. Among her aliases were Miss Fitzallen (while she was a prostitute), Harry Fitzallen (while she was a soldier), and Marian McKenzie (possibly her real name). An arresting officer portrayed her as short, physically strong, well-spoken, and "well skilled in the inequities of the world." Such an individual could be an asset to either army.[32]

Other civilians who violated Article 57 by providing information to the enemy did get caught. Federal court-martial records show that a few civilians were arrested for espionage, although some of those were released, apparently because of the lack of proof; these people represent a small percentage of the civilians who gave information to rebel forces. The same is true for Unionists who helped the Northern army. Rebel court-martial records did not survive the war, but prisoner-of-war documents show that the Confederate army arrested civilians who gave information to the other army, starting with the Battle of First Bull Run. In 1862, suspected Unionists were arrested in Atlanta but then released, and some escaped the city. A tiny number of civilians were executed for spying, but the Southern army, like the Northern army, could never prevent civilians from supplying intelligence to the enemy.[33]

WORKING FOR THE MILITARY

Both armies employed many thousands of civilians, which was common in nineteenth-century societies at war. Article 60 of the Articles of War made it clear that all civilians employed by the military would be disciplined by the military. More noncombatants probably labored for the Confederate side, since the war unfolded in the South, but they labored for both armies, which could boost the local economy. The Confederacy impressed slaves to work for the government, but thousands of white civilians, at least 70,000 by one scholar's estimate, worked for the rebel war department. The Southern government sometimes required its workers to take an oath of allegiance to the Confederacy, although that policy was not consistently enforced.[34]

In 1861 and 1862, white men held a variety of jobs for the Confederacy. Tailors made uniforms for the soldiers, and tanners turned animal hides into leather for multiple military uses. White women labored for the rebel government as well, working as clerks, hospital matrons, and nurses. The Southern military understood that civilian labor was crucial to the war effort. Secretary of the Navy Stephen Mallory advised the commander of the Norfolk naval yard to hire as many civilian mechanics as he needed to "push the work" forward on the ironclads under construction.[35]

Civilians signed contracts with the rebel army to supply the military with almost everything necessary to wage war, and those contracts could be quite lucrative. Some civilians did it for economic reasons, of course, while others did it because of ideology, and yet others for some combination of both motives. Confederate regulations stipulated that wartime contracts would be rewarded via a rigorous process designed to reward low bids, save money, and prevent fraud, but, much like other societies at war, the system could be abused. Civilians who had army contracts sometimes alleged that favoritism and profiteering characterized the decision-making process inside the Southern government.[36]

The rebel military could be an unpredictable employer, showing little consideration for what the average worker needed to make a living. When soldiers seized tools from the blacksmith James F. Brown, they did not return them or pay him for the loss, and his claim for compensation was denied. The army also impressed white male workers on an ad-hoc basis, whether they wanted to work or not. During the Peninsular Campaign, Captain William W. Blackford built a pontoon bridge on the James River in Richmond by impressing over 500 men, white and black, and forcing them to work around the clock for five days until the task was done. The men received a salary and free meals, but the element of coercion is clear. Another white woman, one Mrs. Colvrick, did the washing at Fort Livingston in Louisiana for over a year with no salary. When rebel troops evacuated the fort in April 1862, they left her with nothing to eat.[37]

Moreover, the white Southern workforce was restive, sometimes intractable. Again, like workers in other societies at war, these people took army jobs from a variety of motives. Some wanted to support the Confederate effort, of course, but some employees had no apparent political loyalties, such as a telegraph worker, Mr. Rosewater, who labored for the Confederacy until 1862, when he drifted to Washington to work for the US War Department. Some young men took jobs in Confederate-run factories only because they would be exempted from military service. Despite the stipulations in the Articles of War, the army could not keep all their workers in place; in Louisiana, for instance, carpenters struck for higher wages during the war's first winter. In 1863, when the Confederacy issued its own military regulations, they included almost no protections for civilian workers. They did require that laundresses and other workers would receive daily food rations, too late to help Mrs. Colvrick in

Louisiana. But the regulations spelled out, just as the Articles of War did, that all laborers should be subject to "military control."[38]

The Union army employed white Southern civilians, too, and similar issues arose with their workforce. The exact number of laborers is unknown, since each chief quartermaster was responsible for hiring his own workers, and not all officers kept records. But a single quartermaster, James Rusling, stated that he employed "many thousands" of Southern civilians. In Union-occupied areas, the army commonly required civilian workers to take the oath of the allegiance to the United States before they could work for the military, and many were willing to do so. The worker population was diverse, in every sense. In New Orleans, General Benjamin Butler employed some 2,000 denizens – the native-born, immigrants, men and women – to clean up the city soon after he arrived. Few civilians who labored for the Northern army articulated their motives, but some were eager Unionists, such as the unidentified widow who did washing and cooking for Yankee troops near Memphis. Yet others cared little for ideology. A Tennessean passed herself off as a man and landed a job as an army teamster; after her gender was discovered, she was discharged. She seemed indifferent to politics.[39]

Relations between these workers and the Union army could be fractious, just as they were between workers and the Confederate army. John Spooner, a white man who lived near Chattanooga, found this out the hard way. A native of eastern Tennessee, he moved to the area in 1862, when he agreed to deliver coal and lumber to a Union army camp near his home. For that job, he received generous support: his own blacksmith shop, food rations, clothing, and tools for his workers. Then the army suddenly canceled the contract for reasons the civilian and the military disputed. He claimed it was the "gross favoritism" of a captain who gave the contract to someone else, while an army quartermaster responded that it was the poor quality of Spooner's work. In revenge, it seems, Spooner kept the tools the military gave him. After 1865, the army rejected his attempt to collect money for the unfulfilled contract.[40]

Yet other civilians participated in the underground economy that springs up magically in every society at war. Counterfeit money circulated between quartermasters, banks, and civilians, frequently with the knowledge of the participants, while other persons of indifferent loyalties engaged in illicit trade with the armies, such as the Tennessean who made his living by selling bootleg whiskey to Confederate soldiers. The importance of economic survival is visible in how the neighbors rallied for one Mr. Hudgings, a merchant in Mississippi County, Arkansas. He sold goods to anyone who could pay for them, and his neighbors protested when rebel troops seized his property because, they said, he was the only merchant in the area, he was politically neutral, and the community depended on him.[41]

CIVILIANS IN MOTION

The Southern white population continued to be highly mobile after 1861, despite the efforts of both armies to limit that mobility. In August 1861, the War Department in Richmond began requiring passes or passports for civilians who wished to leave the city; the authorities used the words *pass* and *passport* interchangeably to describe these pieces of paper. War Department clerks started issuing them by the thousands, and within a few years the practice had spread to other Confederate cities. Most people who wanted to travel had to take an oath of allegiance to the Confederacy, which civilians complained about, disliking the inconvenience as well as the similarity to the antebellum passes issued to slaves.[42]

The Confederate passport system did not work very efficiently. The passes themselves were often improvised, as some officers wrote them by hand on pages torn out of ledger books. Civilians managed to obtain blank passes and share them with friends, while others got passes by fraudulent means, the details unknown. "Military authorities" in any location could issue passports, as could any rebel governor, or the occasional self-styled "passport committee," such as one formed in Nashville in 1861, the membership unspecified. Officials could give out passes for personal reasons, such as the officer who gave a passport to a young white woman, Cora Mitchel, because he felt sorry for her. The troops asked civilians in the cities and on the railroads to show their passes, but many people lived in the countryside and traveled by horseback, by carriage, or on foot, and thus avoided detection.[43]

The Northern military used a passport system to control the civilian population in occupied territory, with the same mixed results. From the start of the war, the Yankee army required all civilians in occupied areas to ask a provost marshal for passes if they wished to move beyond Union lines, and many of them complied. Some officers made applicants take oaths of allegiance to the United States, but some did not. The same patchy rules applied to civilian travel out of the Confederacy. Southern civilians could get passes for journeys to the North if they wished, and sometimes they had to take the oath, sometimes not. Friendly Confederate pickets could let civilians travel without a pass into the North, allowing W. H. Krantz, a miller from Virginia, into the Union because he wanted to visit his mother.[44]

From the war's beginning, corruption, incompetence, and everyday sloppiness plagued the federal passport system. In Tennessee, civilians bribed military clerks for passes – 100 American dollars per pass – while other civilians acquired forged or altered passes enabling them to travel within the Confederacy, through the Union-occupied South, and into the North. Sometimes the permission was verbal, with no passes or paperwork involved. After Anne Frobel and her sister Lizzie visited friends in Alexandria, Virginia, in 1861, they could not get permission to return to their country home. They asked a provost marshal and two officers for passes but were refused. They waited in a buggy in Alexandria for several hours before a Yankee soldier hollered at them, "go on," and they were allowed to leave.[45]

Furthermore, many white people continued to travel from the Union into the Confederacy. The two regions were not tightly sealed off after Fort Sumter, as historians once assumed. Northerners wishing to head south applied for passports from the US Secretary of State, many of them stating that they wished to make apolitical visits to relatives, and a minority of applicants received passports. Yankee civilians who were denied passes knew how to obtain them anyway through purchase on the black market from officials who would sell to civilians. Nor were the procedures enforced consistently. As Clara Judd moved from Tennessee to Minnesota and back to the South, visiting kinsmen and seeking work, she traveled sometimes with a pass, sometimes without one, and at least once with a pass obtained from a friend. Despite the blockade, Europeans could enter the region to join the Southern army or take jobs in the government. Thus the armies encountered thousands of people on the move, many of them enigmas, some of them evidently moving with no purpose, others traveling with great determination. The swirling, eddying population was always changing, a sea of new faces who could be either friends or foes, under neither army's control.[46]

HOSTAGES

The armies perceived white civilians as resources in yet another way, as potential hostages. Both armies took civilian hostages, a practice that originated in ancient times and has persisted into the modern era; it was not banned until the Geneva Conventions of 1949. In the past, armies have taken hostages to force the enemy to fulfill an agreement; to exact revenge on the enemy; or to advance specific military objectives. Civilians have also volunteered to serve as hostages for altruistic reasons, but during the American Civil War armies usually took civilian hostages against their will. Hostage-taking occurred all over the South, not just in the border regions, and it happened routinely throughout the war, involving many civilians. The Articles of War and Henry Lee Scott's *Military Dictionary* provided no guidance on how to treat hostages, nor did the *Regulations* of either army. The Lieber Code, issued in 1863 by the Northern army, did. But troops in both armies had a free hand for the first two years of the war.[47]

Hostage-taking was inaugurated in 1861, in the first months of combat. The total number of hostages is unknown, but it reached into the hundreds, if not the thousands. Both armies took hostages for the purpose of changing the enemy's behavior. Confederate authorities were known to zero in on the Unionists in their midst. For example, they arrested a Tennessee farmer named Harrison Self in the fall of 1861 for being a bridge-burner who was loyal to the Union. Southern Lieutenant Colonel Reuben Arnold suggested allowing Self's two sons to enlist in the rebel army and holding Self as a hostage indefinitely to ensure their "good behavior." The officer made this proposal even though he thought Self was probably innocent of bridge-burning. Rebel officers seized hostages in the Border States, such as a physician, one Mr. Smith of Kentucky, and, when they had the opportunity, civilians in the Northern states. Near Winchester, Virginia, General Robert E. Lee told a subordinate to try to seize Northern government officials as hostages to exchange for "our own citizens" taken by the Union.[48]

When the federal army began to take civilian hostages early in the war, their troops showed the same sense of entitlement. They seized both women and men. In June of 1861, troops in Virginia took two adult daughters of a Mr. West as hostages after they found a Confederate uniform in the family dwelling; they planned to keep the women, unnamed, in a fort indefinitely to ensure the father's "good behavior," which presumably meant staying out of the rebel army. They seized members of local elites in the cities they occupied. In Nashville, a Yankee general selected two "wealthy rebels" to hold as hostages in the penitentiary for the return of two Unionists held by the other army in Chattanooga. Some officers, such as Major General Benjamin Butler, wanted the process of hostage-taking to be formalized. After exchanging hostages with Confederate forces at Opelousas, Louisiana, in 1862, he hoped that an agreement could be made to relieve the "pressure" on these noncombatants, but no such agreement was ever reached.[49]

The Northern and Southern press criticized hostage-taking when the other side engaged in it, but both armies treated it as standard practice in their own ranks. Sometimes authorities chose hostages precisely because they were accomplished civilians, although they also picked up individuals by chance, as they encountered them on the march. The two armies incarcerated their hostages in different places – military camps, forts, or hidden away in the countryside, their whereabouts unknown. The officers involved had a great deal of latitude. They rescued hostages before they were formally exchanged, and they freed their own hostages at will. There is no evidence of mass execution of hostages, but things ended badly for some of them. When the two rebel civilians, names unknown, tried to escape from captivity in Nashville, one hostage was recaptured and the other was killed.[50]

As we have seen with other aspects of military behavior, there was an improvised quality to hostage-taking. The armies took hostages to protest the enemy's conduct toward civilians, even if it turned out to be futile. In December 1862, Robert E. Lee advised that a federal army major from West Virginia be held as a hostage to protest the Yankee policy of making rebel civilians take the oath of allegiance in occupied areas. (Needless to say, the US military did not change that policy to accommodate Lee.) Sometimes the armies practiced numerical equivalence – one person taken to exchange for another person – but sometimes they did not, taking a slew of civilian hostages to spring one individual from captivity. Almost all of the hostages were white, although slaves could be caught up in the process. In Missouri, a federal major seized as a hostage the slave of a Confederate civilian, Mr. Adams, to force him to return the slave owned by a white Unionist, Mrs. Joy. Neither slave is identified, and the records do not indicate what happened to them after Adams's slave was taken.[51]

The treatment of civilian hostages varied a good deal. Confederate General Robert E. Lee stated that hostages should be handled with "respect," and Yankee General Adolph von Steinwehr promised that his civilian hostages would share his table and be treated as "friends." He then threatened to shoot hostages if local guerrillas killed any of his troops, which was not very friendly. Some officers permitted hostages to roam around in the towns where they were held, so long as they stayed within town limits, while others put hostages in irons. Regardless of how civilian hostages were treated, few apparently succumbed to what we call Stockholm Syndrome, in which they identified with their kidnappers.

In fact, some hostages developed a deep animus for their captors and a lasting admiration for their rescuers. When a country doctor died in Kentucky decades later, his obituary mentioned his gratitude to the Union captain who rescued him from the Confederates.[52]

In 1862, George C. Rowe of Fredericksburg, Virginia, kept a rare diary of his experience as a hostage. He conveyed overwhelming feelings of powerlessness and a burning resentment against both armies. In his thirties when the war started, he was a successful attorney and a political moderate, serving as an elector for Democrat Stephen Douglas in 1860. He supported the Confederacy after Virginia seceded, but did not join the military. In 1862, Yankee forces took him hostage along with eighteen other men in retaliation for Virginia Unionists seized by Confederates. One August night, an officer with a weapon drawn appeared at his door and took him with other hostages to the Old Capitol Prison in Washington, DC. There he stayed for a month, disgusted at the filthy cell and the execrable food. He mingled with other prisoners, some of whom he liked and some of whom he feared, but the indignity of being held against his will infuriated him. He and his fellow hostages blamed both armies for their plight, Northerners for their "despotic power" and Southerners for taking Unionist hostages. They wrote to Secretary of War Edwin Stanton, asking to be released, with no luck. Then Rowe met with War Department officials, but refused to take the oath of allegiance. He argued with his guards, one of whom threatened to kill him. Gifts from friends and a visit from his wife kept his spirits up until he was released in a hostage exchange in September 1862. After he received a passport, he joyfully returned home.[53]

In the spring of 1863, the North published a new code of conduct for its army, including the treatment of hostages. The author, Francis Lieber, was smart, ambitious, and volatile, a complicated man with piercing eyes in a grim visage. A Berlin native, he fought as a teenager against Napoleon and later in the Greek War for Independence. He migrated to America and took a job in the 1830s at the University of South Carolina. During his twenty-one years as a professor there, he published some influential work on political theory, forging a reputation as a liberal, but his actions on slavery were anything but progressive. He bought several house slaves, claiming that he treated them better than most masters, and he rejected abolition as a federal measure; one distant day, he thought, state-by-state emancipation might happen. He was on cordial terms with the state's slaveowners, among them John C. Calhoun. But he became uncomfortable as secessionist feeling rose in the South, and in 1857, he

FIGURE 2.3 Franz Lieber, war theorist.
Courtesy of the Library of Congress.

joined the faculty at New York's Columbia University. He evidently sold his slaves – although the evidence is not clear – and in 1861, he became a Unionist and backed emancipation. His family divided, with his sons serving in opposing armies.[54]

After 1861, Lieber supported the Republican Party and advocated a vigorous prosecution of the war. He contacted several officers, suggesting that he write a code of military conduct, and in 1862, US General Henry Halleck appointed him to a committee created for that purpose. Lieber wrote most of the document, which bore his name when it was published on April 24, 1863, as General Orders Number 100. The Code consisted of a long disjointed list of articles, 157 in toto, many of them focusing on relations between armies and civilians. Lieber's Code, like his life, was filled with contradictions. On the one hand, he wrote that the army should disturb unarmed civilians as little as possible and spare them as much as the "exigencies of war" would permit. Modern armies must protect noncombatants, he insisted, unlike armies of the ancient world. On the other hand, he argued that civilians of a hostile country are enemies and are therefore subject to the hardships of war. Throughout his Code, Lieber emphasized the prime importance of what he called "military necessity," meaning that soldiers could take any measure necessary to advance the Union cause, including the deaths of "armed enemies" and "other persons." No cruel behavior was allowed, but "deception" was acceptable so long as it did not include "perfidy," a distinction without a difference. In fact, the Code featured so many contradictions it could be used to justify almost any action a soldier might take. His work reflected an uneasy compound of Old World and New, with traces of the Napoleonic Era of Lieber's youth mixed with his Unionism of 1861.[55]

Lieber also declared that hostages were rare in the modern era, a baffling statement in light of the Northern press's coverage of hostage-taking by both armies. He defined a hostage as a person taken "in consequence of a war" or as a "pledge" to ensure the fulfillment of an agreement between the two armies. He further indicated that a hostage was to be treated as a prisoner of war, meaning that he (Lieber's choice of pronouns) should not be punished, treated cruelly, or deprived of food, but he could also be subject to retaliation, just as a prisoner of war could be subjected to it. Regardless of these contradictions, Lieber's Code seems to have had little, if any, impact on the federal military's treatment of hostages. Although it was reprinted and distributed as a pamphlet for men in the field, soldiers and officers almost never mentioned the Code in their correspondence or memoirs. Some of them may have never heard of it. Future generations called the Lieber Code a model for regulating conduct in war, but by the spring of 1863, the army had already settled on its own ideas about how soldiers could treat hostages. Confederates ridiculed the Lieber Code, as we might expect, for its hypocrisy, but they too disregarded its assumptions in their treatment of hostages.[56]

After Lieber's Code was published, the federal army continued to take hostages and treat them as they wished, just as they had before April 1863. Civilian hostages were held in army camps, local jails, and prisons, in some cases hundreds of miles from where they lived. Each side accused the other of treating hostages cruelly. In December 1863, General George Thomas alleged that Confederates held a Unionist hostage in a "loathsome" jail, at the same time that Zebulon Vance, rebel governor of North Carolina, alleged that Yankee troops put female hostages in handcuffs. The armies seized women because of the activities of men, even though the Code suggested that hostages were supposed to be male. In Louisiana, a federal colonel ordered that a local woman, Mrs. Wilcoxen, be taken as a hostage after her husband shot a Yankee private taking food from their residence. The colonel planned to hold her in custody until her husband turned himself in to the Northern army.[57]

Soldiers continued yet other hostage-taking practices, regardless of Lieber's announcement. They followed numerical equivalency, taking five pro-Confederate civilian hostages to exchange for five pro-Union civilian hostages in Missouri, except when they did not: in Louisiana, US General Nathaniel Banks ordered that 100 white men be taken at random to serve as hostages until a federal captain's murder was solved. They still engaged in retaliation, punishing civilians for their relatives' actions. In December 1863, Yankee Major James T. Holmes took as a hostage Mr. D. W. Kimbrough of Tennessee because Kimbrough's son, a rebel officer, captured two federal soldiers; the two Northerners were then freed. Hostages continued to be taken by both armies because of events no civilian could control. Rebel General John Imboden hauled thirty-five hostages, both civilians and Union soldiers, from West Virginia to Richmond, insisting that they be detained for the release of unidentified "Southern sympathizers" held as hostages somewhere in the North. Whether we are discussing smugglers, letter-writers, spies, workers, travelers, or hostages, military policy had a negligible impact on how the two armies interacted with civilians. The same turned out to be true for material resources, starting with food.[58]

3

Sustenance

Soldiers in both armies needed food to survive, and that material necessity had to be met on a daily basis. Hunger was harder to endure than any other wartime deprivation, said Yankee veteran J. D. Bloodgood. In many conflicts, food has been judged the most important supply item needed to maintain an army and bolster morale; as Napoleon remarked, an army travels on its stomach. In ancient times, armies regularly plundered civilians of their viands, but in the modern world, rations were supposed to allow troops to traverse a landscape without living off civilians. Both armies in the American Civil War were expected to feed men with their own supplies, provided by their commissary officers and quartermasters, but neither army was sufficiently well-organized to do that on a regular basis. Like soldiers in other wars, troops in the Union and Confederate armies turned to civilians to meet their need for sustenance, and they often violated policy as they did so. Some of the region's civilians gladly gave food to the armies, especially in the war's early phases, but many more were unwilling to part with victuals necessary for their own survival. Soon the two populations, military and civilian, contended in an increasingly hard fight over food.[1]

The American military had guidelines on foraging, which all emphasized that civilians must comply with the army's demands. The Articles of War, in effect since 1806, were supposed to put some limits on army behavior in wartime, although it was clear that the military's needs came first. Article 52 broadcast that no soldier would leave his post to "plunder and pillage" and stipulated that troops who did so could be court-martialed and sentenced to death. The Articles did not define plunder or pillage, but the *Oxford English Dictionary* defines plunder as the taking of spoils and pillage as the sacking of a place or a person. Article 54 required soldiers and officers to behave in an "orderly" fashion on the march; they could not "waste or spoil" the trees, warrens, ponds, gardens, cornfields, or meadows owned by civilians unless ordered to do so by an army commander; those soldiers who damaged trees, gardens, or meadows without orders could be court-martialed. When the Confederate army formally issued its own regulations in 1863, Articles 52 and 54 were inserted verbatim. And, as we know, Article 56 prohibited civilians from giving food to the enemy. *The Revised United States Army Regulations of 1861* stated that generals had the authority to levy money or contributions "in kind" in the enemy's country when necessary.[2]

Henry Lee Scott's *Military Dictionary*, published in 1861, provided specifics on how soldiers should obtain food from civilians. Born in 1814, Scott had served in the American army most of his life. When the war commenced, he was a lieutenant colonel, but he retired soon afterwards. In his *Dictionary*, he insisted that certain protocols had to be followed on foraging expeditions: officers should travel into the countryside with some troops and a guard; they should seize supplies as needed from civilians, who would be given paperwork for their property; civilians could then redeem the paper for cash or goods promptly, during or after the conflict. War frequently "cripples" agriculture, Scott realized, but troops should deal fairly with civilians whether they were "friendly," "neutral," or "hostile" when taking supplies from them, with no pillaging. Yet he underscored the central message that noncombatants had to relinquish their supplies when asked. Scott used the word "forage" to indicate food consumed by livestock, rather than by human beings, but during the war men in both armies used the word for both forms of sustenance. Both armies appointed boards of survey composed of three officers to judge claims by civilians for damaged property, and boards were established in some US-occupied regions, as well. They were expected to function as a kind of appeals court for civilians, but they left very few records, and we know almost nothing about how they worked.[3]

THE FOOD ENVIRONMENT

In 1861, the daily ration for both armies was enough to keep most soldiers alive, consisting of approximately one pound of meat, preferably fresh beef, one pound of bread, some vegetables, coffee and sugar; as time passed, Southern rations grew smaller, with cuts in 1862, 1863, and 1864. The infantry depended on the ration, which came from commissaries and supply depots at such places as Louisville, Kentucky, for the Union and Columbus, Georgia, for the Confederacy; railroads or wagon trains then delivered the meals to men in the field. Troops in both armies expended numerous calories on a regular basis, and many of them discovered they needed more nourishment than the military gave them. Some of them wanted more fruits and vegetables to ward off scurvy, while others found army fare monotonous or simply inedible. Federal-issued meat was sometimes infested with worms, and some Confederate-issued beef was an odd shade of blue and covered with slime.[4]

Among the several men who served as commissary generals and quartermaster generals in the two armies, Montgomery Meigs, who became the US Quartermaster General in June 1861, was probably the most capable. His role was largely supervisory, however, and the line commanders had much more decision-making power over supply and related questions. The rebel army could never feed all its men, despite the South's bountiful food supply, which historians have blamed on ineffective administrators; the dearth of funds, and an inadequate transportation system. Confederate soldiers blamed the quartermasters, believing that the worst men in the army – the shirkers, the bullies, the alcoholics – ended up in that department. Private John Robson assumed that many quartermasters were dishonest and kept the best supplies for themselves, and Major Michael Harman, a businessman before the war, predicted in 1861 that inexperienced, unsystematic quartermasters would undermine the Southern cause. Many officers certainly lacked the methodical habits necessary for the job.[5]

Throughout the war, the Northern army probably had more food, but its efficiency in delivering food to the men has been greatly exaggerated. The federal military had its own food crises, in which entire regiments had to go without provisions for significant periods of time. Soldiers blamed the shortages on negligent quartermasters, greedy contractors, and incompetent inspectors. The US War Department tried to root out fraud and waste in the system, but the task was overwhelming. Many new quartermasters received little training and were expected to learn on the job. In 1861, Captain Charles Leib, a quartermaster in Buckhannon, Virginia, said they scrambled to get copies of army regulations and then had to persuade officers to complete the paperwork when they took quartermaster supplies; some of the officers simply refused, apparently because it was too much trouble. The bureaucratic outcome was that Yankee soldiers, too, experienced real hunger.[6]

Many things could go haywire as the two armies tried to deliver food for their men in the field, the last, most important point in the supply process. All over the South, commissary wagons were ambushed by the enemy or delayed by inclement weather and bad roads. Railroad cars broke down, ran behind schedule, or were attacked by the foe. Temporary supply depots, established during offensive operations, were destroyed by the other army. These chronic problems in delivering food meant that Union and Confederate troops had to go without rations for days at a time, agony for almost anybody, particularly for men engaged in arduous physical exercise. Federal Private Herman Burhaus asserted that soldiers felt they were "entitled" to decent food from the army.[7]

So the men in both armies adapted to the oscillating food supply. They asked their relatives to give them extra food, as rebel Corporal James E. Hall did; others bartered for grub with pickets from the other army; yet others collected the haversacks of dead soldiers on the battlefield; sometimes they purchased food from sutlers. Federal troops received some food from the US Sanitary Commission, but there was no counterpart for rebel soldiers. Hungry Confederates stole from their own supply trains, just as hungry Yankees stole from their own supply trains. Soldiers who worked for quartermasters, such as Northern Private Henry Aplin, used their positions to cadge some food. He told his kinfolk that he placed false orders for sugar, tea, and molasses and then kept them for himself.[8]

NEW THINGS TO EAT

More frequently, soldiers in both armies turned to civilians for food. They headed out on authorized expeditions, searching for food in the countryside, but administrative problems cropped up immediately. The Articles of War, as well as Scott's *Military Dictionary*, appear to suggest that troops on authorized foraging expeditions should give receipts to every civilian, regardless of their politics, and in the early going, soldiers in both armies sometimes did that. But the troops naturally tended to favor civilians who seemed to be on their own side. In December 1861, US Brigadier General Samuel R. Curtis, a graduate of West Point serving in Rolla, Missouri, told a cavalry officer who seized forage from civilians to give certificates only to "good Union men," which would seem to violate policy, or, in the most generous interpretation, anticipate General Pope's Orders by more than six months. Many soldiers and officers did not care to inquire, however, about civilian politics when they sought food.[9]

The troops' inability to handle the paperwork created yet other problems. Soldiers were expected to use printed forms to record the quantity of goods taken, the date, and the civilian's name, but the paper itself was often improvised. Some quartermasters and commissary officers gave out handwritten receipts done in pencil or allowed wagon masters to sign the papers for them. Other officers refused to keep duplicates of the forms, as regulations stipulated, again, probably because it was too much trouble. Men in both armies did not show much zeal for following procedures on the paper itself. They used the words "certificate," "voucher," and "receipt" interchangeably for the forms given to civilians for the goods soldiers confiscated but did not pay for, even though quartermasters and commissary agents were supposed to use vouchers and soldiers in the field were supposed to give out receipts. ("Certificate" seems to have been an all-purpose word for any military document.) They were not good bureaucrats – in fact, they were very bad.[10]

The difficulties went beyond paperwork, however, involving military behavior itself, for both federal troops and Confederate soldiers. First, let us address Northerners. Lieutenant Colonel Charles Denby proclaimed that the unauthorized confiscation of food would be punished, and sometimes it was punished. Yet military discipline proved to be lenient and sporadic, and it did little to avert wrongdoing. The court-martial records include an infinitesimal number of cases about unauthorized foraging; a random survey of hundreds of files at the National Archives produced exactly one case, described below. Soldiers repeatedly left camp to forage on their own, dodging the pickets and ridiculing the officers they had outsmarted. Several lieutenants tried to keep the troops out of one farmer's meat-house in Virginia, but the troops broke in, anyway, defying their officers and hauling the meat away. Yet other soldiers could not be subdued. Private Cleveland Houser, in camp in Alabama, killed a hog on a nearby farm after he had gone two days without meat rations. Imprisoned in the guardhouse, he admitted that he had done it before, and he did not care if he was punished.[11]

Federal troops applied the word "straggler" to comrades who took food in unauthorized fashion, with the implication that this happened only occasionally and involved trifling amounts of food, but many soldiers were involved and a great deal of food, throughout the conflict. Even before they arrived in the Confederacy, Yankees acted on the assumption that food was there for the taking. In June 1861, Lieutenant Willis A. Pomeroy observed in Hagerstown, Maryland, that Union troops seized all the "eatables they come across." Inside the Confederacy, they did the same. Sometimes they slipped away from camp to forage at night, and sometimes they foraged in broad daylight. They wrung the heads off chickens, milked cows, stripped corn from the fields, and pulled figs off trees. They entered private dwellings and ate the dinner off the table. Soldiers frequently sought out plantations, estimating that the owners had more food than other whites, and they were usually correct. They seized and destroyed most of the 1,500 pounds of meat on a plantation in Dallas County, Alabama. Slaves such as Eliza Evans witnessed much of this conduct, and they sometimes lost food to the armies, but most soldiers took food from whites because they had more of it.[12]

From the war's opening months, federal troops targeted local secessionists as they went out seeking food. They were pleased to take food from such people. In the summer of 1861, soldiers from the First Connecticut butchered a cow in the pasture of such a civilian near Alexandria, Virginia, singling him out even though there was a supply depot in Alexandria. Soldiers took apples from what Private James Pusard called a "secesh Orchard" and milk from what hospital steward Henry Eells called a "secesh cow." True Unionists, they tried to spare when they could. Sergeant Madison Bowler noted that a red white, and blue flag waving in front of a residence could protect the household's food.[13]

Some Northern officers actively encouraged misconduct that violated the Articles of War. When a captain in Lawrence County, Alabama, discovered that a planter had concealed his food-holdings from US troops, he told Private Lewis Oglevie and other soldiers to "take anything we wanted." They eagerly complied, seizing the man's corn, his livestock, and other comestibles. Officers themselves sometimes misbehaved, and men on horseback could be particularly hard to control. In April 1862, five members of the cavalry, including a captain, went on an "unauthorized" foraging expedition near Catlett's Station, Virginia, where rebel cavalry fired on them. Their commander, General Irvin McDowell, reported them to the Secretary of War, but we do not know what became of them. Other officers believed that magnanimous civilians would not hold their conduct against them. General Samuel R. Curtis, who did not follow US policy in Missouri in 1861, hoped in February 1862 that whites in Arkansas would be large-hearted about his army's destruction of food and "forgive" them since the soldiers were genuinely hungry. He added lamely that his troops should follow orders.[14]

Some federal soldiers did feel guilty when the troops seized food from civilians. Private Thomas Evans, who had watched his fellow soldiers forage like "ravening wolves," saw some white girls weeping as federal troops guzzled milk from their spring-house and carried off their butter and meat. His conscience smote him, so he gave them some money from his own pocket. But many others felt that their hunger excused any kind of behavior. Furious because the military did not give him regular meals, Private Ansel Bement did what he called "my first stealing," taking potatoes from Kentucky farms in the fall of 1861. He did not think it was wrong and told his parents about his private foraging expedition. Sating hunger mattered more than anything else, soldiers assumed. Private Moses Parker wrote that he and his friends "stole" an ox in Virginia, killed it, and ate it because they did not have enough rations. "We *took* the beef because we *needed* it," he explained.[15]

The food traffic sometimes moved the other way, as civilians made informal gifts to troops early in the conflict. In 1861, pro-Union whites handed out food free of charge to Northern soldiers in Kentucky, and in 1862, they invited Yankee officers into their homes for meals. Breaking bread together is a timeless symbol of fellowship, and it had been a key feature of antebellum communalism. Such meals delighted federal officers, who understood the gesture. Pro-Confederate civilians gave food to rebel troops in North Carolina and welcomed them into their homes in Virginia for meals, which those soldiers also deeply appreciated. Apolitical civilians gave food to men in both armies, evidently trying to placate both sides if possible.[16]

Civilians who were more entrepreneurial, more pragmatic, or in need of money sold food to the two armies. Starting in 1861, they signed contracts with the rebel military to supply food to the army, and they sold food in bulk to Confederate agents at public markets. These transactions were above board, but many civilians sold food to troops in both armies in surreptitious exchanges in the field. The money involved could be a pittance: after the capture of Fort Henry in Tennessee, some Yankee soldiers began looking for food nearby and paid a civilian fifteen cents for some chickens. But such transactions occurred hundreds of times, with sales to the troops by both pro-Confederate and pro-Union citizens.[17]

Now let us turn to Confederate troops. They sometimes followed procedures, as regulations dictated. Quartermasters had the authority to take supplies when necessary so long as they gave out paper forms and paid for supplies at current market prices, regardless of inflation. Officers serving with Brigadier General Felix Zollicoffer gave a receipt as "instructed" for barrels taken from a Kentucky salt works in 1861. They sometimes followed procedure for small amounts of food. An officer from the Quitman Rifles gave receipts to Arkansan C. M. Cargill for

30 dollars' worth of bacon in 1861. A few quartermasters posted notices in the newspapers, asking civilians to bring their claims forward, and if civilians could not get payment locally, they turned to the Quartermaster General's office in Richmond. The office did pay claims for goods taken by the army, although it required duplicates of all paper forms and it worked slowly, taking many months for claims to be processed.[18]

But Confederate soldiers took food from white Southern civilians, just as Yankees did, without authorization or sanction. They acted as if the region's food supply was an endless larder that should always be available to them. In the summer of 1861, rebel troops occupied Grafton, Virginia, and confiscated all the provisions, eating up "every thing in town," said a federal soldier. Near Hamburg, Tennessee, after Southern troops skirmished on the modest farm of one Mr. Beach in March 1862, they took all his horses, his pork, and his wheat, with no documents and no compensation; then they set fire to his corn crib to cover their retreat from Union forces. In Clinton, Tennessee, an officer known only as "Old Hamilton" took all of Mrs. McAdoo's corn and poultry, leaving no documents and no payment; her son, a civilian, assured her he would try to obtain the right papers. Soldiers took food from slaves on occasion, but they, like their Northern counterparts, typically seized food from white people who had more food.[19]

From the war's beginning, rebel officers struggled to keep their men under control. In the summer of 1861, Colonel Daniel Harvey Hill issued strict orders against his troops foraging on their own near Bethel Church, Virginia, but they ignored him, hunting shoats on nearby farms. In the autumn of 1861, Colonel Patrick Cleburne wanted to show Kentuckians that rebel soldiers were their "friends," but he found out too late that his teamsters and soldiers pillaged food from local families. He was genuinely angry when he realized that other officers who witnessed the plundering did not try to stop it. But even on authorized foraging expeditions, things could go awry. Sergeant John Worsham and some privates left under orders to forage near Rude's Hill, Virginia, and filled two large wagons with corn. Espying some federal cavalry in the neighborhood, they fled back to camp without contacting the civilian owners or giving them any paperwork.[20]

As they fanned out looking for food, rebel soldiers frequently targeted white Unionists, despite Henry Scott's admonition that all noncombatants should be treated justly whatever their political opinions. When Confederate troops could identify them, they punished them for their politics. This happened in the Border States, where a quartermaster seized livestock from a Kentucky family named Frame because a relative was serving as a Yankee officer, and inside the Confederacy, where soldiers plundered the contents of barns owned by North Carolina Unionists. They did not spare women, and they could be vengeful. In Bradley County, Tennessee, troops seized fodder, oats, and corn from a widow, Jane Pettitt, who had eleven children. They gave her nothing for the food, but before they left her farm they burned her family Bible and threatened to hang her.[21]

NEW FOODWAYS, ESPECIALLY MEAT

Yankee soldiers, most of whom had never been in the South before, marveled at the abundance of the region's plant and animal life. They encountered the region's distinctive cuisine, including such specialties as grits and cornbread which were strange and new for these troops. Such dishes were enjoyable, even comforting, to most Confederate troops who had known them since childhood. The few times they invaded the North, rebel soldiers encountered regional customs they found surprising, such as the Pennsylvania practice of serving milk in bowls. Northerners in Dixie used their own slang, such as "flippers" for fried flour cakes, and Southerners said "yams" for what Yankees called sweet potatoes.[22]

Troops in both armies had specific hierarchies in mind as they sought food. They wanted fresh food rather than something from a can, and they preferred bread to hardtack. Most of all, they wanted meat, whether it was beef, pork, chicken, turkey, lamb, mutton, or rabbit. Soldiers fished the region's waterways when they could, but they preferred meat. Since medieval times, it has had more status than any other food, and the maxim that meat gives strength and warriors must have it pervaded both armies in the American Civil War. Men in the ranks took matters into their own hands to get animal protein. Two federal soldiers in the 13th Massachusetts Infantry defied orders against unauthorized foraging and left camp near Goose Creek, Virginia, to look for meat. They shot a ram, dressed it, and quietly brought it back to camp. Many soldiers knew how to store and cook meat, as well. Private Alfred Bellard and his fellows shot chicken and ducks, rolled them in the mud – a nineteenth-century method of preserving meat – baked them, and ate them.[23]

Among the different varieties of meat, the troops wanted beef above all. In his memoirs, William T. Sherman declared that beef, from cattle on the hoof, was the best food for soldiers at war, and soldiers from both armies heartily agreed. Beef was nutritious, Yankee Lieutenant Leander

Stillwell remarked, and it tasted so good; Confederate Lieutenant Albert Goodloe added that his comrades "longed" for it, his motto being "more beef and better beef." (Prime beef, which is high in fat content, is an excellent protein source.) Both armies brought herds of beef cattle with them, although the quality varied, and the bovines did not always keep pace with the armies, so the troops went on official and unauthorized foraging expeditions in search of beef. Rebel General Richard Ewell, a West Point graduate, foraged alone one day in early 1862 and returned leading a live bull with a "triumphant air."[24]

The love of beef manifested itself in army life on a regular basis. Troops in both armies noted the availability of beef cattle when they reconnoitered an area or selected a location for their headquarters. They cried eureka when they found beef left behind by the enemy and wolfed it down. Yankee soldiers consumed some half-eaten plates at a rebel camp where the troops evacuated in a hurry, and rebel soldiers followed suit, snapping up the beef when they came upon an abandoned federal camp. When troops were on the march, they actively looked for beef. As rebel soldiers journeyed through the bluegrass region of Kentucky, they seized the beef cattle first, paying in Confederate money.[25]

Despite this ongoing quest for sustenance, both armies wasted food of all types. Rejecting the antebellum values of stewardship, men routinely destroyed viands to prevent the other army from getting them. Federal troops threw their provisions down wells near Williamsburg, Virginia, during the Peninsular Campaign in 1862 to keep them out of the hands of rebel soldiers. The destruction of food could be an expression of raw power, a deliberate performance in front of civilians, more likely if they lived on plantations. On a North Carolina estate, the residents watched in horror as Union troops killed and skinned cattle, ate what they wanted, and left the remainder behind to rot. Confederate soldiers, too, violated the prohibition on wasting food. While vacating Manassas, Virginia, in the spring of 1862, they scattered flour and other food on the ground to prevent the enemy from consuming it.[26]

Here we have to pause. Why did Confederate troops seize food from white Southerners, including pro-Confederate whites, without following procedure? And why did they waste something as precious as food? After all, they understood how much labor went into raising crops on a farm or a plantation. Maybe they believed the strife would not last long and there would always be enough to eat. Some of them certainly assumed that civilians had to sacrifice everything for the rebel cause. In November 1861, Brigadier General Ben McCulloch wanted every white male "patriot" in Arkansas to burn his grain and his mill rather than let the enemy have them. Other officers thought their appetites had to come first, even if their survival was not at issue. In December 1861, Major John B. Gordon and his troops developed a hankering for eggnog, so they "scoured" civilian households in the Virginia countryside for eggs, which were "exceedingly scarce." But when they concocted their holiday treat, a servant tripped and broke the bowl before they could drink it.[27]

Some rebel soldiers knew full well that civilians were hungry, and some of them deserted precisely because their families back home were going hungry. But that did not seem to translate into consideration for civilian needs in general. Clearly that was true for John B. Gordon, who said that the loss of eggnog undermined his "Christmas cheer." Other Confederate officers felt troubled by the army's behavior and sincerely remorseful at the impact on civilians. Richard Taylor, a planter and son of President Zachary Taylor, owned that the Southern cavalry descended upon the countryside like locusts, hurting "their own people." Yet others tried to rationalize the army's conduct without fully excusing it. Private Carlton McCarthy, an artilleryman, argued that his mates stole food from civilians only because of "terrible necessity," since the army did not provide enough food. Most Southern troops did not seem to recognize the long-term impact of such deeds on civilian morale, much less civilian survival.[28]

CIVILIANS AND THEIR PROVENDER

Some time had to elapse before civilians understood that the armies posed a serious danger to their food sources. In 1861, the press and the rebel government urged civilians to raise food crops to aid the military, and many of them did so. Into the 1862 calendar year, pro-Confederate citizens such as the Humes of Virginia, unwary and generous, still gave food to rebel troops in the area, and Union supporters such as the Parhams of Tennessee were happy to prepare meals for federal troops passing by. But civilians began to realize by degrees that both armies threatened their provisions, regardless of which side they supported. The disenchanted began to focus on their own survival, which they thought more important than helping the military. Mrs. William Randolph, a well-connected Virginian whose family contained numerous rebel soldiers, asked a kinsman how to protect herself from troops who consumed all of her food whenever they visited her home. He advised her to put out the lights every evening and lock up the building.[29]

Most civilians felt greater antagonism for the Northern army, however, partly because more civilians were pro-Confederate, and because the federal army was bigger and needed more sustenance. Most of them did not understand the military bureaucracy, including what kind of information had to be written on which document or where to take the papers they did receive, and they tended to use the word "receipt" for any paper they got from either army. Those who knew enough to take their papers to Yankee quartermasters could not always obtain payment, contrary to regulations. Many people therefore developed a deep suspicion of Northern troops. When a soldier came by Kate Carney's house to buy milk near Murfreesboro, Tennessee, she "blazed out at him." After some Virginians implored soldiers not to take their food, the officers replied that it was a "military necessity," but civilians and troops disagreed on that point. When Mrs. Carroll, a slaveholder in North Carolina, asked a soldier not to take her meat supply because her children had to eat, he responded, "'Ain't we fightin' de war?'"[30]

Civilians began resisting the federal army, trying to protect their food. After a Virginian threatened to set his dogs on soldiers who stole milk from his dairy, they shot the dogs, which would seem to qualify as pillage, but one of the soldiers designated the milk as a "military necessity." Civilians sometimes got into physical altercations with the troops. When a Union soldier tried to shoot poultry belonging to Vianna Arnett, a wheelwright's daughter, she shoved the gun away with her bare hands. (We do not know what happened next.) Other civilians deployed what might be called kitchen weapons against foraging soldiers. Two corporals left camp to take a walk near Owl Creek, Tennessee, and asked some white women at a log cabin for some buttermilk. After the men drank it, they began rolling on the ground in agony, crying that they had been poisoned. The corporals both recovered and limped slowly back to camp.[31]

Most pro-Confederate civilians were stunned to realize that their own troops could take food from them, too. This hard lesson, a sharp shock, was borne in on them again and again. In 1862, civilians in Nashville compared the Southern army's confiscation of their food to a "reign of terror." Mrs. O'Sullivan of Commerce, Missouri, felt so angry that a rebel officer took her food, even though he paid for it, that she followed after him, calling him a "robber," a "scoundrel," and other imprecations as he walked off laughing. From Georgia, a Southern officer's wife known only as Mrs. James offered a somewhat more sympathetic commentary on military behavior. The rebel army was desperate for supplies, and its soldiers became "used to pillage." The war had dulled their sensibilities,

FIGURE 3.1 Women from wartime North Carolina.
Courtesy of the American Civil War Museum.

she thought, and a woman's voice such as hers was not heeded when troops confiscated food.[32]

As these incidents suggest, gender could be a key factor in these exchanges. Food was a woman's domain, cooking her realm of expertise, and most soldiers held in their minds primal associations between females and food. Men in both armies were expected to learn how to cook their own rations, but they missed meals prepared by a woman and the experience of eating at a table with a woman. Some troops, including Confederate Private Edward Moore, deliberately sought out women who seemed "motherly" when they went foraging. Yet traditional ideas about gender proved malleable in wartime. Troops sometimes promised that women would be treated the same as men when soldiers confiscated food, while others took advantage of the women they encountered in the field. Margaret Hildebrand, a Unionist in DeSoto County, Mississippi, did not know that Yankee officers should have given her some documents for her livestock, and they did not offer any. Her brother-in-law later obtained what she called a "receipt" for the property.[33]

Both armies alienated civilians, female and male, by their petty abuses of authority while foraging. It is remarkable how often they damaged kitchenware and cooking utensils during their freelance expeditions. Federal troops in Huntsville, Alabama, entered private homes, demanding to be fed, and then left broken pottery in their wake. Rebel soldiers did the same, even to families who supported their cause. In Hanover County, Virginia, Fanny Tinsley's neighbor willingly gave most of her food to Confederate troops, who then borrowed her crockery and broke it, leaving shards of cups and glasses behind. Men from both armies grabbed coffee pots and forks from households wherever they went, which was galling to civilians, who of course wanted those objects for their own use.[34]

The armies struck at another institution, the local mill, which had been so important in antebellum life. They commandeered mills for their own use, both in the Confederacy and in the Border States, to process grain for their rations. Pro-Confederate civilians were keen to mill flour for the rebel army, laboring around the clock to help them out, although that was risky; Yankee troops arrested a local miller named Weston near Front Royal, Virginia, for supporting the rebels. But federal troops took over mills even if the owners were pro-Union, and they sometimes destroyed them, as they did the Hoyts' mill in Ravenswood, Virginia. That of course undermined the food supply for civilians, who could not process their own grain.[35]

A battle of wits ensued between civilians and soldiers in both armies. Some civilians figured out how to disarm the troops, symbolically speaking. When five Northern soldiers left camp in central Tennessee seeking food, they headed for a plantation where the owners gave them a warm welcome, a fine meal, and some beer. After this collation, Enoch Colby, one of their number, did not have the heart to take more food from them, the original purpose of their expedition. Civilians with unusual self-control tried meekness and submission. Cornelia Parsons, a plantation mistress, kept silent when a US soldier barged into her house near Opelousas, Louisiana, and scooped the meal off her table. She managed a smile, and her quiet demeanor finally shamed the soldiers into leaving. Other civilians employed passive-aggressive tactics to take advantage of the troops, including men in gray. Some white farmers, unidentified, deliberately sold rancid pork to members of the Army of Northern Virginia.[36]

Yet other civilians began concealing their food from the armies. Food hoarding has a long history, and the practice intensifies in wartime. In 1861, civilians began hoarding salt, although the Confederate newspapers, such as the *Richmond Whig*, abjured them to stop. Some civilians hoarded food for the purposes of speculation, but most of them seem to have done it for their own survival. Southern Brigadier General Humphrey Marshall reported in May 1862 that hoarding civilians in Russell County, Virginia, were entirely focused on self-preservation and unwilling to help the rebel cause in any way. Yet other civilians, having realized that both armies could seize their food, concealed their stores from them both. A farmer in Travisville, Tennessee, hid his corn supply from troops in both armies for six months before some Yankee cavalrymen discovered it.[37]

Despite these multiplying threats to the food supply, some civilians continued to abide by the longtime patterns of communalism. The South contained islands of plenty, typically on plantations where wealth and good luck protected the household from want. The Breckinridges, a pro-Confederate family of Botetourt County, Virginia, lived in one such household. Into 1862, they dined well, enjoying such luxuries as dessert, and they invited guests into their residence. Other people who still had a lot of food shared it with relatives, good neighbors, and good friends. But hunger eventually began to reach into the most affluent families. Charles Denby, a Yankee officer, noticed in 1862 that an elderly Alabaman couple lived in a mansion of twenty-two rooms but had almost nothing to eat.[38]

By the winter of 1861–1862, white civilians began to worry about the scarcity of food, and they learned to cut back or do without. Although Jefferson Davis called for days of fasting for the Confederate cause, no civilian, not even the most fervent rebel, wanted to fast on a regular basis. Mary Houston, a middling slaveowner in Virginia, recalled that in the war's second year her family started to experience real privation. Many people gave up coffee and tea, or began using substitutes, parched corn for coffee and blackberry leaves for tea. They consumed less meat, as it became harder to find and more expensive. Members of the plantation elite had to adapt, eating food they had shunned in the past. One slaveowning family, the Williamses of South Carolina, fed their children pork fat in the hopes it would keep them warm in the winter. The meal "disgusted" them, their daughter said, but they ate it.[39]

GENERAL POPE'S ORDERS OF 1862

In the summer of 1862, the federal army articulated a new policy on the army's consumption of material resources. The fighting had gone poorly that year, preeminently with the failure of McClellan's Peninsular

FIGURE 3.2 Union General John Pope.
Courtesy of the National Archives and Records Administration.

Campaign, so in July 1862, General John Pope, head of the Army of Virginia, decided to take a more aggressive tack. Pope, who grew up in Illinois, graduated from West Point in 1842 and served ably in the Mexican War. In his politics, he was an anti-slavery Republican. He came east after serving in the western theater with some success; he knew military regulations; and he wanted to revise them to unleash the army's full power. Open-faced with round dark eyes, he was ambitious, bombastic, a little gullible, and, he later claimed, the mouthpiece of Secretary of War Edwin Stanton.[40]

On July 18, 1862, General Pope issued General Orders No. 5, declaring that the army would live off the country, taking what it needed from civilians. He further declared that officers would seize property, including food, but only under orders, and they would issue "vouchers" for confiscated property, payable at the war's conclusion if the owners could demonstrate they were loyal to the United States from the voucher date to the war's end. Thus he overturned the idea that all civilians should be treated the same regardless of their political views. President Lincoln tacitly approved of Pope's Orders, and on August 16, 1862, Secretary of War Stanton issued General Orders No. 109, which confirmed Pope's ideas. (Pope insisted later that the Secretary drafted his orders in July 1862.) Stanton asserted that military commanders could seize any property they needed to prosecute the war, so long as it was done "in an orderly manner" and nothing was destroyed with "wantonness or malice." Detailed records would be kept on the property seizures for future compensation for civilians loyal to the United States. Pope's Orders initially applied only to the Army of Virginia, but after Stanton endorsed them, the entire federal army was expected to adopt them.[41]

This policy change, which was trumpeted with much fanfare and announced in recruitment posters, had little impact on military behavior in the field. As early as August 1862, John Pope fumed that soldiers were misinterpreting General Orders No. 5 as a license to mistreat civilians and take their property, but he was removed from major command after he lost the Battle of Second Bull Run that month. General George B. McClellan thought Pope's Order would turn the army into a gang of thieves, but commanders more successful than McClellan, such as Ulysses S. Grant and William T. Sherman – called by one scholar the "destroyer" generals – did not even mention Pope's Orders in their memoirs. Among men in the ranks, some troops supported Pope's program, but what is most striking is the silence. Very few soldiers wrote anything about either Pope's Orders of July 1862 or Stanton's iteration in August 1862, probably because they had been living off the land since the war's inception.[42]

Northern troops violated General Pope's axioms right away by continuing to forage without orders. Taking food at will was already normalized, woven into daily routine, long before Pope came along. When soldiers did not get adequate rations, they started looking for food on plantations and farms. Private Cyrus Stockwell witnessed this unauthorized foraging one night in Tennessee in the fall of 1862, despite orders to the contrary, and added, "no one cares." Unsanctioned foraging was forbidden but widely practiced, as Lieutenant Abner Small understood in

November 1862. When troops in the 16th Maine Volunteers felt hungry, nothing, not "threats" from their officers or "even leveled muskets" would prevent them from hunting for food, he wrote. Men still saw the right to take food from any source as a fundamental privilege of being a soldier. In February 1863, Melville C. Follett and four other soldiers foraged in the countryside near Murfreesboro, Tennessee, taking sugar, walnuts, and anything else they wanted. He commented that he had never felt "so free from restraint" since he joined the military.[43]

Federal troops routinely ignored Pope's other stipulations on authorized foraging trips, neglecting, for example, to take civilian political views into account even though he decreed that Unionists – and only Unionists – should receive paperwork. Private John Billings acknowledged that many foraging soldiers did not care very much about discovering whether noncombatants were loyal or disloyal. In the fall of 1862, civilian Henry Haviland saw troops seize poultry, goats, and beehives from white civilians in the Border State of Kentucky, without any inquiries on that point. Soldiers were known to confiscate food from Unionists who had already *given* meals to other federal troops, which disturbed their more thoughtful comrades. Daniel B. Allen, a drum major from Illinois, posed the question in November 1862, "Can it be possible that the weal or woe of our country is dependent on such characters?"[44]

After General Pope's Orders, the Yankee army still had difficulty getting the right papers to men in the field. Even though Pope used the word "voucher," some officers still employed the words "voucher" and "receipt" as synonyms, and sometimes they did not have any of the correct forms, be they vouchers, receipts, or certificates; sometimes they did not fill them out completely, omitting key information such as the amount of food taken. Officers dashed off receipts on the back of used envelopes, pieces of stationery, or, in one case, the bottom of an old passport. Even if soldiers had the right forms, they did not always follow policy. Henry Eells admitted that quartermasters sometimes gave out documents for confiscated food but more often did not, and he predicted that even civilians with the proper forms who swore allegiance to the United States would have a hard time getting compensated.[45]

Neither Pope nor Stanton specified exactly how property-owners would be compensated *during* the war, but those civilians who received papers commonly took their receipts, vouchers, or certificates to the office of the nearest Yankee commissary officer or quartermaster. There they sometimes obtained cash reimbursements for the confiscated property, or, on one occasion, a cow to replace the animal a Florida woman lost to

FIGURE 3.3 Yankee hospital steward S. Henry Eells.
Courtesy of Harvard Art Museums.

the army. At other times, they received nothing at all. Soldiers gave out receipts early on to local people, including Confederate sympathizers, near Yorktown, Virginia, for the value of livestock and fowl they confiscated. But, as Lizzie Jackson Mann recalled, those civilians received documents exactly once for those items, and after that the troops issued no more paper.[46]

After Pope's proclamation, Northern soldiers in the field showed the same brazen disregard for procedure. On unauthorized expeditions, they visited farms at night and took chickens and other kinds of meat, Private Alfred Willett remarked. The troops were not "very particular" about keeping records, Corporal Oliver Oglevie said as his regiment seized corn, tore down a corn crib, and confiscated fifty geese and a dozen pigs from a Tennessee household. Soldiers were known to engage in such foraging trips even when they had supplies available and foraging put them in jeopardy. An Illinois outfit left camp in November 1862 to do illicit foraging in Springdale, Mississippi, on an "extensive scale" even though supply trains had arrived and Southern cavalry were roaming in the vicinity.[47]

Numerous *authorized* foraging expeditions took place, just as they had before Pope's Orders, and Yankee officers did hand out paper for the food they confiscated. Major Hiram Strong participated in one such expedition in December 1862, when a quartermaster led a long train of wagons guarded by three regiments into the Tennessee countryside. The magnitude of the food-gathering, even when it was done per regulations, nonetheless wreaked serious damage on the agricultural economy. In September 1862, troops went foraging near Nashville and brought back 150 wagons filled with food. Foraging had an ever-growing impact on an escalating number of civilians. In November 1862, the quartermaster wagons rumbled through Stafford County, Virginia, with soldiers confiscating enough livestock to feed 15,000 men. They emptied every farm in the area.[48]

Regardless of the shifts in official policy, civilians continued to fear Northern troops. They tried to hide their food, just as they had before July 1862. In Wilson County, Tennessee, white residents saw the Yankee cavalry impressing food and livestock – which local civilians bluntly called "stealing" – and they hid their animals when they heard troops approaching. Other people attempted to do the same. An elderly white woman in rural Virginia managed to put a pig inside a closet, but three soldiers broke into her house, found it, slaughtered it, and ate it. The troops' sense of entitlement was the same. Cornelia McDonald was terrified when soldiers demanding food surrounded her house in Winchester, Virginia, and started breaking the windows with their fists. They called out for breakfast, shouting that they would smash her furniture, too, if she did not feed them. She locked the front door, but they climbed in the windows and started carrying away her provisions.[49]

We can see some uneasiness about military practice in the writings of Lucius W. Barber, a private who enlisted in Company D, 15th Illinois Volunteer Infantry. Hailing from Marengo, Illinois, he was strongly pro-Union, so he volunteered in the spring of 1861. More observant than most people, he was a good writer, and he had a sense of right and wrong. He served in the battles of Shiloh and Corinth in 1862, and in September 1862, he was promoted to corporal. By the time his company reached Holly Springs, Mississippi, in November 1862, Barber thought the men in his company had become too "bold" while foraging. They would slaughter a white man's hogs before his eyes, and if the man protested, Barber wrote, "cold steel" would "put a quietus on him," which sounds as if they either killed him or threatened to kill him. Barber recoiled, saying that such conduct could not be justified. He saw federal troops plunder everyone, rich and poor, young and old, and even though some citizens hoarded their provisions, he believed that others were truly starving. He had witnessed white women and children on their knees begging Yankee soldiers not to take their last mouthful of food. These troops made him feel ashamed, he wrote, and he tried to protect distressed civilians whenever he could.[50]

Confederate officers excoriated Pope's Orders on the seizure of private property, as we might expect, starting with the top commanders. General Robert E. Lee thought the Orders contemptible, while General James Longstreet castigated them as unmanly and immoral. Officers of lower ranks could be even more critical. James L. Clements, a captain from Arkansas, compared Pope to the Devil himself and alleged that "brutalities" followed in his wake. The most typical reaction, however, was silence, in their wartime correspondence and postwar recollections. Richard Taylor and John B. Gordon, who both became generals, failed to mention Pope's Orders in their memoirs, although Taylor dismissed him as a mediocrity and Gordon called him a braggart. But very few Confederates made the obvious point that the Southern army already engaged in similar behavior.[51]

In the autumn of 1862, the Confederate military continued to forage with alacrity. On their authorized foraging trips, soldiers drove out into the country, requisitioning what they needed, while other men defied orders against foraging, evading the guards and heading out to find food on their own. If a soldier found something to eat despite orders against foraging, Corporal George Neese recalled, his comrades prudently did not ask him where it came from. Troops seized food from many civilians, but they preferred Union sympathizers, taking all their food when possible. Rebel officers tried to put a halt to illicit practices, just as they had before Pope's Orders, reminding the men to cease their depredations. Brigadier General Dorsey Pender deplored the way his soldiers could "clean out" an orchard in half an hour, showing no respect for private property. One fall day in Virginia, he actually had to smack his men with his saber to halt the pillaging.[52]

Civilians continued to resist the rebel army's seizure of their food whenever they could. Near Tupelo, Mississippi, an elderly white man pulled a gun on two Confederate soldiers doing freelance foraging on his farm, but they wrestled the gun away from him, broke the weapon against a tree, and forced him to take some food for them back to their camp. Women, too, could take direct action. A Tennessean, name unknown, whose husband was serving in the US Army, went "wild" with anger when rebel soldiers killed her chickens and cooked them inside her house; as they began eating, she hid their muskets, pulled a gun on them, and marched them to the nearest federal camp. The story was repeated with much hilarity in Union circles. Other civilians may have gone beyond that and attempted to kill troops in the enemy army. In April 1863, a rebel captain heard that a Unionist in Little Rock, known only as Mr. Christian, tried to pay two white women to poison Confederate soldiers.[53]

Many civilians recalled 1862 as the year that serious food shortages began. That April saw the first Confederate draft, which absorbed more of the region's white men, even as more slaves hurried away to the Northern army, reducing the size of the workforce. Moreover, the territory that the army could exploit for supplies began to shrink. In this context, civilians began to experience hunger in a new way, not just during sieges at such places as Vicksburg, but in daily life across the region. They became fixated on food, talking obsessively about it, as have ravenous people the world over, and they became willing to eat almost anything. Mrs. Owen of Tennessee picked up morsels of meat that fell off an army wagon after Yankee soldiers foraged through her farm. In the autumn of 1862, crowds of white women and children showed up at federal camps begging for food. That fall, soldiers reported what we would call food deserts, in such places as Bolivar, Tennessee, where all the food was gone.[54]

CONFEDERATE REGULATIONS

In January 1863, the military formally issued its official *Regulations for the Army of the Confederate States*, a somewhat redundant gesture since the army had followed antebellum US regulations, at least in theory, since the war started. These *Regulations* published the Articles of War verbatim from the old US regulations, just as the Confederacy did in 1861, and the volume included Articles 52 and 54, which declared that food was to be taken from civilians only when necessary, with no wastage, spoilage, or needless destruction. The volume added the statement that the rebel army's "wanton destruction" of private property was "disgraceful" and on a par with the enemy's behavior. Commanders had to end this misconduct to protect "our" citizens, which probably meant pro-Confederate civilians, although that was not spelled out.[55]

The old-new *Regulations* of 1863 had a glancing impact on rebel deportment, which is by now no surprise. The more scrupulous quartermasters, such as Charles D. Hill, gave out receipts when they foraged from civilians, usually with no reference to their politics, but many more did not bother with paper forms. As the cavalry from Hampton's Legion galloped through Virginia in March 1863 taking meat from households along the way, Joseph Waddell, a civilian quartermaster's clerk, compared them to "a swarm of locusts." Organizational problems and a glaring lack of discipline continued to plague the commissary and quartermaster departments, despite efforts by Quartermaster General Abraham Myers and other administrators. After a commissary sergeant, W. C. Brown, stole food from a Mississippi farm, his captain reported him for it, but he was not disciplined. Privates needing food resorted to the same measures they had taken in the past. In Tennessee, soldiers from the 25th Alabama Infantry had to fend for themselves when supply wagons failed to appear, so they dug up potatoes in a meadow, cooking and eating as the hours passed.[56]

Driven by their own necessity, civilians began to adapt to the new food regime. They bargained with each other, accepting food as payment for lodging, and with soldiers, trading pies for corn, although that violated military regulations. They resurrected old ways of cooking, making molasses from maple trees as their grandmothers did. In 1863, a Confederate recipe book, collected from articles in Southern newspapers, encouraged civilians to show their patriotism by making substitutes for apples, oysters, and cream out of crackers, butter, eggs, and corn in sundry combinations.[57] Civilians, believing that their own survival was at stake, went to ever greater lengths to obtain sustenance. A Virginian who lived in a log cabin walked 8 miles to purchase some corn and hauled it home on her back. Thefts of food, which happened occasionally before 1861, became increasingly common, as civilians stole from each other; white Southern women engaged in prostitution for food; and more crowds of beggars, adults and children, appeared in the Confederacy – all phenomena that have happened in other countries at war. One Northern private, Asa W. Marine, thought the sight of children begging for food was worse than seeing the dead on a battlefield.[58]

Some institutions did respond to the growing problem of hunger in the region's population. By the fall of 1861, several Confederate cities began distributing food in so-called "free markets" for the poor, and in 1862, some Southern states began to provide rations to widows and soldiers' wives at reduced prices. Churches opened charity kitchens and did what they could to feed the hungry. Individual officers in both armies gave food to needy civilians, although there was no consistent policy in either army. Rebel troops sometimes gave away commissary stores to civilians when they evacuated a place, while Yankee officers tried to help. Colonel Isaac Burrell, serving in occupied Galveston in 1862, shared army rations with starving women and children because "Common humanity" required it. But these efforts could only do so much. Colonel James A. Garfield saw these measures as temporary, expecting civilians to rely on their neighbors if they needed assistance.[59]

IMPRESSMENT

Ironically, the Confederate Congress made official in March 1863 what its army had been doing since 1861, allowing the seizure of private property for military use. This bill, known to the public as the Impressment Bill, passed on March 25, and it stipulated that whenever exigencies required the army to take food or other property, an officer could impress it so long as a certificate was issued on its value. The bill included some protections for civilians; it did not specify those civilians had to be pro-Confederate, although that is the implication. Every state had to set up a board with the authority to set prices paid for this property; the military had to leave enough food to sustain the owner's family; the government had to pay for property that the army lost or destroyed; finally, any officer who violated the bill would be reduced in rank to a private. The War Department promised to reimburse civilians based on its schedule of prices for various goods. In addition, the Congress provided that when an officer and a civilian differed on the value, a third civilian would act as an "umpire," again, confirming previous practice. Rebel troops had already employed a few umpires before the spring of 1863, for instance, to decide the value of sailing vessels seized by quartermasters.[60]

Most of the white Confederate public vehemently opposed the Impressment Bill, despite the clauses designed to protect civilians. The protests, loud and vociferous, began right away in the spring of 1863. The *Chattanooga Daily Rebel* cried that impressment officers had committed "outrages against justice," often against the poor, while the wealthy contrived to evade impressment of their property. Individuals mounted legal challenges to the bill, objecting that the government did not have the right to take food (and timber) for the armies, but they lost in court. Civilians complained at public meetings that officers impressed whatever they wanted, while others objected that the bill could prompt neighbors to inform on each other. Several state legislatures passed laws trying to regulate the confiscation of civilian goods, which had little to no influence on how soldiers behaved in the field.[61]

In the spring of 1863, just as the Impressment Bill passed, civilians in the grip of unbearable hunger broke out in food riots. These riots have tended to occur in cities, with many female participants, and that was true for the Civil War. In Richmond, some 500 women surged from store to store on April 2, "howling," according to a bystander, and knocking people down in the streets as they sought food. Other riots broke out in Mobile, Atlanta, Macon, Salisbury, North Carolina, and High Point, North Carolina. There were probably more riots than the press reported, because, as a Richmonder noted, the newspapers tried to hush up the story. Other Confederate journals blamed the disturbances on criminals, spies, or immigrants, while civilian G. S. Smith blamed white Southern Unionists. The riots demonstrated that current policies were failing, but the rebel government and its army did not recalibrate their policies. The military's demand for food continued to be relentless.[62]

HUNGRY PEOPLE

Just as the South's civilians began rioting for food in the spring of 1863, the Northern military proclaimed Lieber's Code. The sections on food are riddled with contradictions. Francis Lieber avowed that it was legal to "starve the hostile belligerent, armed or unarmed, so that it leads to the speedier subjection of the enemy." He further stipulated that soldiers could withhold food from the enemy and take sustenance from the enemy's country, but he added that private property could be seized only because of "military necessity" to support the US Army, and property of the "unarmed citizen" should be spared whenever possible, especially that of "loyal citizens." So Lieber seemed to tolerate starvation of pro-Confederate civilians as a war method, or maybe only as a last resort, except when it might injure private property or unarmed persons, if they were Unionists.[63]

Lieber's Code did not affect the Union army's confiscation of food, in any event. By April 1863, foraging customs were too deeply entrenched in army practice to change, and the size of the Yankee army kept increasing, so its demands for food grew apace. Officers issued general orders barring pillage from civilians, as well as thefts from quartermaster stores, and soldiers who foraged without permission were arrested, but most of them got away with it. Troops still foraged as they wished, without handing over any paper to civilians, and their officers ignored it, sometimes literally turning their backs to look the other way, cavalryman Charles Bates admitted. They foraged from Unionists, despite Lieber's prohibitions against it. In fact, more soldiers came to assume that all civilians were "damned 'secesh'," as they shouted at Margaret Hildebrand one day in Mississippi. She was actually pro-Union, which she proved to the Southern Claims Commission after 1865.[64]

The negligible impact of Lieber's Code is vividly rendered in the case of US Captain John K. Clark from the 7th Regiment, Illinois Volunteers. In the fall of 1863, he was court-martialed for his behavior in Giles County, Tennessee, where a quartermaster dispatched him and some troops to forage at a plantation. The men got drunk and seized food indiscriminately, and the owner remonstrated, but the soldiers did not give him any receipts. Charged with disobeying orders, Clark pled not guilty. The court concluded that he allowed his men to "pillage and plunder," which was not only "criminal" but "disgraceful." Clark showed disdain for the Articles of War and military discipline, the court found, and such an officer was unworthy to hold a commission. Soldiers who plunder and pillage, and officers who allow it, are "*bandits*," the court continued, and they should receive the "severest punishment known to law," held up to "public execration" to be "loathed, scorned and despised by all good officers, soldiers and law abiding citizens." The language is so blistering that we might expect Clark to receive a harsh punishment, but he did not. The captain was found not guilty, although he had to pay a 50-dollar fine and listen to a reprimand read aloud at dress parade, whereupon he returned to duty. The contrast between the tough language and the lenient punishment is risible. The court did not refer to Lieber's Code, which was published six months before Clark's trial began.[65]

Instances of actual starvation, which Lieber's Code did permit, emerge in the historical record. Scholars have shied away from the word "starvation," perhaps because it seems too ghastly for a war fought inside the United States, but soldiers began to use the word frequently in 1863, and their observations should not be dismissed as hyperbole. Yankee Colonel Daniel McCook gave food to a famished widow who came to his quarters begging for something to eat. She had not eaten in three days, and, he added, pro-Union families near Chickamauga, Tennessee, were "absolutely starving." In 1863, white civilians all over the South, too, began using the word "starving" to describe the region's population. The press depicted gaunt white women with "wild, glaring eyes" and languid children with "pinched" faces and "shriveled" limbs – a textbook definition of starvation. Healthy adults can survive about sixty days with no food, and for those who die, starving is physically painful, involving emaciation, premature aging caused by protein deficiencies, and the blank stare known as the "mask of famine." Starving people are subject to emotional outbursts of euphoria, sorrow, and rage, which helps explain the howling women of Richmond.[66]

Such conditions were the result of policies in both armies, but most Confederates showed an aversion to the moral questions involved, just as their counterparts did in the Union army. Troops condemned soldiers in the other army for taking food from vulnerable civilians, but there was not much difference in how they behaved. Rebel soldiers adhered to their own regulations in haphazard fashion when they invaded the United States in the summer of 1863. Robert E. Lee's army foraged freely in the Northern states, taking what they wished, which local civilians resented just as civilians did inside the South; perhaps as a joke, one rebel officer gave Confederate scrip to Pennsylvanians for the food he confiscated. Officers did unauthorized solo foraging there, as did Rebel Captain Walter Whitted. He foraged at a tidy farmhouse because, he said, his hunger had to be appeased.[67]

Confederate soldiers did much the same back in the South, with the same results. After the Gettysburg campaign, the troops had to return to Dixie with its "meager" food sources, John B. Gordon commented in a deflated tone. Inside the Confederacy, they continued to take victuals as needed from civilians. In the fall of 1863, troops seized over 100 ears of corn from a field near Chattanooga and floated them over the Tennessee River to their camp; they never clapped eyes on the owner, much less gave him or her any receipts. Private Sam Watkins, one of these foragers, wrote that rebel soldiers engaged in these unauthorized expeditions "thousands" of times. In Arkansas, rebel troops defied their officers and killed hogs belonging to civilians in Arkadelphia, Washington, and villages nearby. Their captain, William M. Rust, nonetheless defended them, explaining that some of his troops were sick and all of them were hungry. Furthermore, his men felt "confused" because civilians had once freely shared their food with soldiers. With much indignation, he stated that they did not deserve the name-calling they now received from the citizenry. If Rust could not fathom why white Southerners were no longer generous toward the troops, he was incapable of connecting cause and effect. Such administrative and moral confusion brought predictable results, in the racking hunger among civilians for whom his soldiers were fighting. The same kind of behavior would surface when troops in both armies needed timber.[68]

4

Timber

Both armies needed a lot of timber, and they turned to the South's extensive woodlands to meet those needs. That timber grew on land owned by private individuals, state governments, and, before 1861, the federal government, which owned millions of acres in the South. After secession, the rebel states confiscated the public lands, and the Southern Congress then made the states cede to the Confederacy all property, including forests on public lands, that they took from the United States; Jefferson Davis communicated the same message to his governors. Hundreds of thousands of acres remained in the hands of railroad companies, planters, farmers, and assorted other individuals. But troops in both armies showed little recognition of either private ownership or government ownership of the woodlands. Instead, they assumed from the war's onset that they had the right to take whatever timber they needed. Soldiers defined the taking of wood, whether it was trees clustered in a glade, fences zigzagging across a farm, or planed lumber stacked at a mill, as part of foraging. Timber could be very valuable in wartime, US Major General Abner Doubleday perceived, and other armies have used a great deal of timber in other conflicts. Just as troops in the Civil War took it for granted that their need for food superseded the civilian need for food, the troops assumed that their need for timber surpassed the civilian need for timber.[1]

The Articles of War, with their emphasis on responsible soldiering and civilian acquiescence, covered the use of timber. As we know, Article 52 barred "plunder and pillage" by troops while foraging, and Article 54 required soldiers and officers to behave in an "orderly" fashion on the march; they could not "waste or spoil" the trees, gardens, or meadows owned by civilians unless ordered to do so by an army commander. In other words, they could not freelance when collecting wood or damage the forests at will. When the Confederate military formally issued its own regulations, both these articles were inserted verbatim. The expectations were the same for both armies.[2]

Henry Lee Scott's *Military Dictionary* covered the foraging of timber, as well as food, and the same procedures were supposed to be followed for gathering wood: an officer had to be in charge, paperwork had to be issued, and civilians regardless of their political views would be treated fairly. Scott went beyond the Articles of War, however, by summarizing decades of army practice regarding the woodlands. He put forth a practical, unromantic view of the forest, positing that it existed to supply timber for human beings. Soldiers should use wood to build roads, living quarters, breastworks, parapets, palisades, stockades, abatis, and chevaux-de-frise, the barricades used to obstruct cavalry. He offered specific advice to the troops, suggesting that they choose timber from the middle of a forest and make use of both mature wood and green wood, depending on circumstance; pliant green wood could be used for fascines, long cylindrical bundles of brushwood. He recommended choosing young trees with trunks 6 to 18 inches in diameter to build corduroy roads. He praised all types of pine, which he believed highly useful for constructing buildings.[3]

Scott's advocacy of using timber as needed dovetailed perfectly with the antebellum idea of the "round forty," that is, the practices of squatters on public land who grabbed wood and then moved on. He was either unaware of or indifferent to the views of ex-President James Madison, agricultural reformer Edmund Ruffin, and a few other writers who had urged more active conservation of timber and other natural resources before 1861. Inherent in Scott's book is the assumption that wood could be obtained from anyone, at any time, and he encouraged the use of a great deal of timber. Even though quartermasters were in charge of lumber, fuel, soldiers' quarters, and general supplies, Scott believed that all troops should have a knowledge of carpentry sufficient to build their own quarters, even advising soldiers to pry bark off trees so it could be flattened and dried to use in construction. He suggested that troops should be able to construct a wooden bridge within one hour and to build portable sawmills capable of producing 3,000 feet of timber daily. He self-consciously linked military policy to the frontier period in the nation's history, advising troops building their quarters to put up balloon frames as builders did "in our western country."[4]

WOODWORK

As Scott remarked, infantrymen called "pioneers" usually did the important work of cutting down of timber. The term, so redolent of the frontier era, conveyed simultaneously patriotism, urgency, and wastefulness. When the Confederate army published its own military regulations in 1863, it used the same term for the same activities, defining pioneers as soldiers who removed obstacles to the army's progress, mended roads, and erected defenses. The South and the North had their respective frontiers in earlier generations, so the term resonated for men in both armies. In both armies, pioneers were supposed to be detailed from different companies in a regiment, furnished with tools, and put to work. Their service for both armies began immediately with the outbreak of the war. The South's topography, including the location and quality of its timber, was a significant factor in the military effort by both armies.[5]

Federal quartermaster James Rusling believed that all troops hated doing pioneer work, and some men in both armies did find it dull, too much like farm labor at home. The work could be grueling, as men sometimes wielded axes all day and into the night. Yet other men found the exertion invigorating. Soldiers respected a nimble "axeman" who could identify useful wood in a forest, chop down trees, and split trunks efficiently, skills that were just as valuable in wartime as in peacetime. Both armies valued this labor, sending troops to protect pioneers at work, although some pioneers carried their own guns. Throughout the war, they were known to fire occasionally when enemy troops came into view.[6]

The idea somehow developed that white men did pioneer work in the Union army, while slaves did pioneer work in the Confederate army, perhaps because a few veterans asserted this false notion in their memoirs. In fact, the racial composition of the pioneer forces varied a great deal in both armies. In the Northern military, some officers attached black men to white pioneer units and paid them for their work, while other whites organized black men into pioneer parties without mustering them into the US Army; both slave men and freedmen worked for the military cutting wood. In the Southern army, some white men worked as pioneers, and some black men did too, but it is not clear if they were slaves or freedmen hired or impressed by the military.[7]

Moreover, thousands of white soldiers in both armies foraged for wood but were not always designated as pioneers. On an authorized foraging expedition, officers chose their men, gave them axes, and sent them out to start chopping; the number of men varied, as few as eight or as many as 100. Throughout the war, sappers and miners did the labor of pioneers without being designated as such, as did engineers and mechanics. Soldiers cut wood as part of fatigue duty, of course, but many troops cut and hauled timber without being called pioneers or put on fatigue duty. Officers divided up the labor in an improvised fashion. Ulysses S. Grant once advised William T. Sherman to send his pioneers or other "good men" to cut trees and provide fuel for steamboats in Louisiana. Soldiers asked friends and relatives to send them axes from home, so they could take wood whenever they wished.[8]

IN THE FIELD

As soon as the war started, Union troops began acting on the concept of military necessity when it came to taking wood. This was especially true for one of the army's prime tasks, constructing forts. In the first months of the contest, Yankee soldiers felled many trees to build fortifications in eastern Virginia, and by August 1861, miles of forest encircling the town of Fairfax had disappeared. By the end of 1861, the federal army had taken down "grand forests, centuries old," to build fortifications in that part of the state, a Yankee soldier told army nurse Mary Livermore. The same process happened all over the region, as the infantry did most of the work taking down wood. Union troops cut down "all the timber" near New Madrid, Missouri, Confederate General Gideon Pillow observed, as they constructed defensive works there in the summer of 1861.[9]

Just as important, Yankee soldiers acted on their own, gathering wood in unsanctioned foraging trips. When they camped in August 1861 in Fayette County, Virginia, they burned many fences on the plantation of the widow Ellen Tompkins without notifying or compensating her. Private John Billings recalled that for months before General John Pope issued his orders in July 1862, the soldiers viewed all timber (and all food) as "perquisites," and officers did not interfere when they acted on their beliefs. Many officers either approved or overlooked such conduct. Although US General John Abercrombie commanded troops to refrain from seizing fence rails from civilians near Aldie, Virginia, a colonel told the men to take them anyway to build fires one cold night. With a happy shout, they ran forward to comply.[10]

Southern troops did the same thing, however, seizing and destroying timber before serious combat started. Well before the Confederate army published its own military regulations in January 1863, numerous accounts by soldiers and civilians show that rebel troops shared Scott's assumptions that the material world had to yield what their army needed, even if that meant seizing property from other white Southerners. In the war's early months, rebel soldiers began cutting down forests and destroying fences all over the South. They too acted under orders. In the summer of 1861, Captain W. H. Werth prepared for the Battle of Big Bethel by cutting down trees to obstruct the road, throwing down all the fences nearby and clearing yet more trees so he could maneuver a howitzer into position. In the fall of that year, Private Adam Kersh saw his unit take down 150 acres of timber to build log cabins and fortifications in Virginia. By December 1861, rebel forces had cut a full mile of timber in front of Fort Pillow, Tennessee, and placed the logs crosswise to obstruct approaches by the enemy.[11]

Rebel troops, like federal soldiers, seized wood on unsanctioned foraging trips. Their version of the "round forty" revealed the same acquisitiveness, and they did not always give out the expected paperwork. In November 1861, some troops took a day's supply of logs from a pile on some recently cleared land, according to soldier John Worsham, with no idea on who owned the lumber. Soldiers took fence rails for their firewood, as Captain William W. Blackford and his comrades did on a snowy night in Virginia without a word about who owned the rails. Distance from an army camp did not necessarily protect civilians from losing timber, because troops roamed through hill and dale for sizable distances hunting wood. Soldiers who camped near Raleigh, North Carolina, walked for a mile to find timber for their cabins, which they seized without acknowledging that private citizens might own it.[12]

Troops seeking wood sometimes targeted civilians because of their political views, despite Henry Lee Scott's admonition in his *Military Dictionary* that friendly, hostile, and neutral people should be treated the same. This was true for both armies. By word of mouth, rumor, or observation, they could sometimes discern which people were pro-Confederate, and some federal soldiers deliberately selected rebel property when they chopped down trees. In the lower Mississippi River Valley, they took down the orange groves on three plantations owned by rebels. Confederates serving in Kentucky seemed to enjoy seizing wood from pro-Union inhabitants, Private Andrew Richardson admitted in 1861. But many troops were working too rapidly to ascertain the political views of local people, rushing to take fence rails or cut wood, sometimes within minutes of arriving in a particular place. Edward Bagby, a civilian in Virginia, saw fences disappear wherever the armies stopped on the march.[13]

Some officers in both armies tried to follow regulations and give out documents for the timber they confiscated. Rebel Captain Charles D. Hill certified a claim for twenty-four cords of wood taken from Willis J. Bunkley, the sum of 72 Confederate dollars payable by any rebel quartermaster. Federal Colonel James B. Fry insisted that procedures had to be followed and the correct forms used when his soldiers confiscated fences from the residents of Huntsville, Alabama. But not all officers were so scrupulous. Yankee troops cut wood for four days on Anne Frobel's plantation in northern Virginia, taking most of the trees on her property in the summer of 1861. Her sister asked US General John Sedgwick for what she called a "certificate" for the timber, and he promised she would receive one although she was openly pro-Confederate, but it never arrived. Such negligence, done deliberately or by accident, as well as blunders, inefficiencies, and indifference, can be found in the military bureaucracies on both sides.[14]

In the winter of 1861–1862, the armies withdrew as custom dictated to their winter quarters to rest until spring. Officers searched the woods for an appealing location in or near a forest, as Henry Lee Scott advised, and there the troops began cutting down trees for log cabins. The work was time-consuming, taking up to several hours for one cabin. Scott's *Military Dictionary* indicated that at least forty-eight trees were necessary to build a cabin, sometimes more, depending on the building's size. The quarters were supposed to be laid out neatly by rank, although men sometimes threw up the buildings willy-nilly. They furnished the interiors with furniture they carved from wood taken from local forests. The troops also built chapels and barracks out of wood as necessary.[15]

Many soldiers knew something about domestic forestry and the use of wood because they had grown up on farms. Some men in both armies worked as carpenters before 1861, and some of them knew the language of carpentry, such as "shakes," an archaic term for shingles. Lumberjacks, sawyers, and millers had their expertise, of course, but some bootmakers knew enough to chop down trees properly. City dwellers, store clerks, and university students knew little to nothing about timber, but they had to learn how to cleave wood, just as soldiers had to learn how to cook. Troops acquired other skills, including how to gather kindling and how to make fires, when necessary, with green wood.[16]

These soldiers encountered a wooded landscape of formidable complexity. They studied it closely, paying attention to forest placement, estimated acreage, and the forest's proximity to roads, streams, and rivers. Troops in both armies could recognize a variety of species, such

as red oak, sassafras, tulip poplar, and evergreens of all kinds. They
knew the folklore about various trees, such as the fact that tea made
from white oak bark could cure digestive disorders and that dogs
did not like hickory trees. They continued the venerable custom of
carving their names onto trees, as federal soldier John N. Ferguson
did, inscribing his on a beech as he passed through a Tennessee village
in 1862.[17]

In their perception of the woodlands, troops from the North and
South shared the ideas of most antebellum Americans. They believed
that productive farmland interspersed with trees and meadows was
pleasing to the eye, particularly "wooded and undulating" landscapes, as
New Yorker C. W. Boyce penned in reverie about Virginia's Shenandoah
Valley in 1862. Soldiers in both armies, many of them farmers or farmers'
sons, noticed which trees flourished in which kinds of soil, and they could
identify original forests that appeared to be centuries old. Indeed, lightly
settled forest were found almost everywhere in the region in the war's
early years.[18]

The South was full of pine, Henry Lee Scott's favorite wood. The
pine is an indicator species, meaning that it dominates the environment
almost everywhere it appears, and an evergreen, capable of growing to
great heights. The tree can live hundreds of years, and it sinks taproots
deep in the ground. The pine is native to the region and includes such
varieties as loblollies and slash pines. Longleaf, the most common variety, was also known as yellow pine, Southern pine, pitch pine, and
Georgia pine, and it was much sought after for its tensile strength, high
resin content, and resistance to disease. In 1861, the *Brooklyn Eagle*
noted that the seceded states had taken with them the nation's best pine
forests, as indeed they had. Many soldiers recognized the ubiquitous
pine, which grew throughout the region from Virginia to Texas.[19]

Just as soldiers believed that there was a food hierarchy, with beef
at the top, they believed there was a timber hierarchy, with pine at the
top. The troops preferred to use pine for their quarters and campfires,
because the trunk was relatively easy to fell and the heartwood kindled
easily. Both armies liked to build their quarters near or in a pine forest,
so they could have full access to its resources. Soldiers also relied on a
pine forest's density to move furtively toward the enemy or to conceal
batteries that were under construction.[20]

Troops in both armies favored pine for more personal uses. They made
a fermented drink from pine boughs, and many also knew that pine could
serve medicinal purposes. US General William T. Sherman believed that a

FIGURE 4.1 Pine Cottage, built by Union soldiers.
Courtesy of the Library of Congress.

concoction of pine leaves, which are actually filled with Vitamin C, could
ward off scurvy. (Rebel troops sometimes employed the regional term
"pine tags.") Yet other soldiers preferred the pine for aesthetic reasons.
Maybe because of the pine forest's familiarity, rebel troops felt safe when
quartered within its canopy. A Southern writer called the pine God's gift
to humanity because of its manifold uses, which is, paradoxically, one
reason the pine forests disappeared quickly.[21]

Both armies practiced what is now called "clear-cutting" for all forests,
not just pine, removing every tree on a site. The term dates from the
1920s, but the practice goes far back in human history. Starting in 1861,
soldiers engaged in routine clear-cutting in many places. In the fall of that
year, before the Battle of Carnifix Ferry, West Virginia, rebel troops took
down a mile of forest and built wooden breastworks in the space, and
near Fort Monroe, Virginia, federal troops "cleared off" all the trees as
they made camp, Yankee Private Alfred Bellard said. They also cleared
forests to expose the enemy to view. Confederate soldiers chopped down
all the trees on a point of land near the Potomac River to prevent the
Union artillery from crossing it unobserved.[22]

We might expect that Confederate troops would be more reluctant to take timber, more aware of the damage to the terrain and the people living on it, but this was not always the case. They mowed down the forest, tree after tree, just as Northerners did. Near Bolivar, Virginia, rebel soldiers "wantonly destroyed" 20 acres of woodland in early 1862, onlookers said. In the spring of that year, other troops cut down the forest for 100 yards on each side of the road to Williamsburg, Virginia, to make abatis. Even religious men appeared to be unwilling to face the ethical issues, particularly regarding what they were doing to the civilian population. Corporal Randolph McKim, a future chaplain, boasted about the roof on his cabin made from trees "felled by our own hands," with no reference to who owned the trees.[23]

A few Confederate soldiers did express some uneasiness, laced with guilt, about the taking of so much timber. During the Peninsular Campaign, after troops near Richmond burned many fence rails on local farms, Private J. W. Stipe insisted that they had no other choice. "Wet, without axes, what could they do," he queried. Lieutenant Albert Goodloe regretted seizing fence rails from civilians who were "our friends," but said that soldiers had to build fires to endure the cold weather. But most troops maintained a thundering silence about the ethical issues involved or the practical consequences of what the army was doing to civilians. Private Carlton McCarthy used the passive voice to depict rebel troops cutting timber: trees "rush down," then campfires "start," as if no human agency was involved.[24]

In fact, rebel soldiers mentioned the destruction of the woodlands in an offhand fashion, as if it was a routine feature of warfare. Did they think that the region's wood supply was inexhaustible, as some people did in the antebellum era? Even if they believed that, what about the rights of private property? Did they expect that the issue of confiscated timber would be resolved after the war? If so, they did not elaborate on these points in their wartime writings. Some of them even implied that soldiers were superior to civilians. Private Arthur P. Ford boasted that soldiers learned how to kindle a fire with wet wood during a rain, which he believed few civilians could manage. All too many of them seemed unaware of the impact on civilians. After an officer set fire to a jumble of fence rails in a trench in North Carolina, it was jokingly dubbed the "roasted ditch," which the owners probably did not find amusing. Southern commanders, with a few exceptions, permitted such destructive acts. Major General Stonewall Jackson, one such exception, insisted that his men replace fencing they burned without his permission in early

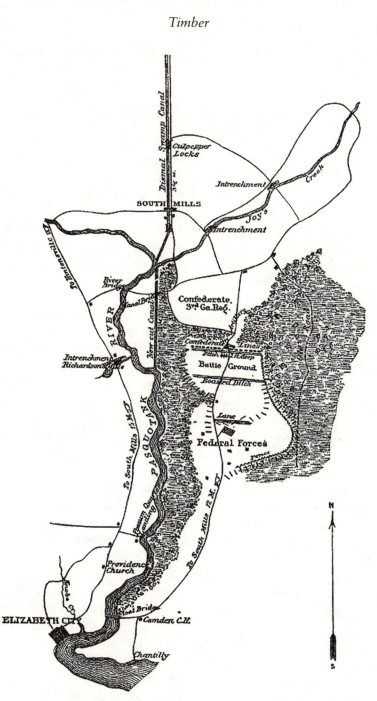

FIGURE 4.2 The "roasted ditch," North Carolina, April 1862.
From the *Official Records of the War.*

1862, and he threatened to punish an entire regiment if it happened again.[25]

MORE CAMPAIGNS, SPRING 1862

When the spring came, and the two armies vacated their winter quarters, soldiers found it difficult to abandon the cabins they had worked so hard to build. Some enterprising fellows sold their huts to civilians for cash as they departed, while other troops burned their quarters to render them useless to their opponents, since soldiers were known to return to their old quarters if military campaigns brought them back to the area. Dozens of wooden villages, instant ghost towns, nonetheless dotted the countryside. Civilians sometimes scavenged the abandoned quarters for timber and then hauled it away.[26]

As they plunged into the spring campaigns, both armies continued to destroy a lot of timber. Southern and Northern troops hacked their way through leafy forests and undergrowth to create pathways for the armies. Both armies constructed more fortifications, which could grow to enormous size. Some forts had the dignity of names, such as the Confederate Fort Magruder in Virginia, while others were thrown swiftly together and then abandoned as the armies departed, the wood wasted. Whenever they paused on the march, squads of men headed out into the countryside to pull down fences to make fires. They burned a great deal of wood, some 1,900 fence rails on a single property, the Whiting farm in Moorefield, Virginia, within three weeks in the spring of 1862.[27]

As these big armies campaigned through the spring and into the summer, their assault on the South's woodlands continued unabated. When federal troops constructed a bridge over the Rappahannock River in Virginia, "Lumber was taken wherever it could be found," US Brigadier General Herman Haupt remarked, adding that his soldiers sometimes gave receipts to the civilian owners although he was "not certain" they always abided by procedure. The troops could inflict damage on trees but leave them standing. Northern soldiers near New Market, Louisiana, stripped evergreen trees of their boughs and branches to make some rough carpets for their tents. Confederate troops could be just as voracious. In the vicinity of Newbern, North Carolina, they felled timber "in every direction" to halt the progress of Union forces.[28]

Some troops praised the visual beauty of the Southern landscape, whether or not they were natives of the region. Men in both armies could feel moved by the tranquility of little groves of trees, the blooming profusion of a springtime orchard, or the sheltering shade on village streets. US Colonel Thomas W. Higginson declared that the Barnwell plantation in low-country South Carolina, with its long avenue of live oaks, was the loveliest place he had seen in the region. Seneca Thrall, a federal army doctor, admired the well-tended plantation grounds and decorative trees in Lake Providence, Louisiana, calling it the most beautiful place he had ever seen.[29]

But the aesthetic appeal of the forest made little difference when the armies had to harvest timber. Northern Private Roger Hannaford lauded Hanover County, Virginia, as "nobly timbered," even though his unit then proceeded to consume much of that timber. Union Colonel Nathan Dudley confessed that destroying the decorative trees on a Louisiana plantation was the most painful act of his military career, but he cut them down as ordered. Rebel soldiers were no different. One Confederate soldier reveled in the beauty of cedars growing near Fredericksburg, Virginia, but then proceeded to chop them down to build a cabin.[30]

William Le Duc, a federal quartermaster, appreciated the value of timber and the beauty of a forest, but he too seized wood as needed. Born in Ohio in 1823, he grew up on farms all over the Midwest. He knew how to build a zigzag fence and construct a log cabin; as a schoolboy he helped his father build a frame house. In adult life, he practiced law in Minnesota, but he was not very political, and he joined the army in 1862 only after a friend suggested that his methodical habits would make him a good quartermaster. So he visited Washington, DC, with letters of introduction and obtained his appointment from Secretary of War Edwin Stanton. He joined the Army of the Potomac and initiated his service with the rank of captain in Virginia in May 1862. He started exploiting the local wood supply immediately. When his men needed light to build a bridge one evening, he took rails from a fence nearby and set them on fire, with no mention of the civilian owners and no paperwork for them. He had been in the service for about two weeks.[31]

Troops in both armies began to comment in 1862 on the war's destructive impact on the physical environment. They noted the acres of stumps left behind by the troops and the standing trees devoid of bark because soldiers had pried it off. A Yankee private, William Parkinson, bewailed that so many trees that had been "killed," in a rather obvious metaphor, near Corinth, Mississippi, when rebels occupied the town in 1862. Soldiers in both armies castigated the enemy for threatening or damaging the countryside, claiming that the enemy had transformed the terrain into

FIGURE 4.3 Federal Quartermaster William LeDuc.
Courtesy of the Minnesota Historical Society.

the antithesis of what a landscape should look like, but both armies did their part in the damage.[32]

In the major battles of 1862, the armies wreaked tremendous damage on the forest in a single day, sometimes within the space of a few hours. This has been true for most wars in the modern era. Men in both armies felt awestruck as the percussions of battle transformed the physical environment, which is why so many of them wrote about it. At the Battle of First Bull Run, Confederate physician D. B. Conrad represented the trees on the scene as "mangled." At the Battle of Shiloh in April 1862, soldiers watched giant trees twist in the gunfire until their limbs thudded to the ground. These scenes, in which flying shells cut everything in their path and ruined great stretches of woods, were both terrifying and grand, Northern soldier Lucius Barber remarked.[33]

Both armies committed deliberate acts of arson, which grew more numerous in 1862. Both sides used what is called broadcast fire, a free-burning fire that is rarely deployed in modern societies because it is so hard to control. Southern General James Longstreet told his officers to set fire to timber near Richmond in June 1862 to surround the enemy with smoke and heat; "fire the timber all around," the order read, and "make it thorough." Fires in pine forests can easily turn into infernos because of a process called fuel continuity, as flames burn rapidly through layers of debris on the ground, the undergrowth, and the overstory, and the region was full of pine. After watching his comrades burn "almost every thing combustible" – forests, fences, and housing – Union Major Samuel T. Wells remarked that armies desolated the physical world for friend and foe alike. All this took place during the "soft war," so-called, before military policy formally changed in summer 1862.[34]

Some Union commanders nevertheless tried to follow official policy on foraging as outlined in the Articles of War. They made soldiers give documents to white Southern civilians whatever their politics might be for the seizure of fence rails and other goods, with reimbursement promised for some time in the future. General George B. McClellan sternly reminded his officers to issue the "most stringent instructions" to eliminate the theft of fence rails in the Peninsula in May 1862 and to purchase wood as needed from the owners. Other officers tried to protect the female relatives of prominent politicians, such as the elderly Mrs. Clement Clay of Alabama, if they had personal ties to the family. Charles Denby made sure that Yankee troops did not abscond with her fences because his father-in-law had known her son Clement Clay, Jr., in the US Senate, although her son was then serving in the rebel government.[35]

The Confederate army also seized timber directly from the civilian population. From the war's beginning, troops commandeered lumber mills from civilians and ordered them to produce lumber for the military. They told Peleg Clarke, Jr., who lived near Fredericksburg, Virginia, that he would face arrest and loss of the property if he did not comply. Officers took wood directly from civilians in Richmond, the capitol, and from people they met out in the field, and they also purchased lumber from the public. The military advertised in the newspapers so they could buy wood from the citizenry, specifying willow, for instance, for the powder factory in Augusta, Georgia.[36]

A small number of civilians benefited directly from signing contracts to deliver wood for the rebel military. Surprisingly, a few white women, such as Ellen Elmore, and a few free black men, such as Horace King, obtained these contracts, but most of the recipients seem to have been white men. Those civilian contractors supplied thousands of cords of wood and feet of plank, and they could make a nice profit, so much so that individual planters sometimes approached officers in their neighborhoods to suggest putting a contract together. That could be risky, however, since federal troops arrested civilians who contracted to provide wood for the Southern government and then confiscated the mills, just as Southern troops arrested civilians who did the same for the Union.[37]

CIVILIANS, THEIR FENCES, AND THE FOREST

In the first year or two of the war, white civilians of all political loyalties gladly helped the armies in wood matters. Confederate sympathizers let rebel soldiers sharpen their axes on grindstones on local farms, and they consulted with rebel troops when soldiers asked them if planks had been augured correctly. Southern Unionists aided the Yankees when they could, defying the rebel forces. Mr. B. B. McKenney of Lancaster County, Virginia, voted in 1860 for the "Union candidate" (probably John Bell, who won the state) and opposed secession; in 1861, he managed to fulfill a business contract and send many cords of wood to his business partner in New York. Apolitical civilians seemed content to do business with anybody. Before he was arrested by federal forces, a roustabout named John McGonegal plied the Mississippi River and its tributaries cutting wood for anyone who would hire him.[38]

Other civilians actively resisted the confiscation of their timber and fence rails. Sometimes there was a verbal confrontation. When Northern troops arrived at a farm near Alexandria, Virginia, they confiscated food and then started pulling down the timber. The owner, an unidentified white woman, asked an officer, "have you no[t] laid waste enough," to which he replied that military necessity required it. Other civilians took precautions to save their property. They could not hide a stand of trees, but they could hide parcels of wood. As Yankee soldiers arrived in a neighborhood, local people hurriedly took their fences down and concealed them from the troops. But the rebel army could be just as demanding. During the early months of 1862, Fannie Hume's aunt lost most of her fences to a Southern brigade passing by her Virginia farm and managed to save her garden fence only after "much difficulty," presumably by arguing, pleading, or abject begging.[39]

Civilians in some parts of the South began reporting wood shortages in 1862, as well as rising prices for timber in both town and country.

A few local governments took note of the deprivation and extended help to the needy. The city of Mobile, Alabama, gave small amounts of wood to the impoverished as a charity, and the municipality of Fredericksburg reimbursed civilians for the loss of cordwood, fencing, and timber during the Yankee shelling of December 1862. But most civilians had to cope on their own. They collected driftwood on river banks or resorted to chopping down trees in local gardens. Yet other households learned to do without fires in daily life.[40]

By 1862, civilians began to realize that both armies could seize their timber with no warning. Soldiers often cut timber at night, or at the crack of dawn, so that noncombatants discovered what was happening only when they heard a ruckus in the yard. A young white woman saw rebel troops serving in Virginia with James Longstreet burn many of the local fence rails as they passed by one night in April 1862. Civilians feared the Union army more, however, because the US Army was bigger and had greater physical needs. When soldiers took down some 2,000 dollars' worth of fences from their farm near Alexandria, Virginia, the owners called them "vile creatures," but the timber was gone.[41]

Civilians could sometimes obtain reimbursements for wood they forfeited to the rebel army. The Confederate Quartermaster General set up such procedures in 1861, and an incomplete Register of Claims covering some Virginians has survived. The register, dating from 1861 to 1864, lists several dozen claims for timber that was damaged, burned, or seized by the Southern military. Rebel Congressman Muscoe Garnett, for example, owned a plantation in Essex County and received 115.28 Confederate dollars for thirty-six cords of wood taken from his estate on March 29, 1862. Other payments could be more substantial, as high as 2,600 Confederate dollars, but the claims process was time-consuming, taking as long as eighteen months, and required approval by quartermasters or their assistants. Applicants whose claims were approved could get payments from any rebel quartermaster, but civilians whose claims were rejected got no explanation. The payments were welcome, of course, yet civilians still lost money because of the time lag in payments. Timber had so many uses on a farm, and it took several years for saplings to reach maturity. And the underlying premise, that the army came first, remained securely in place.[42]

In the tradition of communalism, white Southern civilians were still willing to help each other with timber shortages. The familiar customs from the antebellum era lasted in some places into 1862. Many people felt an abiding sense of obligation for their relatives, and they gave firewood

FIGURE 4.4 Women in wartime Cedar Mountain, Virginia.
Courtesy of the Library of Congress.

to kinfolk who needed it when timber was scarce. Civilians who were regular churchgoers donated wood to their places of worship for Sunday services. But well-meaning folk, no matter how generous, could not take care of everyone. Needy civilians resorted to begging for wood, sometimes from the Yankee army. Just before Christmas 1862, some white women showed up at a Union army camp in Tennessee asking if they could have some old boards lying around the camp.[43]

Many civilians expressed a deep anger as the forests started to disappear. Pro-Confederate residents blamed the destruction on the Union army, of course. John Spence, a Tennessee merchant, thought the US Army took far too much from noncombatants and should have left the owners a "reserve" of timber, at the very least. Rebel women, equally offended, articulated a keen sense of the aesthetic loss. In Louisiana, Sarah Morgan cried that Northern soldiers took "all our beautiful woods," and Judith McGuire felt indignant at the failure of rebel authorities to halt the destruction of the Virginia forest. How could "old" white men (her description) bear to see "ancestral trees" taken down, she wanted to know. None of them mentioned that rebel soldiers of all ages took down the forests, too.[44]

When Pope's Orders were issued in July 1862, permitting soldier to live off the land, they had little impact on the federal army's consumption of wood. What mattered more than policy were the army's material needs, which drove the behavior of men on the ground, and those needs continued to be enormous. There had been much destruction of timber before Pope's announcement, and there would be afterwards. Pope stipulated that pro-Union civilians would receive paperwork, and that happened, sometimes. But General Pope disregarded his own policy a few weeks after he issued it, during his retreat after the Battle of Cedar Mountain in August 1862. When his army camped for a week on Mary Jennings' property in Fauquier County, Virginia, they consumed over 28,000 fence rails. Jennings was a Unionist, but she received no compensation for her losses until well after 1865, even though Yankee quartermasters were nearby and Pope had already complained that soldiers were using General Orders No. 5 as a license to plunder.[45]

Individual officers still tried to conform to procedure. Yankee Quartermaster Simon Perkins, Jr., made a good-faith effort to follow regulations most of the time, but he was unable to prevent a civilian contractor from cutting timber on private land contrary to procedure, and sometimes he broke his own rules. While serving in Tennessee, he told a wagon master to simply "take" fence rails if he could find wood no other way. Other officers made good-faith attempts to correct mistakes when the system failed. US Major General James McPherson asked his subordinates to examine the claim of one Mr. Brown, whose lumber was taken from his mill near Vicksburg for "Government purposes." But the bureaucracy as a whole, as an institution, was as inefficient as ever.[46]

In the fall of 1862, General William T. Sherman forcefully reminded white Southerners that armies had always consumed a great deal of wood. He informed the people of Memphis, Tennessee, of this salient fact while occupying the city in September. After they complained about the army's behavior during the occupation, the general stated in a letter to a local newspaper that armies waste and destroy fences, trees, and houses by necessity, nodding toward Henry Lee Scott without quoting him. He promised to do his best to stop plunder, which he thought went beyond the military's legitimate use of resources, and he quoted the Articles of

War on that score, but he acknowledged that armies did a great deal of unavoidable damage to the physical environment.[47]

Furthermore, the material needs of the Union army escalated, as the armies grew larger; in January 1862, approximately 530,000 Yankee soldiers were present for duty, and a year later the total was approximately 700,000. Since chopping down trees was as hard as ever, troops preferred to seize fence rails, and they continued to do so without getting an officer's permission or giving out documents to civilians. Federal soldiers chose Confederate sympathizers when they could, making sure to burn all the fences on a secessionist's farm in Boone County, Kentucky, even though it was located in a Border State. Their hunger for wood could even undermine military operations. Northern troops stole railroad crossties one night for their campfires, prying up dozens of ties in Virginia and hustling them away on a borrowed hand car, which of course left the railroads nonfunctional.[48]

Some federal soldiers, adhering to the antebellum values of stewardship, abhorred the phenomenal waste of wood they witnessed. In December 1862, Private John Potter was "revolted" as he watched a heap of valuable lumber go up in flames in Mississippi. Some troops felt sorry for civilians, particularly when they seized wood from Union supporters, and yet others decided to act on their remorse no matter what political views civilians might hold. Colonel Charles Tilden serving with the 16th Maine Volunteers pitied an old white woman, wrinkled and gray-haired, who came to his camp after Yankee troops seized her fence rails, boards from her outbuildings, a calf, and a tea kettle. Tilden gave her cash from his own wallet and took up a collection from the officers. The colonel, who sometimes indulged his men who violated regulations, thought there should be limits to what soldiers were allowed to do.[49]

When the Northern army settled into winter camps in 1862–1863, the men used a great deal of timber. Again, the scale of the army's consumption of wood is staggering. Soldier Philo Pearce, camped near Fredericksburg, Virginia, estimated that the army used up 200 acres of pine that winter to build their quarters and fuel their campfires. In November 1862, Private Anthony W. Ross estimated that each man in his brigade of 10,000, the 73rd Ohio Volunteer Infantry, burned an average of five rails daily, or a total of 50,000 rails every day. The confiscation of timber reached in every direction, wherever the armies went. For a distance of 2 miles along the Tennessee River near Nashville, and 1½ miles into the interior on each bank, federal troops cut down every tree and tore down every fence for fire wood.[50]

The assumption that military necessity must prevail persisted into 1863, as Yankee soldiers demonstrated the same appetite for timber. As troops journeyed down the rivers in the Mississippi Valley, they landed frequently to take wood from the banks. Captain Cyrus Hussey, who took part in these expeditions, said that his men were "Wooding nearly all day" in Louisiana with "Much pillaging," but had no further comment about the pillaging. William G. Kendrick, another captain, admitted in February 1863 that his men burned thousands of fence rails near Murfreesboro, Tennessee, "without compunction" or "conscience." In these increasingly empty landscapes, an intact fence became an extraordinary sight. Colonel Hiram Strong, scanning the countryside with a spyglass, exclaimed with surprise when he spotted a fence in rural Tennessee in the spring of 1863.[51]

Yankee soldiers continued to waste a great deal of wood wherever they went. Sometimes they wasted timber by accident. Troops from the 13th Massachusetts Infantry set fire to the grassy banks of the Rappahannock River while cooking over a campfire in 1863, and within a few moments, flames raced through the pine trees lining the waterway. Other troops purposely destroyed wood out of a desire for revenge, setting fire to abandoned enemy camps because they heard that Confederate troops destroyed property during General Robert E. Lee's invasion of Pennsylvania in the summer of 1863. The men wasted a lot of wood because of the chaotic, unpredictable nature of military campaigns. One federal unit built their winter quarters near Fredericksburg, Virginia, in 1862–1863, but then were abruptly ordered to go elsewhere before they occupied the buildings, which happened many times during the war.[52]

CONFEDERATE REGULATIONS

Rebel troops, who were of course unaffected by Pope's edicts, remained as hungry for timber as ever. In 1862, before the Battle of Antietam, they made barricades out of fence rails and "whatever they could get," a soldier observed. Some troops clearly felt that their conduct was justified, if not imperative for their survival. Rumors circulated among Confederate soldiers of pickets freezing to death at night, and some of them insisted that the choice was "'Keep the axes going or freeze'," as Brigadier General Elisha Paxton recorded. They continued to take wood from civilians regardless of their political affinities. By the fall of 1862, civilians in Alabama and Mississippi had complained so often about frequent, irregular impressments of wood and other items by rebel officers that the War Department asked the commander, Major General John Forney, for an explanation. There is no record of his answer.[53]

In January 1863, the Confederate military formally enunciated its policies with the *Regulations for the Army of the Confederate States*. They included the old Articles of War, including Article 52 banning plunder and pillage and Article 54 banning the waste or spoliation of trees. Yet their policy mirrored Northern policy on the central idea that its army had to have timber and that soldiers had the right to take it from any source, including from civilians who supported the rebel army. Showing some awareness of the damage being done to the forests, the Confederates introduced one requirement that was absent from Yankee policy: "ornamental" trees on public grounds could not be destroyed unless a chief of ordnance allowed it. Evoking the antebellum creed of stewardship, they deplored the immorality of plundering Southern civilians of their property, not just their timber, calling acts of plunder "crimes of such enormity" that they should result in "awful" punishments.[54]

After the publication of these *Regulations* in 1863, some rebel officers complied with the spirit and the letter of official policy. They gave paperwork to civilians for wood they took from private property, Colonel William Hoke writing up a voucher for five cords of wood burned by his troops near Front Royal, Virginia. Some officers made their men compensate civilians with labor instead of payment. In the fall of 1863, Lieutenant General Richard Ewell required his men to repair any fences they damaged in central Virginia before the command moved on. As the army began cutting timber on private land to build works to protect Atlanta, Major General J. F. Gilmer advised another officer to abide by policy and have the timber's value assessed by two appraisers and an umpire, a "good plan" Gilmer had already followed.[55]

Again, a few rebel soldiers hinted at some uneasiness about the relentless demands of the military, even as they met those demands. One physician explained that he had to "trespass" to obtain wood for his hospital near Chattanooga, and Private Louis Leon admitted that he and his comrades "stole" fence rails from civilians to make fires one chilly night in North Carolina in 1863. Soldiers realized that the absence of fences made it hard for farmers to plant or raise crops, but they took the fences anyway, and not always for the most compelling reasons. Archibald Atkinson, Jr., a surgeon, watched his unit take down a "good" rail fence in Caroline County, Virginia, so they could cross a ditch one summer morning in 1863.[56]

But most Confederate soldiers followed the cold-eyed axiom that the military's needs came first. They cut and hauled a vast amount of wood while building winter quarters, chapels, and, in a supreme irony, some arbors for shade on a warm day. They chopped down trees to slow the enemy army's advance on the roads or railways, piling up logs and setting fire to them. They took their assumptions with them when they left the Confederacy. In July 1863, after Robert E. Lee's loss at Gettysburg, his troops retreated toward Virginia and took down barns on the Maryland side of the Potomac to build a pontoon bridge over the River.[57]

Rebel troops exhibited their usual indifference to who might own the timber in the landscape. While serving at Chattanooga, Private Jesse Andrews and his captain had no tents for shelter, so they climbed into the nearby hills to cut timber to build their own shanty, with no reference to the owners, much less any paperwork issued to anybody. Men in gray toppled trees from many different properties in a short period of time. They chopped down enough timber to cover "10,000 little hill[s] and ravines" near Port Hudson, Louisiana, one witness said, to halt the advance of Northern troops in 1863. The army still wasted a great deal of wood because of the vagaries of combat. After building forts and shelters at Missionary Ridge in the fall of 1863, troops had to abandon them all because the Union army bested them in combat.[58]

Just as we saw with the destruction of food, some rebel officers appeared to be so eager to hurt the enemy that they were blind to the repercussions for local white people. Colonel Wirt Adams learned that enemy ships on the Mississippi River were running low on fuel, but "fortunately," he told his superior, he had burned some 10,000 cords of wood during a previous visit to Greenville. That would hurt the Yankee fleet, he believed, but he made no comment about the effect on civilians. When trains packed with Confederate soldiers moved through the region, they stopped to cut up random fence rails to supply the engines and then chugged away. After the Battle of Chickamauga, Southern troops inflicted a "great deal of the destruction" on the Gillespie farm nearby, seizing many fences and much timber. Since none of the Confederate court-martial records survived, we do not know how many soldiers were punished for such actions, but Southern troops took resources as needed, with no protections for ornamental trees. The Confederate policy declared in 1863 had little effect on rebel troops, much like Pope's policy shift of 1862 on Northern troops.[59]

A LAND WITHOUT TREES

By the start of 1863, outright deforestation was under way in various parts of the region, although it happened in disparate places at different points in time. In early 1863, federal troops cleared the woods for 2 miles around the town of Jacksonville, Florida, for purposes of "safety," Thomas W. Higginson related. In Stafford County, Virginia, where the Union army used much timber to build their forts, Yankee soldier Austin Stearns said there was not a tree in sight when he camped there in the spring of 1863. Soon afterwards, a journalist portrayed Stafford County as a tundra with no forest, only blackened, burned-over earth that resembled nothing so much as a giant race track in the countryside. The damage inflicted on the forest was both intentional – the result of deliberate actions by both armies – and collateral – an accidental byproduct of war.[60]

Wherever it transpired, deforestation killed off wildlife – mammals, birds, amphibians, and fish – and created what people described as vistas with an unsettling, far-reaching silence. Clear-cutting was particularly damaging to pine forests, even more so on mountain slopes, including the mountains surrounding Chattanooga, where the federal army cut down most of the timber in the fall of 1863; in woodlands containing small streams, the loss of the forest can increase siltation. US Major General Ulysses S. Grant contemplated the siltation process in the fall of 1863, when copious amounts of mud flowed down the mountainsides as he traveled near Chattanooga. Decades of exploitation were packed into a few years, the damage being concentrated in certain places with a lot of heavy fighting such as northern Virginia and central Tennessee.[61]

Deforestation created the perfect conditions for oceans of mud. Since mature trees of different species can suck up 100 gallons of water from the soil daily, the destruction of thousands of trees left the earth saturated with moisture. From the war's first winter, mud baths appeared wherever large number of soldiers camped. The marches and countermarches of the armies, the footfalls of thousands of men, pounded down the bare earth, compacting it and preparing the way for more pools of mud. When the skies opened and the rain fell, the resulting muck was stupendous. Army vehicles, trapped in the mud, had to be left behind. Horses sank up to their shoulders in mud holes, and animals drowned in them as shocked onlookers watched.[62]

The nature of the mud challenged the descriptive powers of most soldiers. Confederate Major Robert Stiles, who watched little green frogs spring up from the churning mire, had never seen anything like it, while Union soldier J. M. Godown deemed it "mud unfathomable." Mud baths in any war can depress soldier morale and serve as a vector for bacteria, including tetanus and anthrax. In the American Civil War, more mud necessitated the use of yet more wood to cope with mud, in a vicious cycle. Yankee troops used more trees to corduroy the muddy roads, even as rebel soldiers took down saplings and underbrush for makeshift bridges over mud holes. General Ambrose Burnside's infamous "Mud March," in which he led the Union army around for two days in January 1863 in the sticky precincts near Fredericksburg, Virginia, occurred in a place with much deforestation.[63]

The financial losses from deforestation are impossible to calculate, whether it was timber stands upended or farms scuttled. To cite just one instance, the US Army cleared land to build Fort Rosecrans, some 200 acres in size, located north of Murfreesboro, Tennessee. A federal soldier riding through the town in April 1863 saw that even the door-yard fences had disappeared. Some of the timber came from the plantation of William Murfree, a descendant of the town's founder. He lost over 100 acres of timber from his 610-acre plantation – worth in his estimate some 45,000 US dollars in 1860 – to Yankee soldiers building the fort, which brought his estimated losses into the thousands. He documented the loss and requested compensation, but as of December 1863, the local board of claims had not acted on his petition. He thought he might never get any payment.[64]

Deforestation indirectly threatened the health of the civilian population as well. As the landscape was hollowed out, white Southerners lost its medicines, such as snakeroot, much prized for its healing qualities. By the fall of 1861, they were already experimenting with substitutes. Some of them shared the results in the newspapers, writing that concoctions made from dogwood root, wild cherry root, and oak root worked nearly as well as quinine in treating illness. They drew upon folk knowledge from bygone days, much of it preserved by women. From Columbus, Georgia, a white man discovered that peach roots could substitute for calomel and tartar, a method used by what he called "old ladies."[65]

The psychological impact of deforestation was equally profound. Trees played a role in community memory for many reasons, among them the fact that trunks were sometimes inscribed with the names of local people. White residents in Culpeper County, Virginia, felt devastated to see the totems of childhood destroyed, and they gave vent to outbursts of "sorrow" as Northern troops chopped down their cedars. As the Union army cut down the woods to build fortifications near his Tennessee residence, John Spence found the resulting wasteland ugly and disorienting, with the "original landmarks" obliterated for miles in every direction. William Murfree's daughter, the writer Mary Noailles Murfree, was in her early teens during the war, and these experiences left a deep imprint on her young mind. Her autobiographical novel, *Where the Battle Was Fought*, set in Tennessee in the year 1871, begins with a featureless landscape still ravaged by the conflict, with nary a tree, shrub, or fence in sight.[66]

Confederate officers nevertheless expected the white Southern public to keep sacrificing the woodlands and its resources for the cause. In 1862, when surgeon Francis P. Porcher began researching his book, *Resources of the Southern Fields and Forests*, he drew on many conversations with private citizens for their knowledge of plants and trees and their creative solutions to the shortage of medical supplies. But Porcher made it clear that the book, which appeared in 1863, was intended to aid soldiers, not civilians, and he seemed oblivious to how the Southern army was destroying the forest's valuable resources. Other officers called on the public to make ever greater sacrifices for the cause, advertising in newspapers to ask the public to donate tree bark for medicinal purposes. Major General Thomas Hindman urged civilians in Arkansas to cut down all the trees lining all the roads to delay the enemy's advance. If necessary, Hindman conjured the public, "burn everything."[67]

In 1863, civilian disillusionment with military destruction of timber reached new depths. Noncombatants found the rebel army's behavior disturbing, regardless of their political loyalties. Myra Carter, an ardent Confederate who ran a farm near Cleveland, Tennessee, was stunned to see rebel troops taking down fences and in general behaving *"very badly."* When they asked for dinner, she turned them away. David Deaderick, who reluctantly supported the Confederacy, also became disenchanted with the armies. A storekeeper, county clerk, and small-scale slaveowner, he lived through the rebel occupation of Knoxville, Tennessee, from the spring of 1861 to September 1863. He watched the Southern army confiscating private property owned by both Unionists and secessionists, and the explanation he heard, "military necessity," he would not countenance. But when federal troops arrived later in 1863, they behaved the same way. Both armies torched buildings and cut timber, Deaderick put forth, and he felt betrayed by both sides. Apolitical civilians also blamed both sides. Josephine Roedil, a Virginian with kinfolk in the North, excoriated both armies for the blasted landscape, devoid of trees, surrounding the town of Winchester in 1863.[68]

The communalism evident in the early part of the war began to fade in 1863. Physical resources once taken for granted dwindled, forcing most people to focus on self-preservation. Matilda M. Champion of Mississippi protested when other civilians charged high prices for cordwood, which she thought was unfair. In the wintertime, a North Carolinian proclaimed that timber, like food, was imperative for human survival, so that people who raised wood prices were engaging in nothing but extortion. A few traditional customs persisted. Whites who fled their dwellings cut firewood wherever they saw it on the roadside without asking anyone's permission, said Josephine Hooke, a judge's daughter. Here was a vestige of the antebellum "round forty" but in an environment of desperate scarcity rather than easy abundance. The armies would render yet more damage to the built environment, especially the private home.[69]

5

Habitat

After 1861, the private home became an arena of intense physical, logistical, and psychological struggle between civilians and armies. The house was supposed to be a sanctuary, the ultimate safe place, but, as has happened in so many conflicts, the war put paid to that idea. Both armies came to view houses in utilitarian fashion, as locations where they could set up quarters, treat the wounded, sleep, harvest building materials, hide from the enemy, or use as platforms from which to shoot the enemy. Since houses could impede an army's locomotion, they could also become objects to be destroyed. From the war's inception, the two armies occupied, reoccupied, dismantled, and destroyed many homes. Civilians often felt profound emotional attachments to these buildings, some of the most meaningful and valuable structures in the landscape. They believed that if the home was destroyed, then it seemed as if anything could be destroyed. The Articles of War covered the private home: Article 52 barred soldiers from committing acts of "plunder and pillage," while Article 54 stipulated that troops could not "waste or spoil" civilian homes; soldiers who damaged houses without orders could be court-martialed. But, as we have already seen with the food supply and the woodlands, policy had little impact on behavior in the field.[1]

Troops moving through the South encountered many kinds of houses in the landscape, which were a revelation to most Yankee soldiers. From the start of the war, they wandered away from camp and gazed upon the housing, noticing how buildings were constructed, their size, and their design, such as the wide verandahs common in rural Virginia. On the march, they took note of what Captain George L. Wood depicted as "formidable" mansions with all the accouterments, and they were fascinated

FIGURE 5.1 Grigsby House, Centreville, Virginia, Headquarters of
C.S. General Joseph E. Johnston, 1862.
Courtesy of the Library of Congress.

by these homes. But attraction could be mixed with repulsion. Seneca
Thrall, an army physician, declared that the "Aristocrat" on his fine
estate exploited working-class people of both races. Troops did not show
the same fascination with the abodes of non-elite Southerners, but they
sometimes entered mid-sized houses, noting the layout of the rooms, and
they felt free to evaluate them, too. Austin Stearns inspected a yeomen
farmer's log cabin, which he disdained for its plain furniture, lack of glass
windows, and lack of privacy. The homes of poor white people, they
dismissed as small and dirty, no matter how much they might resent the
planter elite.[2]

Most Confederate soldiers found the built environment deeply
familiar, so they had less to say about the structures they passed. When
they did describe private homes, they noted the building's age, size, and
the placement in the landscape – "antique" dwellings in one locale, and

the houses scattered around a village in another, Corporal George Neese remarked. Captain William W. Blackford, an engineer before the war, made further distinctions between a "pretty country house" and a "rambling" house constructed at different points in time, with no political commentary. Troops also noticed the objects within, eager to glimpse a clean, spotless bed or hear a piano playing. Very few rebel soldiers of any class background mentioned the homes of poor whites.[3]

Regardless of their opinions of various private dwellings, troops in both armies made full use of those houses. Well before General Pope's Orders in July 1862, they seized homes to serve as hospitals, observation posts for the signal corps, headquarters, or living quarters. Northern troops sometimes took over the modest homes of yeoman farmers or millers, but they preferred mansions, and their Confederate foes had the same preference. Both armies were following Henry Lee Scott's advice in his *Military Dictionary*, as he urged officers selecting houses for military purposes to choose substantial buildings made of brick with a good view of the countryside. Plantation homes suited these requirements perfectly: they were large, sometimes made of brick, and frequently built on hilltops.[4]

For both armies, the brick dwelling was the ideal, the top of the housing hierarchy for its sturdiness and, paradoxically, because bricks could be harvested for many purposes. Most bricks were handcrafted from soft surface clays and fired in local kilns. For families who could afford it, brick was popular in home-building for its subtle range of colors and its resilience. Brick houses also signified affluence and commitment to a location, and they were built to last. The residence at Virginia's Berkeley plantation, for example, was 135 years old when the war commenced. Bricks had other advantages in wartime, for they were fireproof, waterproof, and easier to carry than stone.[5]

The two armies made use of the brick house whenever possible. In the summer of 1861, rebel soldiers took over Wilmer McLean's home for their headquarters because the brick demesne on a hilltop near Manassas, Virginia, was exemplary for military uses. They used other brick mansions for their field hospitals, even when the owners were pro-Confederate, and they sometimes shielded themselves behind these buildings. In October 1861, they hid behind a sizable brick house during an artillery exchange with federal troops in Virginia, the home absorbing the fusillade. Yankee troops took possession of such houses and used them as a base to fire upon the enemy or as a haven to rest between military engagements. They jimmied bricks from vacated homes for different uses, such as constructing fireplaces in their quarters. Much like beef, brick was a valuable resource, and much like the pine forest, the brick house was exploited to the full.[6]

YANKEES AND THE BUILT ENVIRONMENT

From the very beginning, in the war's first weeks, federal officers took an empty mansion as a sign of loyalty to the Confederacy. In the spring of 1861, Major General Charles W. Sandford selected a Virginia estate as his headquarters precisely because the white family had fled the premises. Soldiers tried to spare Unionists whenever they selected buildings for military use; sometimes they could identify these civilians from neighborhood talk. Private Charles Lynch heard that pro-Confederate civilians referred to Cabletown, Virginia, as "Little Massachusetts" because so many Union supporters lived there. They sometimes identified themselves, joyously displaying the Stars and Stripes when US troops arrived.[7]

Taking over private houses meant that Yankee troops sometimes had direct contact with civilians, of course. Before Pope's Orders of 1862, they asked permission of the owners, but they usually took over the building whatever the answer might be. When they dealt with residents who had famous kinfolk, they routinely assumed that those people were pro-Confederate. In March 1862, Northern soldiers ordered C. F. Lee, a cousin of Robert E., out of his Virginia home, giving him a day to vacate the structure before a Union general arrived. (Soldiers took over Robert E. Lee's estate, Arlington, a few days after the family departed in the spring of 1861.) Yankee officers in all parts of the region were supposed to give out vouchers for the housing they confiscated from peaceful civilians whether they were pro-Union, pro-Confederate, or neutral, although not all officers did so, as indicated in the many exasperated reminders from their superiors.[8]

When Northern troops took over private homes as their quarters, they sometimes allowed the residents to stay. Again, individual officers made the decision on their own. They moved into Cornelia McDonald's house in Winchester, Virginia, in April 1862, while she went out for a walk; the wife of a lawyer who owned two slaves, she returned to find soldiers from the 5th Connecticut Infantry camped in her yard. Colonel Charles Candy permitted her to stay in the house and took one room, her absent husband's office, for his own use. In other instances, homes were turned into public spaces. Near Fredericksburg, Virginia, officers hung a banner reading "headquarters" on the brick mansion of secessionist

Horace Lacy, while local people strolled in to talk with the officers. During combat, frightening intrusions could happen abruptly, without warning. When troops took over a house in June 1862 to shelter the wounded during General George McClellan's attempt to take Richmond, the family gathered in one room, trying to avert their eyes from the horrible sights unfolding before them.[9]

Prior to the policy change of July 1862, Union officers put guards in front of some houses on occasion, but soldiers managed to loot from them, anyway. They took books, pictures, and jewelry, some of which they sold for a profit; other objects they took to retaliate against the planter class; and others they kept as souvenirs. They took yet other things for pragmatic reasons, including stoves to use in their winter quarters. All these acts of plunder violated the Articles of War, and some troops did get arrested, but so many soldiers plundered that it proved impossible to halt. US Brigadier General Thomas Williams wearily observed that his troops seemed to think pillaging was not only "right" but an "accomplishment." Soldiers who objected to the pillaging of houses could find themselves cursed by their comrades and accused of sympathizing with the enemy.[10]

As they traveled through the landscape, Northern troops exploited the home itself, scavenging the edifice for its physical resources. Houses of all types and sizes were a great source of raw materials, containing supplies that could be repurposed to help the armies. Well before July 1862, cavalrymen pried rafters and girders from an "old house" to build a bridge over the Chickahominy River. Other soldiers took cypress logs from a "cabin convenient" to build a bridge in Lauderdale County, Tennessee. Sometimes more than one home fell to military needs. In February 1862, an engineer pulled down multiple houses on Daufuskie Island, South Carolina, board by board, and used the wood to build platforms for his batteries.[11]

The Yankee army did more than confiscating, looting, or scavenging: they also burned houses. Long before July 1862, the armies destroyed many homes without receiving orders to do so. Colonel Samuel H. Dunning's troops took it upon themselves to burn deserted houses with no orders in Romney, Virginia, after they set fire to a mill and a hotel as ordered. Other troops committed arson under orders, as well. In the fall of 1861, soldiers put a torch to homes near Cheat Mountain, Virginia, and then feinted toward Confederate pickets nearby to draw rebel soldiers into battle. Sometimes, the motive was retaliation, which occurred even in the Border States. In Talbot

County, Maryland, soldiers burned a house because the owner joined the Confederate navy.[12]

Northern soldiers engaged in what might be deemed preventive arson, well before General Pope made his declarations. In January 1862, US forces torched a plantation home and outbuildings at Port Royal, South Carolina, because rebel soldiers had staked out the grounds to build a battery, which had not yet been constructed; the civilian owner had already disappeared. Some of the fires were set by a single undisciplined soldier. Stewart Van Vliet, a brigadier general who was also a quarter-master, complained that an unknown "incendiary" in his army set fire to the village of White House, Virginia, in June 1862, in defiance of his orders. Yet other officers in the field felt bad when their men burned abandoned homes without permission, but they chose not to discipline those soldiers.[13]

CIVILIANS, THEIR HOUSES, AND THE NORTHERN ARMY

From the war's outset, affluent whites who were related to prominent rebel officers did indeed flee their homes. But citizens from all backgrounds ran as the Northern army came closer, and they were motivated primarily by what they heard about the army's conduct. Martha Read, for one, claimed that Northern troops had burned eighty-five houses in Hampshire County, Virginia, in the war's first year, and other civilians believed the worst about military behavior. These fears prompted entire communi-ties to depart, as did the villages of Dover and Pittsburgh Landing in Tennessee when Ulysses S. Grant's army drew closer in February 1862. The image of the thieving, burning Yankee was embedded in the public mind by the war's first winter.[14]

Leaving could nevertheless be a difficult decision for many people precisely because of the primordial attachment to the home. The pro-spect of going away was "agonizing," Fannie Hume wrote, since it could mean leaving forever. Love of the home, more than political conviction, could dictate who stayed, as could inertia, fear of the unknown, and the lack of an alternative place to live. Citizens from manifold backgrounds chose to remain at home when the Yankee army appeared, whether they were Unionists, the apolitical, or pro-Confederate. In fact, rebel Colonel Samuel Fulkerson advised his relatives to stay if they wanted to save the house, warning that the federal army would take everything in it if they left.[15]

The assumption that all civilians who fled home must be Confederates appears all the more irrational if we examine the history of a single family, that of Phillip Otterback of Fairfax County, Virginia. The owner of nine slaves, he, his wife, and most of their relatives were pro-Union. They lived on his mother's farm when the war broke out, and they stayed for the rest of the 1861 calendar year. In February 1862, some Confederate soldiers burned the farm's outbuildings and threatened to kill Otterback. After that, he gave up. He made contact with the crew of a US vessel sailing the Potomac River, and they agreed to take the family to Washington, DC. A few weeks later, two white men in his employ fled to the federal navy, saying that rebels had destroyed the farm. There is no word on the slaves, who may have run away to the Union lines. Otterback's forsaken house stood mute, his political opinions unknown and unknowable to any army passing through. There was no way to learn the backstory, so to speak, for an individual dwelling.[16]

Many of the civilians still at home were women, anxiously peering out the windows at the soldiers. Most men in antebellum America felt obligated to protect women, but they also expected the opposite sex to be apolitical. Officers assumed that the female relatives of Confederate soldiers shared their menfolk's views by default and insisted that they had to leave their houses. But there was no policy on the issue, and the decisions often depended on the personalities involved. Women living alone could, paradoxically, use their solitude to protect themselves. One middle-aged spinster, name unknown, begged to stay when officers told her to exit her home in November 1861 so they could use it for their headquarters, and they relented. Defiant women, however, could arouse special antagonism. In June 1862, federal troops passing through Jackson, Tennessee, saw a white woman standing in front of a house turn her back and call them "Yankee fools." One Colonel Marsh then ordered that the domicile be turned into a military hospital. He relented on the condition that the owner – another woman, not the one who turned her back – kneel down and ask his pardon, which she did. Regulations did not cover this particular exercise of military power.[17]

Unionist civilians, by contrast, were frequently willing to let Yankee soldiers use their homes for military purposes. Men and women went far beyond the social invitations in the war's opening phases, permitting their houses to be used for such purposes as espionage. In the fall of 1861, a "Union man," unidentified, allowed eight federal soldiers to hide in his home so they could spy on rebel soldiers near Cross Lanes, Virginia. Unionists were happy to offer their houses as way-stations for soldiers in the vicinity. One white woman, her name unknown, gave US Lieutenant Colonel John Nevin a bed in her cottage when he felt ill as he rode down a country road. He spent the night, sleeping deeply, and her family concealed his presence until he left the next day. Civilians with no definite political beliefs cultivated friendly relations with Yankee officers, trying to protect their houses from being taken over, and in a few cases in Alexandria, Virginia, they seem to have succeeded.[18]

REBEL TROOPS AND THE BUILT ENVIRONMENT

Early in the war, when Confederate officers decided to occupy private residences, they sometimes gave out paperwork to the citizenry. Regulations did mean something. In 1862, Captain Charles D. Hill provided vouchers to a civilian for a home he transformed into a blacksmith shop and another building he used for officers' quarters in Richmond. Another captain, John Adams, paid rent for a dwelling near Memphis fronting the Mississippi River to serve as a military prison. Neither officer made any reference to the owners' politics. But it was clear, nonetheless, that the military's needs would take precedence. Assistant Quartermaster Algernon Cabell rented a house in Van Buren, Arkansas, on the most favorable terms imaginable. The handwritten document, which he called an "indenture," allowed him to occupy it at his pleasure and pay 50 Confederate dollars a month to the owners when he had "funds on hand," whenever that might be.[19]

Furthermore, rebel commanders in the field improvised their own rules about the selection of private homes for military uses. Major General Jeb Magruder had specific ideas about which buildings should be seized and used as hospitals. A Virginia native and West Point graduate, he was nicknamed "Prince John" for his courtly manners. During the Peninsular Campaign in April 1862, he commanded his soldiers to choose structures in this order: first, houses occupied by men only; second, public halls; third, hotels; and fourth, houses with families containing both men and women who would, as a last resort, be "forced to give up their residences." Magruder implicitly acknowledged the significance of the home, and domestic values in general, although he did not necessarily abide by them, for he and his wife lived apart for much of their marriage. Perhaps his Virginia birthplace made him take these precautions, but none of them were in the Articles of War or Scott's *Military Dictionary*. So much was left up to individual officers, in both armies.[20]

From the first months of the war, Confederate soldiers plundered private dwellings. They took material objects for practical reasons, just as Yankees did. In July 1861, they broke into a residence and took coal oil and matches so they could burn down some bridges in Virginia. They sometimes focused on Unionists, pillaging their households in North Carolina; by the fall of 1861, their reputation was so bad that female Unionists started screaming when they saw rebel troops approaching their homes in Chattanooga. But Southern troops plundered civilians, regardless of their politics, just as Northern troops did. They were known to take what they wanted or needed, even though Confederate regulations banned plunder. As rebel forces withdrew from Nashville in 1862, some of the units pillaged from "friend and foe alike," prompting one denizen to ask, "what may we expect of our enemies?"[21]

Confederate soldiers exploited homes, the buildings themselves, starting in the war's first year. They, too, put aside antebellum views on stewardship. In the fall of 1861, they ordered white families to leave their houses in Sullivan's Island, South Carolina, and then pulled the structures down to prevent the enemy from using them. The same thing happened in the Border States. Brigadier General J. P. McCown, who served on the Kentucky–Missouri border in March 1862, summarized his actions there succinctly: "Houses burned and torn down, as occasion required." Over time, the troops developed a rather nonchalant attitude toward the destruction of the habitat. In Tennessee, one Confederate unit set fire to a brick home to get it "out of the way," rebel soldier John Jackman said.[22]

Yet the cultural background shared by rebel soldiers and local white people did make a difference, sometimes. Individual soldiers genuinely sympathized with civilians fleeing their homes. John Worsham uttered sorrowfully in 1861 as he watched families leaving Virginia, "Here is war, real war." The fact that some troops served near their homes could put a brake on their behavior. Rebel cavalryman John Porter cantered past a Kentucky house one evening and saw through a window his cousin's wife sitting at a table reading a book. This domestic vision, so evocative of peace, made him long for the war's end, he wrote, and the glimpse of his kinswoman probably made him less likely to scavenge, loot, or burn such a dwelling. We can also hear faint echoes of antebellum prohibitions about harming women. But most Confederate soldiers kept silent on the topic of how their army treated private houses.[23]

Some rebel officers tried to contain their troops and put an end to the blatant destruction of the built environment. They condemned those who set fire to buildings in violation of procedure, calling it an act of depredation, and they had the Articles of War read aloud to men in the ranks.

In 1862, Major M. M. Kimmel decried his soldiers' abuse of all civilian property in Holly Springs, Mississippi, and subtracted the damages from the military payroll. He insisted, too, that the Articles of War be read to all the troops and reminded them that the Southern army should not be "a terror to our own country." Confederate court-martial records have not survived, so we cannot know the number of soldiers who were punished for malfeasance. But the frequent disregard for regulations suggests that rebel soldiers defied their officers, just as Yankee soldiers defied their superiors.[24]

CIVILIANS, THEIR HOUSES, AND THE SOUTHERN ARMY

Some time had to pass before such behavior registered with pro-Confederate civilians. The realization dawned on them at different times, but they went through the same painful process they experienced with the Southern army's seizure of food and timber – understanding eventually that military necessity took precedence over everything else. Before that, typically in the war's first year or two, these civilians welcomed rebel troops into their homes. They were glad to care for a wounded soldier who needed a roof over his head or give shelter to troops in their houses. Neutral civilians felt the pressure to help men in the Confederate army. Private Edward Moore, a slaveholder's son, talked his way into a log cabin, insisting that the husband and wife let him and his mess-mates stay overnight. The wife parried, trying to persuade them to leave, before she finally acquiesced.[25]

Watching rebel troops seizing food or cutting down the forest was alarming enough, but an assault on the home was perceived as an attack on the family itself. Charles W. C. Dunnington lost much of his house to rebel soldiers in the fall of 1861, which must have been particularly distressing because he had a sense of history, co-founding a historical society before the war. The residence near Dumfries, Virginia, was home to Dunnington, his wife, and their seven children; they owned one slave, who apparently ran away in 1861. The structure had two stories and six rooms, with a covered porch, and it was surrounded by outbuildings. When the family was away from home, a Confederate captain disassembled the kitchen, an office, and a shed, and took the doors, window sashes, and weatherboarding from the house. The officer used the materials to construct his quarters a few miles away but left no paperwork on the confiscated property. The Dunningtons returned to find the place so damaged that they could not afford to rebuild. "My wife grieves," Charles Dunnington protested, for the house, her birthplace, which was constructed by her father. He would sue the army if he could, but the local courts were no longer operating. He believed nevertheless that taxpayers like himself should have been protected, and he wondered if he now lived under "military despotism."[26]

Other civilians discovered with a rude shock that Southern troops could indeed take apart the buildings on their property. If pro-Confederate civilians reacted with outrage to the behavior of Northern troops, they reacted to the same actions by rebel soldiers with stunned disbelief. In South Carolina, during the first winter of the conflict, rebel soldiers yanked doors and shutters off plantation mansions for firewood. William Grayson, a resident of the area, erupted that "our own people" were as bad as the Yankee army. Other civilians lost their homes because of the Southern military in sudden, dramatic fashion. Near Yorktown, Virginia, rebel forces shelled the house of slaveowner Mrs. Farrenhold, where she lived with her niece, forcing them to move into a log cabin once occupied by her slaves. A Yankee reporter declared that rebel troops knew she supported secession, but they shelled the house, anyway.[27]

When pro-Confederate whites asked the Southern army, their army, for help in protecting the built environment, they could be harshly rebuffed. In February 1863, F. W. Powell and several neighbors in Middleburg, Virginia, asked cavalryman John Mosby, who was then a scout for Magruder, to quit his warfare on federal troops because Yankee soldiers had threatened to burn the town, including their homes, in retaliation. They obviously hoped that some kind of solidarity still existed between the Southern military and white civilians. Mosby's indignant response – "I unhesitatingly refuse to comply" – revealed a great deal, perhaps unintentionally, about the Southern military's attitude toward civilians and their property. He swatted away their request as a "degrading" compromise with the enemy, adding that he was not responsible for the current state of affairs since his troops had never occupied Middleburg. A month later, in March 1863, Mosby became captain of a band of partisan rangers, but mainstream officers showed the same disregard for the interests of the civilian population.[28]

FEDERAL BEHAVIOR AFTER POPE

After General John Pope's Orders appeared in July 1862, there was no bright line, no sharply contrasting chapters before and after, because the army's need for physical resources remained the same. Just as we saw with food and timber, most soldiers presumed that their needs came first. Pope's Orders of July 1862 included provisions on how soldiers could treat private dwellings (No. 7), on who could remain in those houses (No. 11), and whether houses would be guarded (No. 13). General Orders No. 7 declared that federal troops had permission to destroy houses if the residents within fired on them. General Orders No. 11 allowed "male citizens" who took the oath of allegiance to the United States to remain in their homes; if they refused to take the oath, they would be forced to go south beyond federal lines. In General Orders No. 13, Pope stipulated that guards would no longer be put in front of houses or other private property. He added that the Articles of War and military regulations would provide "ample means" to restrain troops from indulging in misconduct.[29]

Despite General Orders No. 7, federal soldiers persisted in scavenging wood from private homes for military purposes, just as they did before Pope issued his orders. This happened at random, with scant regard for the owners' political views; sometimes it happened under orders. Troops disembarked from Union ships on the Mississippi River to hack logs out of houses to fuel their steamboats because the area woodyards were exhausted, William T. Sherman explained. Privates were known to act on their own initiative, once taking down a kitchen wall in a Virginia home before officers arrived and put a halt to it. The troops continued to single out the houses of high-profile Confederates. In December 1862, the Virginia residence of James Mason, the Confederate diplomatic representative to England, was razed and the rubble carted away, leaving nothing but a big hole in the ground.[30]

Federal troops burned houses after July 1862, just as they had before then, again, whether or not anyone fired a gun at them. They sometimes set fire to homes to punish outspoken civilians. Yankee Henry Eells, now a doctor, knew that federal soldiers deliberately torched private residences and barns in Tennessee if the owners complained about the military's confiscation of their food. Other troops burned houses for health reasons, with no information about the owners' ideological views, destroying homes that served as hospitals for smallpox patients. Many structures could be obliterated in a single expedition. In Arkansas, Lieutenant J. N. Gillham burned as ordered two deserted mansions, the slave quarters on both estates, a cotton gin, an overseer's house, a stable, two barns filled with corn, two storehouses, and forty-four other buildings, including some filled with unginned cotton – all of it destroyed because rebel troops were nearby, and all of it done in the space of two days in May 1863.[31]

Most houses burned easily because they were constructed at least in part of wood. Planter homes, even those made of brick, had timber frames, and most other residences were constructed of pine, cedar, and other highly flammable softwoods. Most homes, whatever their size, contained some wooden furniture and some accelerants, such as kerosene in lamps and turpentine in medicine chests. In fine, they were tinderboxes. Yankee soldiers, many of them farmers or farmers' sons, knew something about fire. They paid attention to wind patterns and put kindling on the appropriate side of the building, and they started with the wooden wings, or ells, when they torched a building. Other federal troops started fires by lighting beds inside the dwellings. Houses could burn very quickly: one residence in Tennessee burned down two hours after Union troops set fire to it.[32]

Some men in the Yankee army felt troubled by the burning of so many homes, believing that the troops had lost their moral bearings. Captain Van Bennett found it hard to see attractive houses in Holly Springs, Mississippi, "willfully and uselessly destroyed," and he pitied the families turned out into the night. Some officers agreed, but not many of them acted on their concerns. Colonel Thomas W. Higginson watched his colleague Colonel James Montgomery torch houses in Georgia and South Carolina contrary to military regulations, which he thought despicable, but he made no formal protest. Army physician Seneca Thrall saw his troops burn at least thirty homes in Tennessee, which he believed unethical even though he was stoutly pro-Union, but he too made no official complaint. He felt relieved in December 1862 when commanders finally began punishing the wrongdoers.[33]

Northern troops did sometimes get punished if they committed arson without permission from their superiors, which violated General Orders No. 7. Their officers seemed to believe that torching a house was worse than looting a house, and they did flex their authority. Members of the 3rd Indiana Cavalry were arrested in 1863 for burning a town in central Tennessee contrary to orders. A handful of court-martial cases involved house arson, and one Captain Owen was dismissed from the army for burning two residences in Missouri without orders while he was intoxicated. But many, probably most, of the soldiers who burned homes without orders got away with it. Officers sometimes lost control of men in the ranks, which could happen to no less a person than Brigadier General William T. Sherman. In July 1863, he realized that his men set fire to numerous buildings in Jackson, Mississippi, despite the presence of guards, leaving much of the town "ruined."[34]

Federal soldiers continued to burn houses to ferret out civilians or guerillas who fired on them, as General Orders No. 7 did allow. They set fire to the home of Confederate Colonel Charles Hopkins on Georgia's Sapelo River after someone on the property shot at them. Officers in such situations took it for granted that they had a wide remit. In December 1862, after parties unknown on the Arkansas shore fired at Northern soldiers traveling down the Mississippi River, the troops landed and burned down all the houses in the area. Five months later, in April 1863, Union troops did the same at a different point on the Mississippi after an unidentified person fired at them. As Private Newton Scott recorded, they disembarked and torched "Every thing that would Burn," not just the house with the sniper.[35]

Pope's Order No. 11, requiring men to take the oath to remain in their homes, was not enforced consistently, either. Sometimes the issue was a turnover in personnel. In Franklin, Tennessee, a civilian doctor, J. S. Parks, swore allegiance to the United States in August 1862, but for unknown reasons a Northern lieutenant who arrived the next spring ordered him to leave his house anyway. Noncombatants of both genders were forced to take the oath, although the Order specified men only. After federal troops confiscated Mattie Porter's house in Memphis, she told an officer that she was apolitical, but she still had to take the oath in 1863 to get it back. Local officers enforced the requirement haphazardly, for women and men. An unidentified widow in Louisiana took the oath to the Union "under protest" but was allowed to stay on her plantation, as were her neighbors of both sexes who refused to take the oath at all.[36]

Contrary to Pope's General Orders No. 13, Yankee officers still put guards at some private dwellings whatever the owners' politics might be. And contrary to his hope (expressed in the same order) that the Articles of War and military regulations would eliminate pillage, soldiers and officers kept on pillaging from houses. After July 1862, the troops brought out towels, butcher knives, and quilts, taken for obvious practical uses, and some officers condoned or encouraged the pillaging, as they had earlier. Captain James Stillwell, a chaplain, identified a Kentucky mansion as the home of rebel officer William Preston Johnston and urged the troops to "help themselves at this house." In May 1863, Colonel Henry Morrow asserted that the army had the right to take "anything and everything" from civilians. That right was "beyond dispute," he believed, although he understood that plundering in Virginia's Northern Neck was alienating the white Southern public. As Morrow might have predicted, only a tiny number of pillaging soldiers landed in the court-martial system, and most of them, such as Captain George Bingham, were released with reprimands. General Pope said again in January 1863 that soldiers misinterpreted his orders as license to rob and plunder, which he rued as very much to his "discredit."[37]

CIVILIANS AND THEIR HOUSES, AFTER POPE

After Pope's Orders were issued in July 1862, white Southern Unionists still tried to help federal troops, just as they had before July 1862. These men and women welcomed Yankee soldiers into their homes and sometimes gave them shelter. US Colonel Charles Cummings said that a "good Union man," name unknown, invited ailing soldiers to lodge in his Virginia residence. Strongly committed Unionists were ready to do more. In Pleasant Hill, Virginia, R. L. Symington and his neighbors asked a federal brigadier general to use their town as a "Military Station" because they had enough houses to accommodate the officers.[38]

At the other end of the political spectrum, Judge John Perkins, Jr., was willing to sacrifice his Louisiana residence to keep it out of the hands of the Northern army. His relatives owned property all over the Mississippi River Valley, and the judge had a luxurious plantation, Somerset, near Carthage. The costly home was surrounded by ancient trees and extensive flower gardens, according to John Wilkins, a federal soldier who saw the estate in 1863. As Union troops approached Somerset in April of that year, Perkins burned down his own mansion to prevent the enemy from occupying it. He must be "bitter," Wilkins observed, in something of an understatement. Perkins, a fanatical secessionist who served in the Confederate Congress, must have known that rebel statutes allowed compensation for citizens who voluntarily destroyed their own property so the enemy could not obtain it. He escaped his own arson uninjured, but there is no record of any funds he may have received. Most civilians were not willing to make this kind of sacrifice for any political cause.[39]

White women of all political views dreaded the loss of the home, the site of so much labor and suffused with so many memories. During the war, they, more often than men, delineated the interiors of their houses – the position of certain objects, the unique "old fashion [*sic*] things" from previous generations, as Martha Crump portrayed them – and the war made women more self-conscious about their homes. Mary Pearre, a young schoolteacher, saw federal troops pillaging her neighbors in central Tennessee, and in 1863 she felt inspired to write a paean to the residence she shared with her sisters. Here she read, prayed, and visited with kin-folk and friends in rooms she loved, "everything in its place," the carpet bright and the flowers on the mantel. The war also changed her views of the local elite. She no longer wanted to live in a mansion on a big estate after seeing how Northern troops treated families who lived in those houses.[40]

Some female civilians got into physical altercations with Union soldiers over access to the home. A group of planter women stood in the doorway of their house in Lamar, Tennessee, body-blocking a sergeant as he tried to enter, but when he threatened to burn it down, they relented, and the officer walked in to search for rebel soldiers. Some pro-Confederate women were willing to risk their lives to save their dwellings, and on a few occasions, in such places as St. Joseph, Louisiana, they succeeded. Plantation mistress Anna M. Farrar and several women defended their homes "by their presence," refusing to leave in June 1863 when Northern troops burned other properties close by. Their tactic succeeded for some reason, as it did not for other civilians, and their homes were not torched. Sheer chance could sometimes make the difference. Martha Pollard, a yeoman farmer's wife in Tennessee, left her house after some privates announced they would set fire to it in ten minutes, but federal officers came by and stopped them, saving the building.[41]

Most white men did not want to see houses destroyed, either. They did not always express the deep feeling for their homes that women did, but they saw houses as significant material assets, and in some cases, they had designed the buildings themselves. They thought armies had no right to destroy houses for any reason, but few of them had encounters with soldiers in their homes, since many pro-Confederate men left to fight the war. The few who stayed home tried to take matters into their own hands. John Long, a boy in Tennessee, watched federal troops dismantle his house in 1863 and use the lumber for their breastworks. He ran over to protect the building, but the soldiers held him back. Elderly men, still living at home, came to a fatalistic acceptance of their inability to fend off the Northern army. One Virginian watched the troops take his house down, brick by brick, to build fireplaces in their winter quarters. He told a Union soldier that "the d – Yanks would unpave hell itself" if they wanted to do it.[42]

With so many houses going up in flames, civilians male and female inev-itably fell into harm's way. Some officers gave residents advance warning, if only a few minutes, before they put the torch to their homes, but some did not. Mose King, a slave who witnessed such a conflagration, saw federal soldiers burn down a planter's house in Mississippi with the family inside; the master and mistress burned to death. When a dwelling caught fire in Gallatin, Tennessee, with the occupants inside, a Yankee chaplain did nothing, because, he averred, they were secessionists. When civilians had the opportunity, they did some frantic bargaining with Northern soldiers to save their homes. After troops entered his house in Tennessee in 1863, filled it with kindling, and prepared to fire the building, merchant Chesley Williams told them about some rebel pickets in the area. That turned out to be enough to spare his residence.[43]

Some civilians discovered that blood, gore, and dead bodies had invaded the home itself. They found permanent bloodstains inside houses that had been used as hospitals, and when the battles ended, blood literally soaked the earth and filled the ditches around local buildings. Soldiers expired in front of private homes and inside of them, during and after battle, and their bodies were hastily buried, singly or in groups, close to where they fell. Dead men filled front yards, backyards, and fields, the bodies put in shallow graves. An overpowering stench emanated from the corpses, as microorganisms broke down body tissues and released foul-smelling gases. Nineteenth-century Americans believed that the smell of death could cause illness among the living, which was not in fact possible, but the prospect frightened civilians. They abhorred the smells emanating from dead people and dead animals in the landscape, which could spoil a house in and of itself, making it unlivable.[44]

Long after Pope's Orders were promulgated in July 1862, an abandoned house remained, by definition, a secessionist house. Most federal soldiers continued to assume that all departing civilians must be Confederate supporters. This assumption, repeatedly contradicted by plain fact, was ever more widely accepted in the Yankee military. The affluent Georgians who fled their homes before the invading army in 1863 were "consummate fools," as well as secessionists, Captain James Stillwell scoffed. Another federal soldier, coming upon the deserted town of Sartaria, Mississippi, remarked that the inhabitants must be secessionists "or they would not run from us." The unoccupied houses did not stay empty for long. Other civilians took over these domiciles because the region had an increasingly large population of homeless people who needed shelter. White Northern civilians who came south, such as government agents, schoolteachers, and the wives of high-ranking officers, moved into abandoned homes. Julia Dent Grant, spouse of Ulysses S. Grant, resided in an empty house while visiting her husband in the fall of 1862, and she pitied the absent owners.[45]

CONFEDERATE POLICY

There was no turning point for the rebel forces, no crisp division before and after January 1863, when Confederate military issued their own policy on the built environment. The *Regulations for the Army of the Confederate States*, published in Richmond in January 1863, simply confirmed existing practices and reiterated the vintage Articles of War. The *Regulations* included Article 52 and Article 54, taken verbatim, with the same threat of punishment by court-martial. But the Southern regulations differed from Yankee policy in one respect. They went a step further in condemning wrongdoing by the rebel military, remonstrating that plundering or marauding of any kind was "disgraceful," criminal, and merited an "awful" punishment.[46]

After the Confederate *Regulations* appeared, rebel officers sometimes followed their procedures. They paid rent on houses they used for their headquarters or offices. Major William Barnewall, Jr., handed over 30 Confederate dollars a month for a home on St. Michael's Street in Mobile, Alabama, in the spring of 1863. They paid some claims for other privately owned buildings, such as hotels, that the military took from civilians. On rare occasions, officers returned houses to the owners after they had been selected for officers' quarters. When one Mrs. Loeb asked that a Confederate general give back her residence in Canton, Mississippi, he not only returned it but reimbursed her immediately for damage to the property. Maybe he wanted to protect a homeless woman; maybe she was an uncommonly persuasive individual.[47]

Other Confederate soldiers persisted in their destructive practices, which were routine long before the *Regulations* were proclaimed. Southern troops exploited the habitat to the full, under orders or on their own initiative. They used vacant homes as their headquarters, the politics of the owners unknown, and they could leave the buildings "much abused," admitted Jedediah Hotchkiss, a topographical engineer with the Confederate army. As their regulations permitted, they burned houses, torching handsome dwellings around Jackson, Mississippi, in July 1863 because Yankee soldiers had taken shelter there and the flames would prevent nighttime attacks by the enemy. Southern troops also invaded the privacy of the home, charging into residences without notice searching for Union men.[48]

In fact, rebel troops still targeted Unionists for mistreatment after the appearance of the *Regulations*. In the fall of 1863, a Southern general deliberately positioned his troops around the home of Virginia planter

FIGURE 5.2 Home of John Minor Botts.
Courtesy of the Library of Congress.

John Minor Botts to draw gunfire toward the structure, a large, plain wooden building, painted white with a stately portico. Botts, believed to be loyal to the Union, refused to leave his mansion, and the soldiers eventually gave up and withdrew. Rebel troops still burned the houses of Unionists, and they engaged in other forms of intimidation. They seized furniture from pro-Union households, in one case selling it and using the profits for what a federal soldier called a "blow-out" of a party near the Mississippi River in 1863. The furniture sale violated Confederate regulations on profiteering, as did the merry-making.[49]

That did not stop Confederate officers from denouncing what they saw as the other army's misconduct. Daniel Harvey Hill, now a major general, launched into a tirade in March 1863 about the Union army's damage to the region's housing. Hill, a South Carolina native and graduate of West Point, served in the Mexican War, all the while developing a deep antipathy toward Northerners. As a college professor in the 1850s, he hated Yankees so much he found ways to ridicule them in a book he published on algebra. When the war broke out, he quickly joined the Confederate

FIGURE 5.3 John Minor Botts and family, Culpeper, Virginia.
Courtesy of the Library of Congress.

army, and he served with General Robert E. Lee before being sent to North Carolina. In early 1863, when Hill was serving at New Bern, he received a message from US Major General J. G. Foster about prisoner exchanges. Hill answered that federal soldiers had burned the homes of the rich and poor, as well as churches, barns, stables, and whole villages, adding that Foster was the "most atrocious house-burner" in the world. Hill insisted nonetheless that the Confederate army had the right to burn much of Plymouth, North Carolina, an event that Foster had criticized, and he bellowed back, "It is no business of yours if we choose to burn one of our own towns." Foster's answer is unrecorded. The hypocrisy of such criticism, and the related issue of what both armies did to the civilian population, escaped General Hill.[50]

Other rebel officers made it clear that they agreed with Hill, openly defying Southern courts who tried to restrain them. As we know, the Confederate court system was very weak. The government never appointed a Supreme Court to serve as a final arbiter in legal disputes, although the rebel Constitution provided for its creation, so state and local courts had to grapple on their own with discord between the military and civilians. In November 1863, Colonel Wyatt Aiken dismissed a state superior judge's decision that he did not have the authority to seize a home and a tavern to use as hospitals in Macon, Georgia. After the owner (Mr. McLean or McLane) sued the colonel, Judge O. A. Lochrane decided in the owner's favor, concluding that the law did not allow the seizure of private dwellings. Lochrane, an Irish immigrant, supported the Confederacy, but he thought that military power had some limits. Aiken rejected the decision completely. He replied in the local newspaper that the Confederate wounded had to have shelter and he planned to compensate the owner eventually, sometime after the soldiers departed. "Necessity" required him to take the house, and he would trust his own discretion to impress private property as needed. Aiken, for all his high-handedness, was only stating actual practice. On a day-to-day basis, there were few constraints on the rebel army's behavior.[51]

HABITAT LOST

Such conduct was indeed shocking to most civilians, especially for the South's white women, who found the invasion of the privacy of the home very hard to bear. When Confederate troops entered a Louisiana house uninvited in the spring of 1863 seeking draft evaders, they cursed the residents, including the women, who objected to their presence. Gender conventions intended to protect women mattered less and less as time passed, which some women reluctantly had to admit. Priscilla Bond, a planter's wife in Louisiana, outlined the misdeeds by federal troops – white Southern civilians driven from their homes, houses pillaged, women robbed at gunpoint – but acknowledged that citizens in the Border States feared the arrival of Southern troops for the same reasons.[52]

Some pro-Confederate civilians gradually came to see that there were few differences between the two armies. Slowly but surely, the image of the pillaging rebel soldier took root in the public mind. Edmund Ruffin, the eccentric planter who had advocated secession before 1860, became deeply disillusioned with the Southern military. The owner of much land in Virginia, his native state, he literally fired the first shot at Fort Sumter. But after 1861, the two armies trampled repeatedly over his Virginia properties. In the spring of 1863, after several of his homes were damaged, he decided that Confederate troops were thieves, just like Yankee soldiers. As both armies marched through his land in Tennessee, David Deaderick came to the same conclusion after both armies stole from his house. The

FIGURE 5.4 Priscilla Bond of Louisiana.
Courtesy of Louisiana State University.

danger posed by Southern troops is illustrated by the last days of W. A. Withers. A merchant in his sixties known by the honorific "colonel," he owned no slaves and lived alone in a fine house near Jackson, Mississippi. In July 1863, as the armies did battle all around him, Withers was killed, probably by stray gunfire, and when Confederate forces evacuated the area, they burned down his house.[53]

The ethic of communalism, engrained in white Southern culture before 1861, lasted for a while, at least, regarding the habitat. When Addie Patterson's father joined the Confederate army while he was constructing a new house in South Carolina, a neighbor finished the residence for him. Many civilians felt true sympathy for people who lost their homes and tried to help their fellows. Near Raymond, Mississippi, a physician lent his comfortable house free of charge to friends who fled their own dwelling as the federal army drew near. In Louisiana, a neighbor begged

Rebecca Wadley (Sarah Wadley's mother) for shelter for herself and her four children as they dodged the Yankee army in May 1863, and even though Mrs. Wadley had a family of her own, she felt obligated to take them in.[54]

But there was a limit to communalism about housing, just as there was for the sharing of food and timber. Early in the war, local fire companies attempted to douse the homes torched by the armies, but the number of burning buildings overwhelmed them. In the face of the war's mounting upheaval, generosity wore out and goodwill became exhausted. Refugees fleeing the Yankee army did not always get help when they asked acquaintances, friends, even kinfolk for shelter, much to their dismay. Certain civilians discovered that the profit motive trumped everything else. One family, who had permitted friends to live in a house free of charge, suddenly informed them they might have to move so the dwelling could be rented to people who could pay. Mrs. C. M. Stacy, one of the tenants, responded that it was hard to trust "any body scarcely these days." As community ties deteriorated, white civilians began pulling down neighborhood buildings that the armies left untouched for the raw materials within.[55]

Many villages inside the South were destroyed by the war's grinding friction, with no obvious culprit. The fighting destroyed numerous hamlets in eastern Virginia, so that by the spring of 1863 a traveler encountered a lunar landscape of muddy roads with no houses and no people visible for miles. In other parts of the region, entire settlements were left in shambles. Moscow, Tennessee, a thriving little town in the spring of 1862, lost most of its housing by the spring of the following year. Two years of military occupations reduced Centreville, Virginia, to a few haggard buildings by the summer of 1863, with abandoned Confederate forts ringing the town. One rebel newspaper described the South's broken houses as "Pope's handiwork," but both armies had a hand in it. The 1864 calendar year would bring more such transformations, forcing civilian society to the breaking point.[56]

6

Breakdown

As the year 1864 opened, soldiers and civilians escalated their fierce struggles over the resources of war, and their equally intense struggles with each other. This calendar year would see the opening of major federal campaigns in different theaters – Ulysses S. Grant's effort to take Richmond and vanquish Robert E. Lee; Philip Sheridan's campaign in the Valley of Virginia; and William T. Sherman's drive toward Atlanta – plus hundreds of smaller engagements in the region, all of them combining to use up or destroy a tremendous amount of resources. No more policy pronouncements came forth, but there were some continuities from the war's early years. Neutral civilians still tried to stay out of the way and avoid helping either army. Troops and civilians still disputed the war's root causes when, for instance, US Captain Andrew Curtis lodged with the Ravenels, planters and longtime South Carolina residents. But those spirited debates, which occurred frequently in the conflict's early years, seem to have diminished by 1864. Too much blood had been spilled, and too much treasure destroyed.[1]

In the war's last year, the methods of the two armies completed their convergence. Both armies routinely violated policy and procedure as men seized resources, with an ever-growing sense of entitlement. Some troops in both armies began to assume that they were better than civilians and could take whatever they needed to survive, although there was always the counterforce of soldiers who tried to protect civilians or anguished over the mistreatment of civilians they witnessed. If the armies resembled machines, they were machines with no drivers. And, as the months went by, more soldiers and civilians abandoned what remained of traditional social mores. The communalism that had lasted in attenuated form in the war's early years thinned out. The endless demands of the two armies proved to be too much for white Southern society.

Civilians and troops alike began witnessing strange, uncanny events that broke with antebellum benchmarks on how people should behave and how they should relate to the physical world. Driven to the brink by the war's relentless pressure, some civilians began violating elementary concepts of personal safety, engaging in conduct that defied reason. They also witnessed horrible incidents involving the natural elements, most especially fire, that transformed the landscape in ways that they found hard to put into words. Meanwhile, the massive number of dead people and dead animals left unburied turned fields and waterways into open graves. The startling, the lurid, and the surreal became commonplace in 1864.

PEOPLE

White civilians still engaged in activities prohibited by the Articles of War, involved in many aspects of the war's thrust and parry, and they did so with zeal. They carried on smuggling for politics and profit, in the Confederacy and the Border States. Men and women were arrested for smuggling the usual array of goods – medicine, military supplies, and provisions. Captured civilians, such as one Mr. Thorn, taken in Louisiana, related that some Northern officers knew about the smuggling, and federal officers in turn suspected that Treasury agents connived at smuggling by civilians. Northern journalists denounced smuggling and what they saw as corruption inside the Confederacy, but the Southern press remained mostly silent, for obvious reasons. Yankee troops arrested smugglers of both sexes, fined them, put them in prison, and sometimes executed them, but the smuggling went on.[2]

Consider Mary Polk Branch, a planter's wife, who illustrates how smugglers could evade the system, as well as how self-interest could overcome ideology. In her thirties when the war started, she was highly literate and utterly pro-Confederate. Her husband owned land in Tennessee and Arkansas, in addition to several hundred slaves, and her four brothers served in the Confederate military. But she had pro-Union kinfolk, and she was not afraid to ask them for favors. In 1864, when she wanted to travel from Tennessee to Arkansas to visit relatives, a Unionist brother-in-law somehow obtained permission for her to take illicit articles, including medicine and sugar, hidden in her trunk. She also had important assistance from a US provost marshal, name unknown, who sealed the trunk and her coat pockets, which were filled with tobacco, so they could not be inspected during the journey. Mrs. Branch may have bribed him for his help, since her family still had money, but his motives are unclear. In any case, she arrived in Arkansas with the goods undiscovered.[3]

Civilians defied the Articles of War in other ways, by corresponding with the enemy. Just as they had earlier in the war, they exchanged mail via private couriers, as did civilian George Fuller, whom Yankee troops arrested in Virginia. The armies reacted by arresting any civilian possessing large numbers of private letters. Union provost marshals in Knoxville, Tennessee, seized family missives to make sure they contained no dangerous information, but civilians used onion juice to write messages which were legible only when the recipients held the letters close to a flame. When civilians were caught smuggling letters, they could receive severe penalties. After Joseph Leddy was captured in Arkansas for smuggling letters, the federal army convicted him at court-martial and sentenced him to be hanged.[4]

Noncombatants gave information to the different armies, just as they had in 1861, 1862, and 1863. Ordinary people, typically identified in military correspondence as "citizens," provided details about the coordinates and movements of the enemy, with Unionists helping the Northern army and Confederates aiding the rebel army. In Alabama, an unidentified white man quietly slipped a piece of paper to Yankee Captain James F. Chapman warning him about enemy troops close by. Civilian motives still included a mix of the political and the financial. In Virginia, an Englishman named Mr. Sime gave information to US Brigadier General J. H. Wilson, and, the officer noted, he seemed "well disposed" to the federal cause and might give more if he were "properly rewarded."[5]

Other civilians engaged in more systematic espionage, with lethal results. In January 1864, teenaged David Dodd was arrested in Little Rock for gathering information on Yankee regiments, fortifications, and artillery. A merchant's son, he worked as a civilian clerk for the Union regiment occupying the capitol, and after his arrest, he was soon executed. Civilian spies continued nevertheless to take great risks. From jail in Tuskegee, Alabama, a white woman named Mrs. Keelan tried to smuggle a letter to none other than General William T. Sherman, but it was intercepted; she tried to escape but was caught. The two armies seem to have become more watchful, and more anxious, about civilian spies in their midst. Sherman himself, writing from Nashville in the spring of

1864, believed that numerous spies escaped detection, as they certainly did. Spying for the enemy, it bears repeating, violated the Articles of War.[6]

The two armies were increasingly cavalier in how they treated civilian employees. James Rusling, a federal quartermaster working in Tennessee, exulted in what he called his "vast control and patronage and power," with some 12,000 civilian laborers under his command in 1864. Both armies did have power over workers, and they moved workers around at will, for different purposes. In Richmond, Treasury Secretary Christopher Memminger forced female clerks to leave for Columbia, South Carolina, in April 1864 because he feared a US invasion; when they protested, he threatened to fire them if they did not go as they were commanded. In Georgia that summer, General William T. Sherman declared several hundred factory workers, mostly women and children, to be prisoners-of-war and sent them to the Midwest.[7]

Yet other civilians still traveled around, bent on their own purposes, despite the passport systems set up by both governments. They journeyed through the Union, the Confederacy, and the Border States collecting personal debts and visiting relatives, even as the fighting rolled on. Some of the South's European residents, frightened by the war's rising tumult, decided to leave the Confederacy, and some of them were allowed to travel minus passports, but most federal officials tried to enforce passport requirements for native-born civilians, with the mixed results of earlier years. Yankee soldiers accepted passes that were out of date, possibly because they could not read, as Mary Dickinson speculated in Louisiana, or maybe because they sympathized with female travelers such as herself. Other white people continued to forge passports, some of them very good replicas.[8]

The armies continued to seize hostages wherever they went, for the same purposes: to force the enemy to release their own hostages, to make the enemy refrain from certain behaviors, or to exact revenge. Lieber's Code had little impact on the conduct of Yankee troops, and both armies, Union and Confederate, cast an ever-wider net. Soldiers chose civilians at random, such as the young man, appellation unknown, lounging on the bank of the Tennessee River. He was taken hostage by Yankee Major Lewis Stegman to ensure the "good behavior" of his brother, whom Stegman forced to work as a guide for federal troops. Soldiers took female hostages, including the spouses of high-ranking military figures. Union troops in Smithland, Kentucky, seized Confederate General Hylan Lyon's wife as a hostage for some Northern officers held by the rebel general; the tactic worked, for Lyon immediately released the officers.

The armies seized political figures as hostages, too. Confederate Major Charles O'Ferrall seized two members of the West Virginia legislature, Messrs. Wheat and Bechtol, along with several other civilians, names unknown, and ferried them to Richmond where they were held for the exchange of hostages taken by federal forces.[9]

Civilians became more directly involved in hostage-taking, in ways undreamt of under Lieber's Code. In January 1864, Yankee soldiers went to Winchester, Virginia, under orders to arrest the mayor and hold him hostage for another civilian, but they could not find the mayor, so they chose someone at random, Robert Conrad, who claimed to be too sick to travel. Then another white man, Mr. Ginn, objected that hostage-taking stirred up antagonism toward Unionists such as himself, so the troops left empty-handed. Sometimes civilians initiated the capture of hostages, with deadly outcomes. In the spring of 1864, Unionists in Fayetteville, Alabama, seized a pro-Confederate yeoman farmer, Drury McMinn, so Confederate civilians retaliated by taking Unionist Lemuel Burnett as a hostage. A few weeks later, McMinn and four other men, including a rebel lieutenant, were found shot to death, their bodies tied to some trees. Then a circuit judge ordered Burnett to be turned over to him, but a rebel provost marshal refused to heed the order and took Burnett into his own custody. This last incident reveals not only civilian vulnerability to the army but the continuing inability of the Southern court system to restrain the military.[10]

SUSTENANCE

The quest for food, the great essential, went on with increasing urgency. Federal soldiers repeatedly violated the Articles of War, as well as Pope's Orders, as if they were a distant memory from another time. A seasoned veteran told Private Frank Wilkeson in 1864 to "steal" food from anyone, "food and food and still more food." Yet comestibles became ever more scarce as the fighting wreaked more damage on the region. Some farmers, exhausted and disturbed by the armies' presence, decided to forgo planting their usual crops in the spring of 1864. By that time, more places in Virginia had turned into food deserts, with very little left after repeated foraging by both armies. Some of the most hard-fought campaigns happened there, as thousands of men strained their physical abilities to the utmost. Sergeant Austin Stearns commented that strenuous campaigns left the men very hungry, and, after participating in battle that summer, he never had such an appetite.[11]

The Union army, with more men in the field, continued to forage from the rich and poor, as planter Richard Gwathmey saw in Hanover County, Virginia, with little regard for their politics or the required paperwork. Although the federal army built more supply depots as it took over more territory, the Northern military still could not carry food to all the men in the field. Yankee troops foraged out of genuine hunger. Soldiers in Meridian, Mississippi, outpaced their supply wagons and took food from civilians there to fill their empty stomachs. Other soldiers even took food from human beings to feed their own livestock. Samuel Cormany, who reported being well fed from army rations during the Battle of Cold Harbor, said his men "confiscated" corn from local people to give to their horses.[12]

Some Northern officers wanted to prevent unauthorized foraging, as they had before 1864, promising that troops who took "household stuff," especially food, from civilians would be severely punished. After soldiers foraged local people in Arkansas without permission, Major General Joseph A. Mower ordered that any troops who did that again would be assessed for the damages, which seems to have halted foraging for a time. In the ranks, some men felt compassion for the white Southern population. Private Reuben Wickham realized that there was not a mill or barn standing for 100 miles around Winchester, Virginia. Expressing sympathy for the inhabitants, he had no desire to go foraging in such a desolate place.[13]

But other federal soldiers did as they wished, their conduct sanctioned by their officers. Infantrymen were allowed to "run loose all over the Country" after the surrender of Atlanta in September 1864, robbing fields, barns, and homes, observed Captain Theodore Allen. Troops in other places openly defied their officers. In Missouri, Private John Ritland said that officers told hungry soldiers they could not forage in a Border State, but they seized food from civilians, anyway. When a captain then threatened to deduct money from their wages as a punishment, some privates threatened him in turn, and he backed down. Cruel, pointless behavior by the troops also mars the historical record. In north Georgia, Yankee soldiers fired at sheep in the fields and left the squirming animals there to die.[14]

Yankee troops continued to waste food, despite the straitened circumstances of 1864. This was true even for meat, the foundation of the military diet, which soldiers sought wherever they went. They "Stole" so much beef and poultry from civilians in Virginia that much of it went to waste in camp, Private James Stepter confessed to his wife. In May 1864, in the ultimate waste of food, soldiers ate so much food foraged from people near Malvern Hill, Virginia, that they made themselves sick. After going without rations for a day, they overate and then started vomiting. They had to spend the next day recovering in camp.[15]

White Southern civilians tried mightily, as they had before, to protect their food supply from the Union army. They drove their livestock into local swamps and river bottoms or hid their meat supply inside their houses. When troops discovered their food resources, civilians implored them not to take it, and, on occasion, the troops relented. In Mississippi, Mrs. Brett and her daughters stood in a stable door and refused to let a Yankee soldier take the bay horse necessary to run their farm. For unknown reasons, he gave up and left, but that was rare. As soldiers seized most of his poultry and livestock, Georgian Henry Mack brought out a "protection paper" given to him in October 1864 by a US general (probably George Thomas). The troops advised this yeoman farmer that civilians loyal to the Union would receive compensation "some day" for their losses.[16]

In this context, General William T. Sherman's March to the Sea appears to be less shocking than contemporaries, or historians, once assumed. His famous Order No. 120, issued on November 9, 1864, allowing soldiers to "forage liberally" during the March, was nothing new; troops in both armies had been doing that since the war's first year. His troops had seized a lot of food from civilians earlier that year during the campaign to take Atlanta, despite the officers' efforts to stop it, and now his army consumed a great deal of food on the way from Atlanta to Savannah, again, despite his officers' attempts to rein them in. His March to the Sea became notorious partly because of geography – dramatic events concentrated in one place – and timing, since it transpired within six weeks just after Abraham Lincoln was reelected, and the fact that many of the civilians his army encountered were female. Sherman's deliberate silence during the March ratcheted up public curiosity about his campaign. If he devastated the Georgia countryside, as he commented in December 1864, other foraging parties had done much the same in many places that year.[17]

The Confederate forces did not treat the white Southern population much better. The rebel supply depots had some food, and many of the railroads were still running in 1864, but the bureaucracy could not get viands to the men, letting them go for days with no rations issued. So the troops turned to civilians, now more than ever. The Richmond authorities acknowledged that the War Department was "constantly" employed in correcting "irregularities" in the army's impressment of private property, including food. The military's demands on the public escalated nonetheless. Southern Brigadier General J. D. Imboden publicly called on civilians in March 1864 to donate grain to the rebel cavalry, even though he understood they had already given an "enormous amount" to the army.[18]

Rebel troops continued to feel that their physical needs mattered more than anything else, although no one could pretend that the South's larder would last forever. All the social, cultural, and political bonds that might have held rebel soldiers back from hurting white civilians had frayed by 1864. Sergeant William W. Heartsill knew that his brothers-in-arms had no need to communicate with each other when they needed food, since they were about to forage in "some man[']s field." Soldiers took food from civilians who had been generous with them in the past. Privates from the Confederate cavalry "stole" every item of food they could carry from a plantation near Berzelia, Georgia, even though the owner already donated food to the army. Southern officers could demonstrate contempt for noncombatants. Major W. H. Tunnard and his comrades ridiculed an old white man who came to their camp near Shreveport searching for honey baskets they had foraged from his place. They did not give him any paperwork, even though Tunnard proclaimed his support for the Confederate cause. The major added that hungry soldiers were not "moralists" and would steal grub from any source – from their own supplies or from civilians – to get what they needed.[19]

"We ask to be saved from our friends," Mr. G. M. Barker implored Confederate authorities in January 1864. This noncombatant announced that rebel soldiers in Drew County, Arkansas, seized food from civilians with such abandon that they dreaded Southern troops as much as Yankees. As Barker revealed, the long-expected consequence of the Southern army's behavior began to happen on a large scale that year: the alienation of the civilian population, including those who once advocated the rebel cause. Rebecca L. Felton, a slaveowner's wife who initially supported the Confederacy, declared that there was little difference between Yankee General William T. Sherman and Confederate Major General Joseph Wheeler when it came to foraging, since they both seized food indiscriminately from civilians. Major General Richard Taylor perceived that civilians in Louisiana felt so much "discontent" because of the rebel army's impressment of cattle that they purposely drove their animals into the hands of the Union army. The army's own conduct had finally undermined the military's capacity to maintain public support.[20]

White Southern civilians protested to Confederate soldiers taking their food, much as they protested to federal soldiers. Yet again, these interactions frequently involved men taking sustenance from women. Mary Pearre's kinswoman saw rebel troops sweeping through central Tennessee, confiscating all kinds of food. She went into the field and begged them, "at least divide with us," but the soldiers took the best of the family's livestock. A few women took up weapons to defend their food supply, the ultimate rejection of antebellum gender roles. An unnamed woman, living alone in a log cabin, brandished an axe when a rebel soldier tried to take bacon from her kitchen, so he backed off and let her keep it. Roving packs of hungry females could affect military decisions in ways no one could have anticipated in 1861. In Pierce County, Georgia, white women with guns broke into a Confederate storehouse in 1864 and made off with wagons full of bacon. Major General Lafayette McLaws advised his superiors that the Third South Carolina Regiment should remain nearby in case these civilians caused further trouble.[21]

Regarding the Confederate seizure of food, some officers did follow bureaucratic procedure, even now. When the Southern cavalry camped on a farm near Lenoir, North Carolina, and confiscated food from the owners, they paid "what they thought it was worth," a young woman said. Some white civilians were reluctant to take rebel currency as it lost value, but it was better than nothing at all. Other officers reminded their fellows that actions had consequences. In Arkansas, Captain W. J. McArthur reproached a comrade for allowing the "stealing" of livestock, insisting that civilian property had to be respected. Soon, he pointed out, citizens would prefer the federal army to the rebel forces. Major General Thomas Churchill could only agree, blurting out that depredations by Southern troops were harming the very people who were essential for the Confederacy's success.[22]

Pro-Union civilians, still hanging on in 1864, occasionally offered their fare to Yankee troops passing by, but they, like their pro-Confederate neighbors, had been foraged repeatedly by both armies. Private John Billings and other federal troops admitted that hundreds of Unionist families lost their food to the Yankee army's unending demands. The Southern army was still eager to pillage Unionists, seizing all the food from Drucilla Cameron's residence in Marion County, Mississippi, before they cursed her and threatened to kill her husband. The planter John Minor Botts, who already had his domicile surrounded by rebel troops, watched more rebel soldiers tear up his garden, seize his fences, and take his corn in 1864. He cuttingly remarked that white Southerners should not complain about the behavior of federal soldiers.[23]

Both armies now inspired nothing less than loathing in much of the civilian population. Therefore, civilians did what other people have done during a food crisis and focused completely on self-preservation. Believing that their own survival was at stake, they began assaulting soldiers who foraged in the countryside, and sometimes they killed them. They murdered Yankee soldiers *and* Confederate soldiers, leaving the mutilated bodies on the roads. Some civilians turned on each other, threatening each other over access to food. In 1864, a white man pulled a knife on a white boy, J. D. Goldman, and threatened to murder him if he revealed the existence of his stash of bread and meat.[24]

Famished civilians unable to obtain nourishment began to eat foods that had been considered unsuitable for human consumption before 1861. They turned, as people have done in other wars, to "taboo" or "pariah" foods, including, most horrifying of all, rats. We know that rats carry bacteria, fungi, viruses, salmonella, rabies, and a host of other diseases, but many people in other societies have consumed rats during famines. During the American Civil War, the rodent population grew rapidly, probably because of the increasing number of dead bodies, and some ravenous civilians began to eat rats. In Virginia, a white boy known only as Morton skinned some rats, boiled them, baked them in a skillet lined with dough, and wolfed down his rat "pie," glad to have something to eat in the spring of 1864.[25]

The suffering of hungry people did not go unnoticed. Northern troops seemed to be more aware of the moral issues involved, or at least they articulated such thoughts more often. Lieutenant Elliott F. Grabill excoriated the misconduct of federal forces in North Carolina, writing that his army had degenerated into a "mob," and he said he did not join the military to take the last mouthful of subsistence from crying women and children. Rebel soldiers, by contrast, had less to say about the harm done to hungry civilians, and, when they did address it, they justified their actions in the name of self-preservation. Private Philip Stephenson and his comrades violated procedures and took food from civilians in Mississippi because they had what he termed a "deadened conscience." This was simple theft, he realized, but he asked, "What were we to do? Starve?" Other Confederate troops managed to blame civilians. Private Arthur P. Ford stated that rebel troops defied orders and killed hogs on private property because they were hungry, and the owners deserted their farms and left the animals behind, thus repeating the other army's justification for plundering after the residents disappeared. Many of those civilians left, of course, because they now feared the Southern army as much as the Northern army.[26]

Reports of starvation multiplied in 1864, far beyond the numbers in the past. John M. Thayer, a Yankee brigadier general, discerned that pro-Union families in western Arkansas were on the verge of "actual starvation." Something had to done for them, he insisted. Major General G. K. Warren asked for help from another officer after being beset once again by "starving women and children," adding that "our pillagers keep these people in constant terror." Aid from individual officers, Confederate relief organizations, or other institutions was not enough to alleviate the crisis, and noncombatants perished from hunger, as has been true for many societies at war. In May 1864, civilians in Randolph County, Alabama, wrote to Jefferson Davis to inform him that "Deaths from starvation" had occurred in their county despite their "utmost efforts" to prevent them.[27]

TIMBER

The special weather conditions of 1864 hastened the destruction of the forests. The early months of the calendar year were extremely cold, so that soldiers froze to death as far south as Texas, and in the fall of 1864 the winter came early, with severe frosts in October in Virginia; the low temperatures prompted both armies to use yet more timber. The sheer intensity of the combat also hastened deforestation. During the galvanic fighting around Richmond in May 1864, the woods caught on fire repeatedly, unnerving the troops. Sometimes the forest burned all night, while the wounded suffocated or burned to death. The growing significance of the military objectives, with so much at stake, further increased the consumption of wood. As William T. Sherman hammered his way through northwest Georgia toward Atlanta, and rebel soldiers tried to fend him off, both armies practiced clear-cutting, taking down trees for hundreds of yards. The armies created more mud everywhere they went, inhibiting their own progress as they thrashed their way across the landscape.[28]

Yankee troops who needed timber still sought out their favorite wood, pine, for their fires, for the usual array of military purposes. Regular soldiers, pioneers, and fatigue parties used pine and other species to build their headquarters, breastworks, dining halls, log cabins for medical staff, and wooden walkways between the buildings. As the number of dead soldiers increased, week after week, more wood was needed to provide coffins and grave markers. The army still inflicted damage on the forests, and some soldiers felt bad about it, depressed by such sights as the bullet-riddled saplings on the Chickahominy River, but they adhered to their practical view of the forest, perceiving wood as a resource they had to have. They kept up their continual harvest of fence rails, using them to build bridges in such places as Tippah Creek in Mississippi. They built a portable sawmill in middle Tennessee and processed what a soldier called timber "of the best quality and of all descriptions."[29]

The Union army wasted a great deal of wood, just as it had in the past, much of it by accident. Soldiers constructed breastworks out of fence rails to defend against the enemy, but then the enemy did not show up. They still destroyed timber on purpose, torching the enemy's supplies whenever they encountered them. Major General Lovell Rousseau commented in passing that his soldiers burned a "large amount" of lumber in Auburn, Alabama, while tearing up the local railroad. Other soldiers wasted wood in a reckless fashion that put civilians in peril. They left Murfreesboro, Tennessee, and made big fires out of fence rails in the countryside before returning to town, attempting to deceive the foe about their whereabouts. The fires were still burning when they departed the area.[30]

Federal soldiers often acted on their own, freelancing as they seized wood without consulting anyone. On a daily basis, troops engaged in departures from official policy, bending or breaking regulations, as they saw fit. In the winter of 1864, they stole from their own facilities in Union-occupied territory, filching wood from woodyards and cutting the sides out of boxcars near Alexandria, Virginia. Private William G. Bentley owned that his confreres lost their "scruples" about burning fence rails in Tennessee, taking it for granted that all of the residents were secessionists. Other soldiers cut up trees for more frivolous reasons, chopping off the branches of a chestnut tree near Kingston, Georgia, to get the chestnuts, an action that would have been condemned by most people in the antebellum North and South.[31]

Much of this happened because of the ongoing bureaucratic failures of the Northern army. Routine corruption sometimes played a part. Unionist civilians in federal-occupied Vicksburg saw army clerks profit from illicit dealing in "Govt. wood" and other supplies. Routine carelessness took its toll. Railroad superintendent J. H. Devereux wrote that thefts of timber from the Yankee woodyards near Alexandria, Virginia, took place with the knowledge of indifferent officers who had no sense of duty. The lack of bureaucratic diligence remained a common problem. Federal commanders had to task their subordinates – over and over – to try to control the men and make them follow procedures on confiscating wood from civilians.[32]

Union officers tried, as they had tried before, to persuade the men to follow procedures. Brigadier General J. M. Thayer banned the burning of fence rails near Fort Smith, Arkansas, because, he reminded his troops, such thefts hurt the army, the federal government, and the citizenry; he then made his men issue receipts for property they took, so that loyal people could receive compensation. When all else failed, officers threatened the men with bodily harm. An officer known only as Pennington (probably Colonel Alexander Pennington of New Jersey), threatened to shoot any man who took fence rails in rural Virginia and then stood watch over a fence to enforce his threat. The troops despised him for that, according to Private Roger Hannaford. On rare occasions, soldiers were court-martialed for stealing fence rails, but most of them, such as Corporal Dallas Brewster of Illinois, were acquitted and released. No one, it seems, was really in charge.[33]

The Confederate army, as we would now expect, exploited the South's forests with the same alacrity as their enemies. They could still appreciate the beauty of the woodlands with their towering pines, and they regretted the battlefield damage inflicted on trees, as trunks splintered into tiny pieces during the Battle of the Wilderness, but they were driven by the same overwhelming need for huge amounts of wood. Relying on their pioneer forces, as well as men in the ranks, they too used wood of all types to build bomb proofs, living quarters, and bridges. They took countless fence rails for a variety of uses, constructing barricades near Kernstown, Virginia, before battle, and they engaged in clear-cutting, taking down great swatches of trees all over the region.[34]

Rebel troops wasted wood, just as Yankee troops did, because of the ongoing demands of war. Major General Richard Taylor hoped to outmaneuver the enemy during the Red River campaign in Louisiana by pretending to have more troops than he really had – 6,000 men – so he built extra campfires and then made a lot of noise rolling wagons over downed fence rails. Timber also went to waste because of military incompetence. During Sherman's campaign to take Atlanta, rebel soldiers threw up stockades of wood that had to be relinquished soon afterwards because they were badly constructed. Everywhere they went, Southern forces burned wood belonging to private citizens if that wood could conceivably help the enemy. Between Pulaski and Spring Hill, Tennessee, troops incinerated two woodyards, a sawmill, and three railroad bridges, lighting up the night for miles in all directions.[35]

Confederate officers issued more sweeping orders prohibiting the unauthorized arson of fence rails and other "depredations" against civilians, and they tried to do right, sometimes, by the white Southern population. Major Robert Stiles pulled a revolver on two soldiers who violated his orders and cut timber in the Virginia countryside without permission, relenting only when they agreed to desist. Some officers still gave out paperwork for the wood they seized from noncombatants, issuing handwritten documents to the Hamilton family of Petersburg, Virginia, because the wood was necessary for the "public service." The documents are hard to categorize as receipts, vouchers, or certificates, but the officers, who had no money, promised reimbursement at some unspecified time in the future.[36]

Southern troops routinely flouted their own regulations, however, just as Yankee soldiers did, despite the efforts of their more scrupulous officers. In Tennessee, rebel troops gathered fence rails without consulting anyone and threw them together to protect pickets from the enemy. As other soldiers passed through the state, they pulled the planks off buildings for their campfires. Yet other troops engaged in depredations on a larger scale, which hurt their own supporters. The cavalry took some 11,000 fence rails from widow Jane Garrett of Madison County, North Carolina, in the spring of 1864, but when she complained to the quartermaster with the unit, he did nothing, issuing no paperwork. The Board of Survey in Asheville found that the military owed her 8,900 Confederate dollars for the rails. They noted that she had two sons in the rebel military, but it is not clear if she ever received any money.[37]

Many civilians grieved, as much as ever, for the loss of the forests. In northeastern Mississippi, a preacher said that the impact of the Battle of Brice's Crossroads on the forest and undergrowth was as bad as a fire. Louisa Lovell, a planter's wife in Natchez, had a furious argument with a Northern colonel about whether her family or the US government owned the woods in front of her mansion. She lost, and after she watched the large oaks – "dear old trees" – being cut down, she could have killed the officer who ordered it. Union supporters assigned responsibility in a different fashion. Margaret Lindsley, the daughter of a Tennessee attorney, decried the bleak landscape after Yankee forces took down all the trees near her home, but she did not blame the army per se. Rather, she blamed the destructive forces unleashed by the war.[38]

Civilians made determined efforts to recover some compensation for their damaged forests and fields from the Southern government. In 1864, they were still trying to figure out the system. B. H. Haxall saw a Confederate battalion camped on his farm burn down his woods and

FIGURE 6.1 Fair Oaks, Virginia.
Courtesy of the Library of Congress.

destroy most of his fences; then their horses consumed his entire crop of clover. Months later he discovered that the quartermaster's statement was not enough to document his losses, so he asked a friend in the rebel government for advice on how to press his claim. Those who pursued their claims found that Confederate officers could accept or reject their petitions, with no reason given. Samuel Goode received nothing for the fence rails and wheat destroyed while 910 Confederate steeds grazed on his land for a single day, May 19, 1864. Some civilians gave up and left home to live elsewhere so they could find enough wood to last through the winter of 1864–1865.[39]

HABITAT

The troops continued to exploit the South's built environment as they embarked on the massive military campaigns of 1864. Let us begin with the Yankee army. Wherever they went, the troops described the characteristics of private homes – the princely mansions, the log cabins, the frame houses of middling farmers – and the objects within – furniture, carpets, daguerreotypes on the walls. Yet they still exploited those dwellings whenever necessary. They took over the homes of local people for their lodging, giving the owners short notice to vacate the premises, and they still saw large brick houses as ideal structures for military use.[40]

The looting of private homes went on, although Union troops still occasionally put guards in front of occupied homes owned by civilians, regardless of their politics. The men pillaged homes of all sizes, snatching jewelry, crockery, and the random split-bottom chair. They still harvested buildings for wood, lifting the weatherboarding off structures as needed, and they scavenged for whatever kind of wood they needed in an emergency. When General James B. McPherson died during the Georgia campaign in the summer of 1864, William T. Sherman had the body laid on a door wrenched off a neighboring house.[41]

Swearing an oath of allegiance to the United States did not always make the difference in saving a house, *pace* General John Pope's policy back in 1862. Federal troops sometimes enforced the policy, threatening civilians with eviction if they did not swear allegiance to the United States, and some noncombatants took the oath to remain in their houses. But other soldiers did not enforce policy, for women or men. In Flat Creek, Tennessee, Yankee troops regularly searched Letitia Dobson's home for her husband, whom they suspected was on leave from the rebel army, but, she assured her daughter, she did not have to take the oath. Other military authorities did not bother to enforce their own public statements. In Jacksonville, Florida, the provost marshal declared a deadline in the spring of 1864 for all residents to take the oath or be expelled from the area, but several months afterwards one Mr. Dorman, who refused to take it, still lived in his house.[42]

Federal troops did their best to protect Unionists when they could identify them. After a scouting expedition, Lieutenant A. N. Harris drew a superbly detailed map of the political terrain near Batesville, Arkansas. His map, which was based on close observation of the people and the landscape, indicated which households had contributed officers to the federal army, as well as political divisions within the households. Just as Yankee officers had done earlier, they tried to spare Unionist homes when they chose residences for their lodging or headquarters. They sometimes made an effort to protect their buildings in other circumstance, even if it was difficult in practice. In May 1864, P. G. Bier, an adjutant general for Major General David Hunter, commanded a cavalry officer to burn every building in Newtown, Virginia, and every structure in the countryside between Newtown and nearby Middletown, Virginia, except those belonging to loyal citizens, most particularly a Dr. Owens who had treated the Yankee wounded.[43]

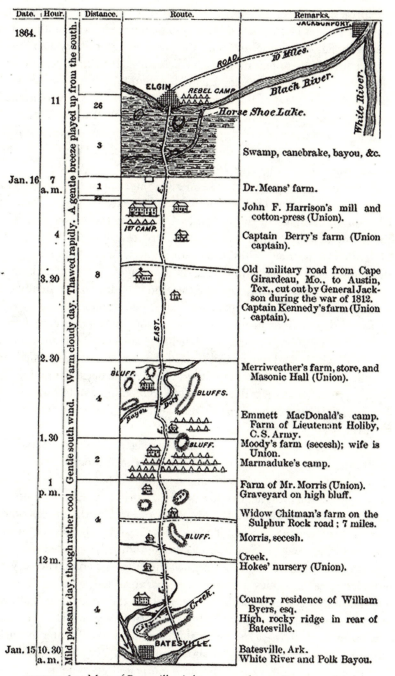

Date.	Hour.	Distance.	Route.	Remarks.
1864.				JACKSONPORT.
				ROAD 10 Miles.
	11	26	ELGIN REBEL CAMP	Black River. White River.
			Horse Shoe Lake.	
		3		Swamp, canebrake, bayou, &c.
Jan. 16	7 a. m.	1		Dr. Means' farm.
			1ST CAMP.	John F. Harrison's mill and cotton-press (Union).
	4			Captain Berry's farm (Union captain).
	3. 20	8		Old military road from Cape Girardeau, Mo., to Austin, Tex., cut out by General Jackson during the war of 1812. Captain Kennedy's farm (Union captain).
	2. 30		BLUFF.	Merriweather's farm, store, and Masonic Hall (Union).
		4	BLUFFS. Bayou Dry	
	1. 30	2	BLUFF.	Emmett MacDonald's camp. Farm of Lieutenant Holiby, C. S. Army. Moody's farm (secesh); wife is Union. Marmaduke's camp.
	1 p. m.			Farm of Mr. Morris (Union). Graveyard on high bluff.
		4	BLUFF.	Widow Chitman's farm on the Sulphur Rock road ; 7 miles. Morris, secesh.
	12 m.			Creek. Hokes' nursery (Union).
		4	Creek.	Country residence of William Byers, esq. High, rocky ridge in rear of Batesville.
Jan. 15	10. 30 a. m.		BATESVILLE.	Batesville, Ark. White River and Polk Bayou.

A gentle breeze played up from the south. Thawed rapidly. Warm cloudy day. Gentle south wind. Mild, pleasant day, though rather cool.

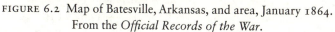

FIGURE 6.2 Map of Batesville, Arkansas, and area, January 1864.
From the *Official Records of the War*.

Northern soldiers continued to set fire to houses, however, often selecting planter homes. As ex-slave Daphney Wright recalled, they chose the big, handsome houses in South Carolina for arson. They also burned down empty homes of all sizes, everywhere, in such places as Simmesport, Louisiana, if snipers concealed themselves within. Officers still took the most utilitarian view of what could be done with the private home. In October 1864, before his famous March to the Sea, William T. Sherman instructed a corps to burn "houses or piles of brush" as they traveled through Georgia to indicate the location of the head of the column, as if houses were interchangeable with brush piles.[44]

Entire towns went up in smoke in 1864, and not just the major cities torched by Sherman. The Northern army burned tiny places, including Clarendon, a village in the Arkansas Delta near the Mississippi River. Every one of Clarendon's 300 residents fled before the army arrived in 1864. Private Leander Stillwell did not know why his comrades burned this ghost town: perhaps they were tired or angry, he speculated; maybe they did it on their own; or maybe they did it under orders. In any case, he surmised that Confederates could have used the houses for cover, so he found their actions justified as a military measure – preventive arson, again. Federal troops burned populated towns, including Ream's Station, Virginia, which had what Colonel Elisha Rhodes called some "fair dwellings" before his men set fire to it. They left the place a smoking ruin. By his own account, Rhodes later told a civilian he would burn a town first – in that case, Newtown, Virginia – and get the order permitting it after the deed was done.[45]

This inferno of destruction excited strong reactions from civilians, most often concerning the private home. White men lamented the destruction of houses suffused with childhood memories, but it was women who gave voice to the most acute sense of loss. Henrietta Lee, wife of attorney Edmund Jennings Lee, felt distraught after one of David Hunter's officers burned her dwelling in the Shenandoah Valley. Her spouse, a cousin of Robert E. Lee, owned some house slaves but initially opposed secession; the family supported the Confederacy after the war commenced. When Henrietta Lee sent a message to Hunter, the words fairly leap off the page. Her father, a Revolutionary War veteran, built the house, and "hallowed memories" gathered around it. She was born there, and Hunter's niece had been a guest there. So why, she demanded, did Hunter burn her house? The general evidently did not reply.[46]

Revenge – pure, raw, and simple – motivated many federal soldiers in the war's last year. William G. Bentley, a private in the 104th Ohio

Volunteer Infantry, admitted that his comrades destroyed buildings in Tennessee in November 1864 because of what rebel soldiers did at Chambersburg on the way to Gettysburg the year before. Some troops had misgivings about the practice, as soldiers always had. Private Charles Kingsley's unit ranged through the Virginia countryside with what he called "no greater purpose than to burn the dwelling of a prominent rebel" to repay the torching of Governor Augustus Bradford's house in Maryland. After they burned a mansion, he doubted that it would help defeat the Confederacy, since "rebels can play at the same game." Private Chauncey Barton (no relation to Clara or Stephen Barton) expressed more anguished objections. He felt sorely troubled as his comrades burned the home of a white woman and her young children as the family watched. He had seen similar acts of arson "hundreds" of times, but he did not like it, he told his sister, even if the civilians were rebels. Yet these remorseful individuals could not slow down the juggernaut.[47]

Confederate troops, riding the same juggernaut of war, exploited the built environment much as their foes did. As they traveled the region, they too noted the plantation mansions with fluted columns, the neat cottages, and the little cabins, along with the numbers of rooms, the trees close by, and the estimated age of the buildings. Despite these commentaries on the habitat, they too frequently disregarded privacy, property rights, and their own military policy when it came to the home. Southern officers took over residences as needed for their headquarters, even if they knew the owners personally and they supported the Confederacy. They constructed their works in private homes, using the dwelling as a core and building around it.[48]

Inside private dwellings, rebel soldiers looted, just as federal troops did. They entered houses in Kingsport, Tennessee, and stole such personal possessions as jewelry, and they pillaged deserted homes in and around Atlanta, taking whatever they liked and scattering books, clothing, and artwork in their wake. They did not always identify themselves to noncombatants when asked. After soldiers plundered houses in Henderson County, North Carolina, one of the homeowners, Rachel Lanning, asked for their names, but they refused to tell her. Then they insulted her neighbor Elizabeth Youngblood, a middle-aged widow who ran her own farm, while sweeping up diverse "small articles" from the premises before they left.[49]

Confederate soldiers persisted in their attacks on the homes of Unionists, Caroline Muirhead, for one, who lived near Murfreesboro,

Tennessee. At the war's outset, she named her infant son Abraham Lincoln Muirhead, a defiant statement of political loyalty if ever there was one. Her neighbors suspected that she might be "dangerous" to the Southern cause, and in December 1864, rebel troops arrested her for repeatedly aiding the enemy's war effort. Then they hauled her into the homes of local secessionists to question her, hoping that these environments would intimidate her, and in the interval her own house was robbed. She was released, but a few weeks later, rebel guards burned her home, her smoke-house, and her cotton crop. The total loss was some 4,000 US dollars.[50]

The Southern military devastated the built environment, wherever they went. One night in September 1864, Joseph Wheeler's cavalry burned the Tennessee home of the Starnes family, putting the torch to it before they awakened the residents to warn them the edifice was on fire. Confederate soldiers pulled down mansions near Nashville before the battle in December because the structures would interfere with cannon fire. (Yankee troops in the area did the same.) Rebel soldiers burned public buildings, torching all of the municipal structures in Martinsburg, Virginia, in May 1864, and they helped obliterate entire towns. In Baldwin, Florida, which was occupied by the two armies at various times, Southern troops set fire to houses and left behind charred heaps of wood, dead horses, dead mules, and an unbearable stench.[51]

A few civilians found that the Confederate army's mistakes could obliterate their homes in one blinding flash. In 1864, such a fate befell Lawrence J. Messerry, the postmaster of Rantowles' Station, South Carolina. Messerry, who supported the Confederacy, lived in an aged two-story residence with a brick foundation, brick chimneys, a shingled roof, and a porch, home to ten people. Rebel Lieutenant John N. Edwards moved powder and shells from a nearby magazine into Messerry's basement without asking the owner, and when Messerry balked, the lieutenant invoked "military necessity," saying that engineers were rebuilding the magazine and he had to store his supplies somewhere. The officer nonetheless gave him no paperwork. Flying sparks from a chimney set the house on fire, and it exploded, the bricks blown to the winds. Messerry cried that troops on the scene did not help him and his young son as they doused the flames; the lieutenant insisted that two soldiers did help. Then other buildings on the property combusted and burned down. No one died – something of a miracle – but the shell-shocked owner wrote to Confederate General P. G. T. Beauregard, asking for shelter for his family. Beauregard issued a written censure to the lieutenant and his commander, but there is no apology on record to Messerry and no evidence that the rebel army provided him with shelter.[52]

How could rebel soldiers allow such things to happen? Military necessity, of course, bad luck, bad judgment, and carelessness all played a part, as Messerry's fate revealed. There is also the motive of personal enrichment. Robert Hudson, a planter in Edenburg, Mississippi, saw bands of Confederate scouts and independent companies plunder homes in his neighborhood, stealing from "our own people" for their own gain. Other men seem to have gone mad with the fury of war and the power they exercised over civilians. Some Texas cavalrymen looted David Morrell's farm in North Carolina, taking his corn with no compensation or paperwork. Then one of the Texans rode his horse into Morrell's house and shot the family dog. Colonel John B. Palmer sent a captain to investigate the matter, but we do not know if the cavalrymen were ever punished.[53]

As we have seen, Southern troops all over the region expressed some discomfort about the damage to local housing. During the defense of Atlanta, Private Philip Stephenson did not want to enter a house he had visited earlier, the owners having fled as the two armies circled each other. Now the furies raged around the "big brick shell, empty and desolate," which made him feel queasy. More frequently, rebel soldiers blamed the Northern army for wrongdoing. George M. Neese, a member of the artillery, decided that the Yankee army ruined Edmund Ruffin's house, even though Ruffin pointed out that both armies damaged his property. Some rebel troops blamed civilians for leaving their homes, thus duplicating the other army's justification for destroying houses. If civilians departed their homes, Corporal William W. Chamberlaine wrote, their dwellings would be pulverized by soldiers from both armies.[54]

Rebel officers did try to rein in their misbehaving troops, threatening to arrest officers and privates who entered homes on the march near Shreveport, Louisiana, in April 1864. Some men were indeed arrested for misconduct. Lieutenant James Kidd, deemed a "very shrewd villain" by another Confederate officer, was arrested with other cavalrymen for robbing civilians in their houses in Tennessee. Brigadier General John McCausland's "outrageous" conduct, including the burning in 1864 of Chambersburg, Pennsylvania, infuriated Brigadier General Bradley T. Johnson, and, what was even worse, he thought, the widespread plundering by his men after they returned to the Confederacy. Such troops could not be disciplined, Johnson declared, and a court of inquiry should be opened. The inquiry apparently never took place, but McCausland maintained that Jubal Early ordered him to burn Chambersburg in retaliation for the federal army's actions. He did not explain the pillaging inside the Confederacy.[55]

The year 1864 witnessed a final breakdown of social mores among members of the rebel army, as Confederates engaged in shocking violations of cherished social practices. These practices included such time-honored customs as the burials of their fellow citizens. In Virginia, rebel soldiers seized a horse from a funeral cortege bearing a white woman's body to her grave, as her relatives and friends watched. Some of these troops showed an open disregard for the physical markers of community and family history. In Cassville, Georgia, they took down tombstones in the local cemetery to get them out of the way as they built their earthworks. No institution was safe. Confederate soldiers broke into a church in North Carolina, looted the building, and penned obscene messages on the walls, seemingly oblivious to the symbolism.[56]

Many civilians decided that there was no longer any difference between the two armies when it came to how they treated physical resources. William Pitt Chambers, a Confederate sergeant major, worried in 1864 that indiscriminate destruction of civilian property by his comrades would only "widen the breach" between the army and the white Southern populace. As he feared, that breach became unbridgeable. In February 1864, white people near Warren, Arkansas, told Rebel Private George Boddie that both armies were equally dangerous. The cavalryman had to acknowledge that the army was making enemies of civilians by despoiling "our own people." Civilians naturally felt that no one was looking out for their interests. In February 1864, the local court in Appomattox County, Virginia, tried to take possession of victuals impressed in the county by the rebel military, but the Richmond government threatened to indict any civilian official who withheld food from the army. Secretary of War James Seddon vowed that the same punishment would be meted out for similar conduct by other civilians. The final rupture between the Confederate army and the white Southern public was under way.[57]

THE UNCANNY

Some civilians began to crack under the compounding pressures of war, engaging in increasingly reckless behavior. In May 1864, a tall, well-dressed clergyman walked right through the Battle of Yellow Tavern, calling out in a booming voice, "'Where's my boy? I want to see my boy.'" The man strode across an active battlefield while troops shouted at him to leave before he disappeared, uninjured, into the woods. Other civilians, harrowed by loss, could no longer reason clearly. During the Atlanta campaign, a white woman darted from one pine tree to another seeking her husband's grave. All she knew was that he had been buried near a pine tree, so she ran on, "nearly crazy," rebel soldier Sam Watkins noted. Other civilians were overcome by trauma, undone. As federal troops made their way through the Shenandoah Valley, a white girl stood at her front door watching the buildings burn on her family's property. She began yanking the hair from her head, repeating the curses she heard from passing troops, and shouting with maniacal laughter.[58]

To many people, it seemed as if the material world itself was coming apart at the seams. Fires burned beyond the control of either army, the flames racing through the landscape with preternatural swiftness. After Yankee troops ignited thousands of cotton bales on the levee in Alexandria, Louisiana, in May 1864, the wind carried the burning cotton fibers all over town. Flames engulfed the village just as the sun was coming up, illuminating the place in an otherworldly glow. The troops grasped at historical analogies for the gothic scenes unfolding before them. In October 1864, Yankee Corporal George Howard stood slack-jawed at a huge conflagration of buildings in Virginia, with the sun piercing the dense smoke while women and children shrieked and old men cursed. He compared it the burning of Moscow during the Napoleonic Wars. Fire and the aftermath of fire staggered civilians as well. Harriet E. Johnson watched flaming pieces of weaponry crash into her yard in Bristol after federal troops set fire to a depot on the Tennessee–Virginia border. She thought the thick black smoke, more awful than anything she had ever seen, resembled the Day of Judgment when the world would end.[59]

As the death toll mounted, the landscape filled up with human body parts, skeletons, and corpses. Civilians and soldiers recorded sights that are difficult to read about, even now, and which must have been even harder to witness. By 1864, most of the battlefields of the South were glutted with human remains. Skeletons were visible at Chickamauga from the battle the year before, the bones exposed after a rain, and later in 1864, yet other skeletons could be seen protruding from hastily-dug graves at Resaca, Georgia. Soldiers watched with ever-renewing horror what the mayhem did to the human body. After an explosion during the Atlanta campaign, Confederate soldier Phil Stephenson saw human viscera rain from the sky and catch in the trees overhead. As if the earth could not hold all the bodies, one Yankee soldier suddenly popped out of a large pool of mud, his leg breaking the smooth surface. His stunned comrades quickly pulled him out, leg first. Amazingly, he was still alive.[60]

As freakish as a leg emerging from a mud pool might be, it was the human hand reaching up from the grave that seemed to haunt many people. Throughout the war, soldiers and civilians commented on the grisly sight of a dead hand jutting up from a shallow grave. Perhaps the outstretched hand symbolized the slain reaching back to the living – perhaps that is why this image became fixed in the collective memory. In any case, the mounting fatalities meant that more people encountered this manifestation of the dead, and the repetition could have a desensitizing effect. Samuel Agnew, a minister in Tippah County, Mississippi, came upon a Yankee soldier's grave in June 1864 while walking down a country lane near his home. The body was stiff with rigor mortis, which sets in three or four hours after death, and a human hand projected out of the dirt. The two armies had fought all around Agnew's home in Tippah County, and several soldiers were already buried in his yard. A thoughtful man who usually took his religion seriously, he said nothing this time about the soul of the departed. Repulsed by the hand's decaying flesh, which had turned black, he worried only that the stench from the corpse would make living people sick. Otherwise, he was unmoved, his pastoral instincts having deserted him. The preacher had seen too many dead bodies.[61]

7

1865 and After

The struggle over the South's human resources persisted into the early months of the new year, as civilians remained deeply involved in war-making. They smuggled goods over the Potomac River and in other parts of the Confederacy, and men and women both were arrested for smuggling and espionage. Civilians gave information to the two armies, Confederate and Union, about the enemy's movements. Noncombatants still worked for both armies. They worked as carpenters, tinsmiths, clerks, and cooks for the federal army, even as other whites labored as messengers and office workers for the rebel military. Noncombatants managed to evade military efforts to control their travels, as they had earlier, by using illicit passports to move between the United States and the Confederacy.[1]

To the very end of the war, both armies continued one of their most invasive practices involving civilians, taking hostages. The troops seized hostages into the spring of 1865, when some of them expired in military custody despite the provisions of Lieber's Code back in 1863. One Mr. Smith, a Unionist, died in Confederate Lieutenant General John B. Hood's custody in Murfreesboro, Tennessee, in March 1865 as he was held with another white man as part of a possible hostage swap with US Brigadier General H. P. Van Cleve. On April 12, 1865, a Northern lieutenant posted near New Orleans suggested taking a Mr. Whitaker hostage to prevent his son from aiding the Confederate cause; the officer evidently did not know of Lee's surrender in Virginia a few days earlier. The possibility of being taken hostage by either army clearly frightened many noncombatants.

Perhaps it is no surprise that a rebel soldier observed that civilians in central Tennessee "seemed to shrink and hide from us" in the war's last months.[2]

The same bureaucratic indifference, or incompetence, marked the operations of both armies in their dealings with noncombatants. Sometimes civilians were spared by irregular military practices. In January 1865, Union soldiers did not require one Mr. Higginbotham, the county clerk in Nassau County, Florida, to take the oath of allegiance because he feared his neighbors would burn down his house if he did. More often, civilians continued to be harmed by the disregard for procedure. In March 1865, Private Edwin Finch of the Yankee cavalry said that when he wanted something to eat or drink in the Virginia countryside, "all you had to do was to go and get it." The impression arises yet again that no one was completely in charge of either army. On April 18, 1865, Confederate Major General Thomas Churchill ordered guards to prevent his soldiers from leaving camp near Marshall, Texas, because they committed "depredations" on local citizens, but the troops defied his orders, so he sent a cavalry patrol to arrest them. Apparently, he too had not heard of Lee's surrender at Appomattox.[3]

Individual men in both armies tried nevertheless to protect civilians, as some of them had done throughout the conflict. They showed the same residual moral sense, a sense of obligation to noncombatants, that had never entirely disappeared from the military. One Yankee officer forced some troops to return household goods pillaged from Sarah Jane Sams in Barnwell Courthouse, South Carolina. In Florida, near the St. John's River, members of the Confederate cavalry captured federal soldiers in February 1865 and made them give back livestock they had just taken from civilians nearby. In Aberdeen, Mississippi, rebel officials announced in February 1865 that they would ask umpires to resolve disputes between troops and civilians over military payments for food, although there is no record of whether the consultations ever took place.[4]

Moreover, the material demands of the armies were unchanged. Rebel soldiers still took food from mills, barns, and stores without authorization, and they still burned commissary stores to prevent the enemy from getting their supplies. They cut down trees in the roads to delay the federal army's advance in the Carolinas, and they inadvertently wasted wood everywhere they went. Members of the Army of Northern Virginia built a chapel from wood seized in the Old Dominion in March 1865, but two days later they had to evacuate the area and leave it behind. The teenaged Mollie Mallay, a housekeeper's daughter in Kentucky, saw no difference between the Confederate and Union armies that passed through her neighborhood in early 1865. They both seized resources of all types so that "evy [*sic*] body Suffers."[5]

The Northern army's demands continued to be voracious. The troops still confiscated livestock from civilians, including Unionist Eliza Cleveland, the poor widow of a yeoman farmer in Claiborne County, Tennessee. They told her in January 1865 that they "*must*" have her sorrel horse, which she needed to make a crop, and they took it. Near Charlottesville, Virginia, soldiers set fire to the fences on a roadside to keep themselves warm one night in March 1865. Lighting each panel of fence with a blazing rail as they marched forward, they left behind a wall of flaming woods that was visible for miles. The troops kept exploiting the built environment, as they had before. As General William T. Sherman's army journeyed through the Carolinas in early 1865, contending with heavy rains, his men disassembled twenty-five empty houses and used the materials to build bridges over the Salkehatchie River. The assumption that military needs took priority remained securely in place for both armies.[6]

The search for food, perhaps the most desperate of all contests, persisted to the very end with desperate results. Hunger prompted soldiers in the two armies to forage ever more diligently from white civilians in early 1865, leaving many communities devoid of anything to eat, even as famished civilians begged soldiers for food. Civilians fired on Yankee troops foraging for food, and in Fayetteville, North Carolina, they killed some of them. During the war's last weeks, hungry civilians died, but not from gunfire. The mayor of Columbia, South Carolina, estimated that over 150 people starved to death in the city after it burned in February.[7]

Not surprisingly, many civilians now comported themselves with hard, cold self-interest, abandoning what was left of communalism of the antebellum order. White men who once supported the rebel cause now did business with the Yankee army, buying domiciles at public auction that had been vacated by their neighbors. Neighbors stole from neighbors, including from people who had once befriended them. Many Southerners had lost the desire to fight. "Even in Mississippi," according to Confederate Sergeant Major William Pitt Chambers, civilians held public meetings in February 1865 calling for reunion with the North. In

the first week of April, civilians in Lynchburg, Virginia, wanted to surrender to some federal troops nearby, but Rebel Major General Lunsford
L. Lomax, who had just arrived in the area, talked them out of it. The
apolitical and the neutral still focused on running their farms and trying
to make a living.[8]

Civilians and soldiers alike witnessed more scenes of the uncanny,
terrible and strange to behold. In March 1865, a house, unmoored but
intact, drifted down the Cumberland River in Tennessee with the corpses
of a man, a woman, and some children visible inside the structure. The
ravages of fire continued unabated, with more astonishing results. After
Yankee troops near Goldsboro, North Carolina, set fire to some turpentine factories, the melted rosin ran down into a creek and floated on the
water's surface for hundreds of yards, crackling and hissing as it rolled
downstream. Other eerie, unforgettable scenes filled the landscape. In the
war's final days, burning boats drifted down the James River in Virginia,
and wagons set on fire by fleeing Confederates flamed in the roads near
Petersburg.[9]

The last drama in the great conflict happened at Wilmer McLean's
residence. This slaveowner had to flee his home, Yorkshire plantation,
near Manassas, Virginia, when the Battle of First Bull Run thundered
into his front yard in 1861. McLean resettled at Appomattox
Courthouse partly because he thought the sleepy village some 200
miles to the west would be safe. His house there was a three-story
brick structure with a long wooden porch, one of the more substantial
dwellings in the area, and after the two armies converged around the
edifice, Generals Robert E. Lee and Ulysses S. Grant conducted the
surrender ceremony in McLean's parlor on April 9. Yankee souvenir-
hunters took the "surrender table," among other objects in the well-
appointed house, and the table passed through the hands of several
owners before the Chicago History Museum acquired it. Yet McLean
blamed the rebel army and the Yankee army in 1865 for the loss of his
first house and the damage to his second. On April 9, he told a member
of Lee's staff, Confederate Brigadier General E. P. Alexander, that
"you," the Southern army, had "ruined" his plantation in 1861, so that
he hoped to never see another soldier from either army. Now, McLean
said, his fence rails were burning up in the campfires of both armies as
the war ground to a close. Even if Lee did not surrender to Grant in his
parlor, the two armies probably would have plundered McLean's house
at Appomattox because the structure was full of material resources
both armies needed.[10]

FIGURE 7.1 Wilmer McLean.
Courtesy of National Park Service.

POSTWAR: PEOPLE

In April and May 1865, when news of Lee's surrender spread through much of the South, most civilians assumed that the war was over. For them, Appomattox spelled the end of it all rather than Richmond's surrender on April 3, Abraham Lincoln's assassination on April 14, Jefferson Davis's capture on May 10, or the capitulation of any other rebel officer. Individual commanders on both sides released most of their civilian hostages without fanfare. Some of the pro-Confederate hostages had to take the oath of allegiance to the United States, and some evidently did not. Into late April, rebel authorities held James P. Crane, a railroad conductor, at Salisbury prison in North Carolina as a "special hostage," probably because he was pro-Union. How he acquired his special status is unclear, but he too was eventually released. There was no state-level or national policy on how to deal with civilian

FIGURE 7.2 Wilmer McLean's house, Appomattox Courthouse, Virginia.
Courtesy of the Library of Congress.

hostages and no public discussion of compensating them. In other societies, civilian hostages have sometimes received public thanks for their
sacrifices, and some of them have obtained postbellum assistance from
government officials and charitable societies, as did German civilians
who were interned in England during World War I, but American
civilians were on their own in 1865. The experience left its mark on
them, whether it was lasting trauma or the sense of triumph that they
had survived an ordeal.[11]

Pro-Confederate white civilians felt shattered when they learned of
Lee's surrender, while Unionists expressed overwhelming joy when they
heard the tidings, "*glorious news*," as one of them exclaimed. (Black
Southerners found it even more glorious, rejoicing at the end of bondage
and Confederacy, as ex-slave Fannie Berry recalled.) Many whites,
including those who supported the Confederacy, were simply relieved
that it was over. People of all political views felt the need to communicate the overwhelming experiences they had lived through. Kate Stone,
living in Tyler, Texas, in May 1865, hosted a long stream of callers,
everyone "too restless and wretched to stay at home." She perceived
that they "must talk it over with somebody." Mail service resumed in

FIGURE 7.3 Kate Stone of Louisiana.
Courtesy of Louisiana State University.

most communities by the summer, and civilians began writing to their relatives, inquiring about the fate of kinfolk who had dispersed across the region.[12]

For months after the war officially ended, the South remained a dangerous place. The legal system no longer functioned in many locations, and independent bands of ex-soldiers from both armies roamed the countryside. In Chester, South Carolina, which had no court system in the spring of 1865, yeoman farmer John H. Simpson guarded his house and his livestock from thieves plaguing the area. Other civilians took advantage of the chaos to seize what used to be military supplies whenever they could find them. In the early summer of 1865, they broke into the Confederate quartermaster depot in Anderson County, Texas, and took what they needed as the lonely quartermaster still on duty tried to fend them off.[13]

The soldier population made more demands on civilians, well after Appomattox. The rebel armies disbanded in April, May, and June in ad-hoc fashion, typically whenever their officers learned of Lee's surrender. Now it was time, as William Pitt Chambers understood, to deal with the "material problems" of civilian life, starting with how to get home. The rebel veterans poured through the countryside, sleeping at night in empty buildings. They asked for food from civilians, who sometimes complied, although ex-planter Dolly Burge locked her door and closed her blinds to discourage them from calling at her residence. The Northern army both gave food and took it away. Occupying forces handed out food to noncombatants who took the oath of allegiance, while some Yankees kept foraging from civilians. Samuel Cormany, a first lieutenant, wrote on April 25 that his hungry troops "appropriated all we needed" from the Virginia countryside. Military discipline in the US Army, which had never been very effective during the war, seems to have deteriorated after combat ended in 1865.[14]

SUSTENANCE

The competition for material resources between armies and civilians went on for months after Lee surrendered. Noncombatants expected the foraging to stop after that, and they were incensed when some Yankee troops kept on seizing and destroying food. One Mrs. Stein of Spring Hill, Alabama, threatened to shoot two Union soldiers who entered her home to forage for food a week after Appomattox. Civilians such as Sallie Clayton, a banker's daughter, were not sure how veterans from either army would behave in the spring of 1865, but they found out soon enough. In Washington, Georgia, ex-Confederate soldiers on their way home in May 1865 seized provender and livestock from local people, including plantation owners. One veteran was spotted leading a mule away from its owner, as a white man followed after him making "useless remonstrances," just like during the war.[15]

The South still had a few enclaves of plenty, such as Montgomery, Alabama, which had seen no serious combat. Louise Wigfall Wright, whose father had served in the Confederate Senate, was glad that town-dwellers had enough food to provide for wayfarers in the spring of 1865. But the agricultural economy had more or less ground to a halt by 1864, with few crops harvested in the fall of that year. After peace broke out, many people still had to make do with dismal, paltry fare, and they still bartered for food, just as they had before combat ended. The crops in the autumn of 1865 were small, so that food scarcity lasted into the next calendar year.[16]

Many civilians were still in danger of dying from starvation. In June 1865, US Brevet Major General J. H. Wilson declared that central Georgia featured a population of 30,000 people desperate for food, some of them at the brink of death. In Randolph County, Alabama, the scene of wartime riots by civilians, white women and children went door to door begging for food in 1866. Multiple reports of starving people led the Congress in 1867 to pass the Southern Famine Relief Bill, which allowed the federal government to give victuals directly to hungry civilians, but food production in many parts of the region did not rebound until the 1870s. A generation would pass before the agricultural economy completely recovered.[17]

TIMBER

The region had some living forests, undamaged by combat, and veterans exploited the woodlands even though the war had officially closed. Federal soldiers cut down trees and took down fences all over the region as the spring passed. Confederate veterans heading home needed wood, too, and they burned fence rails on farms and plantations as they camped along the way. A South Carolinian returned to her place on the Ashley River to find all of her trees, "the work & culture of years," cut down by parties unknown. Other civilians rejoiced to come back and see their groves still standing. One Georgian discovered her "grand old trees" upright with hundreds of names carved on them, material evidence of the flourishing antebellum community.[18]

Yet the much of the South was devoid of trees, with many bare, lifeless landscapes. In May 1865, long stretches of land in North Carolina were stripped of pine forests, the fields empty, with not a fence in sight, which one Yankee journalist called "awful" to behold. Mary Jones of Georgia visited Nashville in 1866 and remarked that the city was full of trenches and fortifications left in position when the shooting stopped. Most of the trees had been cut down, leaving the capitol "hot and glaring," unprotected from the sun. The destruction of the region's forest meant that it took a long time to rebuild fences, of course. In 1866, a traveler did not see a single fence for miles in the area surrounding Gallatin, Tennessee.[19]

Reforestation began when hostilities ceased, initiated by nature itself as new trees sprang up in the wasteland, and by the region's farmers, who strove to replant the woods on their own. There was no organized effort at the state or federal level, although the US government reasserted ownership of public lands in the region and tried with the Southern

Homestead Act of 1866 to make it easier for working-class whites and blacks to buy small tracts of land. The reforestation process is always site-specific, involving such factors as the variety of trees (monoculture inhibits the process), the degree of soil erosion, and human traffic in the location. The South's reforestation was slow. The naturalist John Muir, traveling through the region in 1867, commented that the region's forests still looked as if they had been "slaughtered." But the woodlands did come back, taking about twenty years for most species to rejuvenate. By the 1890s, the region's forests had recovered sufficiently to attract the eager interest of the nation's lumber companies.[20]

HABITAT

In a few places, the South's built environment had survived more or less untouched by the fighting. In August 1865, Huntsville, Alabama, contained some fine homes and a handsome courthouse built in Greek Revival style, but in other parts of the Old Confederacy, entire towns had been wiped out. The infrastructure of Bolivar, Mississippi, consisted of a solitary chimney, standing alone in the summer of 1865, and in Selma, Alabama, the main buildings were in ruins, surrounded by fortifications built during the conflict. Absent any state or federal policy on taking down the various forts, in 1866 farmers outside of Richmond began leveling the works the armies left behind. Other forts were left to decay where they had been constructed, worn down by the elements.[21]

Much of the housing stock was gone in the countryside, as well. In May 1865, Confederate veteran John Porter did not see a single dwelling as he journeyed some 100 miles through northwest Georgia along the track of Sherman's army. A month later, an anonymous civilian recorded that there was scarcely a house visible for miles outside Jacksonville, Florida. The surviving buildings were still at risk, since Northern troops stationed in the region in the early months of peace scavenged them for timber. Homeless white people sometimes took up lodging in the empty houses until the owners reappeared.[22]

Civilians gradually restored the housing stock, of course, but that too was a slow process. A Yankee soldier noted in the fall of 1865 that less than half of the town of Jackson, Tennessee, which had burned during the war, had been rebuilt. The housing shortage meant that white people, such as former slaveholders in Bates family of Missouri, moved into buildings once occupied by slaves. Many whites, especially women, felt deep nostalgia for their old homes, with a sense of loss that lingered for years afterwards. Conversely, refugees who came back to find that their houses had survived felt overjoyed. In June 1865, Elvira Scott returned to Saline County, Missouri, and found her home, which had been used as a military hospital, whole and entire. She cleaned up the bloodstains, and after her husband's mercantile business recovered, they expanded and refurbished the building. She was very proud of their resurrected house.[23]

Many private homes stood next to cemeteries large and small, the dead literally surrounding the living. Row upon row of graves lined the roads near Nashville, observed Harvey Moorehead, a white Northerner who traveled through the area in 1866, and hundreds of other graves filled the landscape between Chattanooga and Atlanta. The effort to identify and rebury the bodies took several years, involving private societies for the Confederate dead and the US Quartermaster Department for the Union dead. Federal officials asked local whites for information about which regiments were buried in which cemeteries, and they sometimes obliged the officials. Civilians too had their confrontations with the human remnants of war, including the unforgettable image of the dead man's hand reaching back to the living. From her window in rural Virginia, Sara Agnes Pryor espied a single hand jutting up from a soldier's grave after a heavy rain in the spring of 1865. Her husband had served in the US Congress before 1861 and then joined the Confederate army; he had not yet returned home. She quickly covered up the hand, his identity and military allegiance unknown.[24]

MEMORY

The collective memory in the postwar South turned out to be as complicated as the war itself. The politically neutral blamed the destruction of the South's resources on that large impersonal entity known as "the war" – that is how John H. Bills of Tennessee chose to describe it. Former Confederates, when the jolt of defeat was fresh, could be more direct. Some of them verbalized the heretical idea that the grim struggle had not been worth it. Mrs. E. M. Izard, a South Carolinian from the old planter elite, cried that the tremendous human and material losses were for *"nothing, nothing, nothing."* Other individuals, some of them from the planter class, said what would soon become unsayable. Heartsick from all the deaths, ex-planter Dolly Burge excoriated the politicians "blinded" with hostility for Abraham Lincoln who insisted that no blood would be shed over secession; they left the South a wreck. Less affluent

Southerners did not conceal their views. In 1865 and 1866, journalist John Trowbridge encountered working-class whites who expressed the fiercest hatred for Jefferson Davis and other Confederate leaders.[25]

Regarding the conduct of the two armies, some white Southerners acknowledged just after the war that soldiers in gray had harmed civilians. Wilmer McLean was not the only one who accused the Confederate army of damaging private property – there were other fleeting moments of candor. The widow of a Virginia state senator, name unknown, told a reporter in 1865 that men from both armies took whatever they wanted from noncombatants. Other civilians, such as Anna Hasell Thomas of South Carolina, asserted that year that rebel forces had pillaged from civilians; the army scouts had been particularly demanding, she said. In the summer of 1865, an unknown person stenciled lines from Samuel Taylor Coleridge's poem, "France: An Ode," onto an oak tree near the James River. The poem, dated 1798, reveals the author's disillusionment with the French Revolution, specifically how the reckless pursuit of political conviction led to havoc and bloodshed. The journalist for the *New York Herald* who read it on the tree trunk could not tell if a rebel or a Unionist had written it.[26]

White Southern Unionists had their own memories, of course, which is common among dissenters who have lived through civil wars. They felt vindicated when the Confederacy was no more, and they wanted to record what they had been through. In 1866, John Minor Botts published a memoir, *The Great Rebellion*, which he dedicated to Ulysses S. Grant. The Virginian denounced secessionists and Confederate politicians for bringing the calamity of war upon white Southerners to benefit the slaveowning elite. When peace came, pro-Union Atlantans tried to build a public monument in the city to Abraham Lincoln, but they could not raise enough money to complete the project. Union supporter Eliza Cleveland was willing nonetheless to declare that the Yankee army, as well as the opposing army, seized goods from civilians without authority or sometimes did them harm.[27]

That was something that pro-Confederate whites soon became unwilling to admit. The moment of candor evaporated, the Southern military's wrongdoing forgotten. This mysterious alchemy, which created a wildly inaccurate narrative about the conflict, began soon after the first shock of defeat had passed. Even though these misrepresentations have happened after other American conflicts and wars in other countries, it is still hard to explain. Could it be that these civilians felt ashamed of their own army? Or did they feel unwilling to assail relatives, friends, and neighbors for their misdeeds? Or was it a massive displacement of anger at the rebel military onto the federal military? After all, abundant evidence of the Southern army's conduct remained in plain sight in the landscape, and some veterans admitted that they had harmed their own people. When William H. Tunnard published his memoir in 1866, one of the first by a Confederate officer, he wrote that his hungry troops improperly seized food from civilians, but he dismissed the subject, asking why anyone would "dwell on this gloomy picture." Other veterans, such as former General Richard Taylor, expressed sincere regret at how the rebel army hurt civilians. Not mincing any words, he stated that Confederate officials had seized food from them as if they were medieval peasants. Sam Watkins, promoted to corporal in the war's last year, recounted examples of rebel soldiers mistreating, exploiting, or tricking noncombatants. He felt some contrition, professing that civilians were at the mercy of soldiers in both armies.[28]

But many Confederate veterans sidestepped the issue of responsibility completely, preferring not to address such large themes, at least in writing. Yet others blamed one federal commander in particular. In 1865, veterans and pro-Confederate civilians already pilloried William T. Sherman as the chief villain, leaving desolation wherever he went. Still other whites went beyond Sherman-hating to demonize the entire Yankee army for the damage visited upon the region. Confederate soldiers they rendered as the gallant protectors of Southerners, whom they portrayed as united in their support for the effort. Veterans and civilians alike drew a veil over the damage the rebel army had inflicted on the white Southern population and the world they inhabited. The platitudes of Lost Cause culture quickly obliterated the history of the army's depredations.[29]

As for compensating civilians for the war's material losses, the authorities took the same decentralized, ad-hoc approach to reimbursement as they had during the conflict. In July 1865, a Yankee captain asked what he should do when civilians in Alabama presented him with wartime receipts from the Northern army. Indeed, what should be done? General John Pope's Orders of 1862, and Secretary Edwin Stanton's endorsement, had promised compensation at some point in time. Here and there a few white Southern civilians received cash payments from federal troops in 1865 for property taken that calendar year, but that seems to have been rare. The same decentralized approach applied to property once owned by the Confederate government. Rebel Quartermaster J. J. Busby purchased 640 acres of land in Texas and constructed a large residence, log cabins, frame houses, and mills on the property. The government never reimbursed him, however, and in June 1865, he still had the deeds. He contacted US Major General F. J. Herron nearby to ask what he should do with the property.[30]

Yet civilians all over the region still hoped that the promise implicit in their receipts, vouchers, certificates, indentures, protection papers, and other documents would be kept. Many presented their claims to the US Quartermaster's Department, while others wrote to the War Department in Washington, DC, enlisting legal help to get their money. In 1867, Attorney R. J. Atkinson tried to obtain payment for six clients who had what he called "regular certified vouchers" for housing rented by the US Army in Tennessee, writing directly to Secretary Stanton, but the outcome is unknown. In 1868, the Tennessee state legislature allowed civilians to apply for compensation for property taken by the two armies. For reasons unknown, the state never paid most of the claims, but a few Unionists obtained small payments at the county level for goods seized by the Confederate army.[31]

The creation of the Southern Claims Commission by the US government in 1871 represents the most thorough effort to reimburse Unionists who lost property to the federal army. The Commission focused on the states of the former Confederacy plus West Virginia; the other Border States were covered by a separate Congressional bill. Some 16,000 completed claims were investigated, and by the time the Commission staff finished its work almost ten years later, they had paid 4 million dollars to approximately 7,000 applicants, with an average payment of about 571 dollars. They considered claims for the entire war, before and after General John Pope's Orders of 1862. Pro-Confederate civilians were supposed to be eliminated, even if they received paperwork from the Northern army, as were the politically neutral. The burden of proof was on the applicants, who had to prove their material losses with documents and personal interviews in Washington, DC, or in their homes in the South. The Commission imposed new, tougher standards after the fact, continuing the bureaucratic confusion of the war itself: Unionists were redefined as those who had been loyal from the war's beginning – although Pope said recipients had to be loyal from the date of the voucher – and loyalty was redefined to mean those who had actively resisted the Confederate cause.[32]

Following these more exacting standards, the Commission gave out payments to ex-slaveowners and non-slaveowners alike, male and female, some European immigrants, and a few African Americans. But the process excluded many people: Unionists who had moved away from the old

Confederacy; those who were too intimidated in the postwar South to admit they were Unionists; those who could not afford the expense of the process; those who did not complete the paperwork; and those who did not vigorously resist the Confederacy from the war's inception. We must remember, too, that only a fraction of civilians who lost property to the federal army ever received any paperwork. Thus only a small percentage of Unionists received any payment from the national government.[33]

Long after the Commission finished its work, white Southerners who were loyal to the Union kept trying to obtain compensation. In 1883, the US Congress allowed individuals to pursue their claims through other means, and some civilians approached the Senate directly. In 1898, the estate of Anna Fitzhugh, mistress of Ravensworth plantation in Virginia, petitioned the US Senate for remuneration for 100,000 cords of wood lost to the army during the war. Even though Fitzhugh was a Unionist, and the Senate formally acknowledged that she was a Unionist, she had rented the land from Mrs. Robert E. Lee, whose heirs could eventually receive any compensation awarded to the estate. (George Washington Custis Lee, Robert E.'s son, retired there in the 1890s.) Therefore, the Senate concluded, the estate should receive nothing. As the decades passed, most Americans in all regions forgot the very existence of people like Fitzhugh, as well as the apolitical who just tried to endure the mayhem. Lost Cause culture, among its many mythologies, broadcast the notion that all white Southerners had advocated secession and supported the war.[34]

Individual Yankee veterans, grappling with the war's moral issues, tried to come to terms with their army's exploitation of the South's material base. Most of them accepted the view cohering after 1865 that all Northern men had served bravely and honorably, and most veterans wanted to remember things that way. A few of them tried to justify the army's behavior. Private John Billings pointed half-heartedly to some tangible benefits left behind in Dixie, such as bridges that had been strengthened by US Army engineers. Others consoled themselves with what they believed to be the toughness of the white male Southerner. General John Pope rationalized his army's onslaught on the built environment by saying that these men accepted the damage the war brought. They bore the loss of their "ancient homes" without complaint, and he admired their stoicism. It is impossible to know if Pope broached this topic with any Southern men, but he probably did not talk to many Southern women. Sixty-three years after the conflict ended, Eugenia Bitting orecalled vividly the "bareness of the place" when she returned

FIGURE 7.4 Ravensworth, home of Anna Fitzhugh.
Courtesy of the Library of Congress.

to see that her house and other buildings were gone. The wife of a prosperous yeoman farmer, she told a friend in 1928, "you can imagine our
feelings."[35]

White Southerners who supported the Confederacy tried, and failed,
to come to terms with larger issues about responsibility. John Muir
encountered people in postwar Georgia who were prematurely aged,
emotionally scarred, and consumed by what had happened to them. This
mild-mannered pacifist from Wisconsin felt no remorse for avoiding military service, and he had some sympathy for the region's whites, but their
bitterness made him uncomfortable. He hoped for better from the next
generation. Many ex-Confederates tried nonetheless to inculcate hatred
of the North in young white people. William D. Gale, a veteran living in
Tennessee, proclaimed in 1865 that he and his wife deliberately taught
their boy such hostility. Using a culinary metaphor, he explained that
their son's "bread is buttered" with the hatred of Northerners. The image
of the ravening Yankee soon consolidated in the regional memory. That
projection was easier than facing up to the destruction wreaked by an

army of white Southerners upon other white Southerners and on the physical environment in which they lived.³⁶

In fact, the war severely damaged the human resources of the white Southern people, especially such intangibles as the good judgment to set priorities and the creativity to solve political, economic, and social problems. After any kind of disaster, whether the cause is human behavior or nature itself, the survivors draw on robust communal relationships to rebuild, but the war had destroyed most of those social bonds. In some ways, this was just as catastrophic as the destruction of physical resources. Pro-Confederate Southerners lost the ability to tell the truth about what had happened to them, namely that the rebel army exploited the civilian population and its material resources to the full, just as the Yankee army did, and, equally important, that numerous white Southerners had opposed the Confederacy from the start and repeatedly helped the federal army. This inability to tell the truth afflicted veterans as well as noncombatants. Basic facts, fully documented and seemingly irrefutable, were virtually erased from the public memory. Over the long term, there was no reckoning on the ethical issues or policy violations on the part of the rebel military. Another century would pass before most whites in the region began to consider a more accurate narrative of what happened to the region's resources between 1861 and 1865. Historians, too, will continue to explore the complexity of the South's wartime experience.³⁷

Notes

INTRODUCTION

1 Federal Census of 1860, Free Schedule, Louisiana, Livingston Parish, p. 219; Diary of Sarah Lois Wadley, September 21, 1861, Collection Description, Sarah Lois Wadley Papers, University of North Carolina, Southern Historical Collection (UNC-SHC). After the war, the parish name was changed to Tangipahoa.

2 Federal Census of 1860, Free Schedule, Mississippi, Warren County, p. 15; Collection Description, Sarah Lois Wadley Papers, UNC-SHC; Diary of Sarah Lois Wadley, January 3, 1861, October 1, 1860, March 27, 1861, October 13, 1860, December 4, 1860, December 31, 1860, January 5, 1861, December 29, 1860, January 3, 1861, July 22, 1861, March 20, 1861, July 14, 1861, July 28, 1861, Sarah Lois Wadley Papers, UNC-SHC.

3 Diary of Sarah Lois Wadley, September 21, 1861, Sarah Lois Wadley Papers, UNC-SHC.

4 Edgar Ely to Mrs. Theodore Fowler, January 24, 1864, Ely Family Letters, New York Public Library (NYPL). On civilians in other wars, see Uglow, *In These Times*; Gibson, *Behind the Front*; Proctor, *Civilians in a World at War*; Tirman, *Deaths of Others*; Merridale, *Ivan's War*; Schrijvers, *Crash of Ruin*; Eby, *Hungary at War*.

5 Bledsoe, *Citizen-Officers*; Watson, *Peacekeepers and Conquerors*; Herrera, *For Liberty and the Republic*; Skelton, *An American Profession of Arms*; Chetail and Haggenmacher, eds., *Vattel's International Law*; Reardon, *With a Sword in One Hand*, pp. 10–11, 15, 19–21, 87, 137; Coffman, *The Old Army*, pp. 42–211; Carnahan, *Lincoln on Trial*, pp. 23, 43, 119; Escott, *Military Necessity*, pp. 17, 93–94; Davis, *Jefferson Davis*, pp. 440, 541, 581. Cf. Witt, *Lincoln's Code*, pp. 2–9, 237–238, who argues that Lincoln deserves credit for Lieber's Code.

6 Dyer, *War*, p. 4; Hickey, *War of 1812*, pp. 129–130; Schrijvers, *Crash of Ruin*, p. 105; Parker, *Global Crisis*, pp. 28–29, 671. On the scholarly debate on "total" war or "hard" war, Royster, *Destructive War*, and Fellman, *Inside*

War, argue that the war had a deeply destructive impact, while Dilbeck, *A More Civil War*; Grimsley, *Hard Hand of War*; and Neely, *Civil War and the Limits of Destruction*, believe that it did not.

7 Goff, *Confederate Supply*, pp. 129–130, 90–91, vii; Wilson, *Business of Civil War*, pp. 3, 191–192.

8 Shannon, *Organization and Administration of the Union Army*, vol. I, pp. 53–103; Hagerman, *American Civil War*, pp. xi–xviii, 58; Huston, *Sinews of War*, pp. 179–187; Wilson, *Business of Civil War*, pp. 191–192; Wiley, *Life of Johnny Reb*, pp. 90–107; Escott, *After Secession*, pp. 54–93.

9 Le Duc, *This Business of War*, pp. 68–69, 84–85; Diary of W. C. Brown, passim, Chattanooga Public Library (CPL); Adams, *Charles Frances Adams*, pp. 147, 135; United States War Department, *The War of the Rebellion: A Compilation of the Official Records of the Union and Confederate Armies (OR)*, Series 2, Vol. 4, p. 951; Eggleston, *Rebel's Recollections*, pp. 208–210.

10 Borch, "Lore of the Corps," p. 1; Witt, *Lincoln's Code*, pp. 269, 273–274; Alotta, *Civil War Justice*, pp. 202–209; Kastenberg, *Law in War*, pp. 193–228. Similar bureaucratic issues plagued the medical departments and Freedmen's Bureau; see Humphreys, *Marrow of Tragedy*, pp. 34–36, 38–39, 129–130, 208–242; Downs, *Sick from Freedom*, pp. 81–82. The Confederate Patent Office operated smoothly because it had a small, experienced staff; see Knight, *Confederate Invention*, pp. 4, 49–52, 204–205.

11 Mitchell, *Civil War Soldiers*, pp. 138, 140–146; Glatthaar, *General Lee's Army*, pp. 176–185; Hughes, ed., *Memoir of Stephenson*, pp. 26, 82; Wills, *Army Life of an Illinois Soldier*, pp. 360–361; Ramold, *Baring the Iron Hand*, pp. 273–276, 286–287; Wiley, *Life of Johnny Reb*, pp. 217–243; Wiley, *Life of Billy Yank*, pp. 193–223.

12 Perrow, *Complex Organizations*, p. 4; Grimsley, "Success and Failure in Civil War Armies," pp. 118, 135; Alvesson, *Understanding Organizational Culture*, pp. 1, 166–167, 172, 183; Hoffer, *To Enlarge the Machinery of Government*, pp. viii, 9–10, 13; Komer, *Bureacracy Does Its Thing*, pp. viii–ix; Schuck, *Why Government Fails*, pp. 4, 13.

13 Escott, *Military Necessity*, p. 72.

14 Wiley, *Life of Johnny Reb*; Wiley, *Life of Billy Yank*; Barton, *Goodmen*; Jimerson, *Private Civil War*; Manning, *What This Cruel War Was Over*; Sheehan-Dean, *Why Confederates Fought*; Noe, *Reluctant Rebels*.

15 Marshall, ed., *War of the People*, p. 83; Simon, *Bad Men Do What Good Men Dream*, p. 4; Lewis, *Impulse*, pp. 163, 166, 174–175; E. H. Hawks to My dear Mrs. Secretary and Ladies, November 26, 1862, Papers of Doctors J. M. and Esther H. Hawks, Library of Congress, Manuscript Division (LC).

16 Stout, *Upon the Altar of the Nation*, pp. 286–292, 321–328, 329–392, 393–394, 401; Dilbeck, *A More Civil War*, pp. 4–7, 128–129, 134–135, 144, 154–155; Livermore, *My Story of the War*, p. 659; Graham, ed., *Under Both Flags*, p. 191.

17 Foner, *Fiery Trial*, p. 143; Williams, Williams, and Carlson, *Plain Folk*, pp. 1–2. Historians differ on the existence and vitality of Confederate nationalism: Rubin, *Shattered Nation*; Wetherington, *Plain Folk's Fight*; Gallagher, *Confederate War*; Faust, *Creation of Confederate Nationalism*;

Thomas, *Confederate Nation*; and Massey, *Bonnet Brigades*, argue that it was strong, while Myers, *Rebels against the Confederacy*; Storey, *Loyalty and Loss*; Williams, Williams, and Carlson, *Plain Folk in a Rich Man's War*; Bynum, *Free State of Jones*; Fisher, *War at Every Door*; Dyer, *Secret Yankees*; Current, *Lincoln's Loyalists*; Durrill, *War of Another Kind*; Beringer, et al., *Why the South Lost*; Escott, *After Secession*; Degler, *Other South*; and Tatum, *Disloyalty in the Confederacy*, argue that it was weak or that Unionist support persisted during the war. Freehling, *South vs. The South*, points out the strength of Unionism in the Border States.

18 Glatthaar, *General Lee's Army*, pp. 176–185; Escott, *Military Necessity*, pp. 165–178; Sutherland, *Seasons of War*; Whites and Long, eds., *Occupied Women*; Ash, *When the Yankees Came*; Massey, *Refugee Life*, pp. 204–211.

19 Harrison, *Rhetoric of Rebel Women*; Jabour, *Scarlett's Sisters*; Gardner, *Blood and Irony*; Edwards, *Scarlett Doesn't Live Here Anymore*; Faust, *Mothers of Invention*; Whites, *Civil War as a Crisis in Gender*; Rable, *Civil Wars*; Elshtain, *Women and War*.

20 Reardon, *With a Sword in One Hand*; Ramold, *Baring the Iron Hand*; Escott, *Military Necessity*; Grimsley, *Hard Hand of War*; Mitchell, *Civil War Soldiers*. For different views on the strength and modernity of the Confederate state, see Bonner, *Confederate Political Economy*, pp. 17, 183–184, 202; Bensel, *Yankee Leviathan*, pp. 233–234. For the scholarship on state formation, see Brooke, Strauss, and Anderson, eds., *State Formations*.

21 Cashin, "Trophies of War"; DeGruccio, "Letting the War Slip through our Hands," pp. 15–35.

22 Brady, *War upon the Land*; Drake, ed., *The Blue, the Gray, and the Green*; Fiege, *Republic of Nature*; Meier, *Nature's Civil War*; Judd, *Second Nature*; Tucker and Russell, *Natural Enemy, Natural Ally*.

23 Hess, *Civil War in the West*, pp. 121, 126, 161–165, 174, 257; Ash, *When the Yankees Came*, pp. 55, 92; Escott, *After Secession*, pp. 109–110; Wiley, *Johnny Reb*, p. 102; Wiley, *Billy Yank*, pp. 233–236.

24 Nelson, *Ruin Nation*; Grimsley, *Hard Hand of War*.

25 Romero, *Gender and the Jubilee*; Cecelski, *Fire of Freedom*; Siddali, *From Property to Person*; Camp, *Closer to Freedom*; Hahn, *Nation under Our Feet*, pp. 13–115; Frankel, *Freedom's Women*; Syrett, *Civil War Confiscation Acts*; Thomas, *Confederate Nation*.

CHAPTER I: OLD SOUTH

1 Ash, *When the Yankees Came*, pp. 4–5; Crofts, *Old Southampton*, pp. 75–101; Burton, *In My Father's House*, p. 75.

2 Memoir of Letitia Dabney Miller, p. 18, Mrs. Cade Drew Gillespie Papers, University of Mississippi, Special Collections (UMIS).

3 Burton, *In My Father's House*, pp. 47, 57, 123; Wyatt-Brown *Southern Honor*, pp. 117–291; William H. Holcombe Diary and Autobiography, vol. I, pp. 1–10, UNC-SHC; Journal of Micajah Adolphus Clark, pp. 32–64, USC; Autobiography of Martha Louise P. Branch, p. 1, Munford Family Papers, Virginia Historical Society (VHS).

4 James M. Deaderick to Dear Cousin George, April 30, 1859, Murrell Family Papers, University of Virginia, Albert and Shirley Small Special Collections Library (UVA); Sarah S. Thompson to Virginia A. Shelby, July 15 [1832 or 1833] Grigsby Collection, Filson Historical Society (FHS); Ann M. Shank to Dear Mat, September 27, 1856, Joseph Belknap Smith Papers, Duke University, David M. Rubenstein Rare Book and Manuscript Library (DU); Cooper-Hopley, *Life in the South*, vol. I, p. 75; Ann Archer to Edward Archer, March 25, 1855, Richard T. Archer Family Papers, University of Texas at Austin, Dolph Briscoe Center for American History (UTA).

5 Kate McLeod to Albert Blue, March 25, 1856, Matthew P. Blue Family Papers, Alabama Department of Archives and History (ALA); Diary of Kate S. Carney, August 3, 1859, UNC-SHC; Livermore, *Story of My Life*, pp. 205–206; "Obituary," Thomas Hardin, *Augusta* [GA] *Chronicle*, October 14, 1853, p. 3.

6 Taylor, *Eating, Drinking and Visiting*, pp. 62–63; Mary R. Kirkwood to Emma Chesnut, July 20, 1841, Cox and Chesnut Families Papers, USC; Green, ed., *Memoirs of Mary A. Maverick*, p. 55; Murr, ed., *A Rebel Wife in Texas*, p. 64; Interview with John Franklin Smith, American Life Histories, LC, http://rs6.loc.gov.

7 Zimring, *To Live and Die in Dixie*, pp. 67–97; Finding Aid, Diary of Jason Niles, July 20, 1863, February 1, 1864, Jason Niles Papers, UNC-SHC; Diary of Joseph Waddell, February 26, 1856, September 24, 1857, Valley of the Shadow Project, University of Virginia (VSP); Stern, *Southern Crucifix*, pp. 2–17, 18–37; Weissbach, *Jewish Life in Small-Town America*, pp. 12–13.

8 Autobiography of Martha Louise P. Branch, p. 1, Munford Family Papers, VHS; Pringle, *Chronicles of Chicora Wood*, p. 18; Born in Slavery, South Carolina, Interview with Anne Broome, p. 105; www.loc.gov.

9 Wolfe, *Daughters of Canaan*, pp. 2–3, 58–64; Glover, *Southern Sons*, p. 25; Batchelor and Kaplan, "Introduction," in Batchelor and Kaplan, eds., *Women and Material Culture*, pp. 2–7; Cashin, "Introduction," in Cashin, ed., *Our Common Affairs*, p. 10; Burton, *In My Father's House*, p. 128; Lerner, *Grimké Sisters*, pp. 41, 54–60.

10 Diary of Hardy V. Wooten, 2: 47, July 9, 1840, Hardy Vickers Wooten Papers, ALA; Testimony of Elizabeth Ann Clary, Case of Doctor Wilson, October 17, 1850, Montgomery Circuit, Quarterly Conference, Records of the Methodist Episcopal Church, Texas State Library and Archives Commission; Ann M. Gale to My dear Son, March 28, 1852, Gale and Polk Family Papers, UNC-SHC.

11 Pringle, *Chronicles of Chicora Wood*, pp. 129–130; Hazen and Hazen, *Keepers of the Flame*, pp. 129–131, 66–78; Outland, *Tapping the Pines*, p. 63; "Local Items," *Alexandria* [VA] *Gazette*, June 16, 1854, p. 3; "State and City News," *Richmond Whig*, April 23, 1855, p. 2; Pyne, *America's Fires*, p. xvi.

12 Klein, *Days of Defiance*, p. 33; Anderson, *American Census*, p. 19; Edwards, *People and Their Peace*, pp. 7, 64–99.

13 Williams, Williams, and Carlson, *Plain Folk*, p. 9; Ingraham, *The South-west*, 2: 171; Perdue, Barden, and Phillips, eds., *Weevils in the Wheat*, pp. 323,

326; Avirett, *Old Plantation*, pp. 118–119; Lerner, *Grimké Sisters*, pp. 41, 53–56, 60; Baggett, *Scalawags*, pp. 21, 71–72; Fladeland, *Birney*, pp. 90–92, 113–123.

14 Recollections of Anna Clayton Logan, pp. 14, 19, VHS; Hilliard, *Hog Meat and Hoecake*, pp. 21, 67, 235, 40–52; Smedes, *Memorials of a Southern Planter*, p. 84; Willis Lea to William Lea, January 11, 1847, Lea Family Papers, UNC-SHC; Matilda Finley to Caroline Gordon, January 14, 1854, James Gordon Hackett Papers, DU. The South exceeded all other regions in the production of corn, a staple of the American diet; Kennedy, *Agriculture of the United States in 1860*, pp. l–li.

15 Counihan, "Introduction," in Counihan and Kaplan, eds., *Food and Gender*, pp. 4–7; Cecil-Fronsman, *Common Whites*, pp. 143–144; Diary of Eliza Robertson, November 30, 1854, December 2, 1854, March 20, 1855, Eliza Ann Marsh Robertson Papers, UNC-SHC; Sharpless, *Cooking in Other Women's Kitchens*, pp. 3–4; Recipe Book of Martha M. Dinsmore, 1829–1857, Dinsmore Homestead, Burlington, Kentucky, www.dinsmorefarm.org/biographies; Diary of Kate S. Carney, July 12, 1859, UNC-SHC.

16 Cecil-Fronsman, *Common Whites*, pp. 1, 103–109; H. H. Harris to his cousin, September 12, 1848, Person Family Papers, DU; Shields, *Southern Provisions*, pp. 8–9, 146; Marks, *Southern Hunting*, pp. 28, 46–48; Ingraham, *The South-west*, 2: 172; Maxcy Gregg Sporting Journal, vol. 2, 1839–1845, April 6, 1845, April 19, 1845, Maxcy Gregg Papers, USC; Rosengarten, ed., *Tombee*, pp. 130–131.

17 F. Devereux to Catherine Polk, December 25, 1844, Josiah Gale to Ann Gale, March 17, 1852, Gale and Polk Family Papers, UNC-SHC; S. R. Eggleston to R. T. Archer, January 25, 1858, Richard T. Archer Family Papers, UTA; Moore, ed., *Plantation Mistress on the Eve of the Civil War*, pp. 62, 77.

18 McDaniel, *Irresistible History of Southern Food*, pp. 57, 58, 171–172; Martha L. Maney to Martha Ann Maney, February 1, 1848, Douglass-Maney Family Papers, Tennessee State Library and Archives (TSLA); Schlesinger, ed., *Cotton Kingdom*, p. 312; Hess, *Carolina Rice Kitchen*, pp. 5–9, 95–96, 102.

19 Horowitz, *Putting Meat on the American Table*, pp. 1–2, 12, 17; Hilliard, *Hog Meat and Hoecake*, pp. 83–86, 125, 40, 95–98; Kemble, *Journal of a Residence*, p. 20; MacClancy, *Consuming Culture*, p. 151.

20 Memoir of Letitia Dabney Miller, p. 7, Mrs. Cade Drew Gillespie Papers, UMIS; Hickman, *Mississippi Harvest*, pp. 25, 38; "Saw and Grist-mill," [Little Rock] *Arkansas Weekly Gazette*, January 17, 1851, p. 4. In the 1850s, steam-powered mills appeared in some communities; Hickman, *Mississippi Harvest*, p. 26.

21 Toussaint-Samat, *History of Food*, pp. 145–146; Amelia Thomson Watts, A Summer on a Louisiana Cotton Plantation in 1832, p. 9, Somerville and Howorth Family Papers, Radcliffe College; Branch T. Archer to Richard T. Archer, October 21, 1853, Richard T. Archer Family Papers, UTA; Strother, "Rural Pictures," p. 170; Eppes, *Through Some Eventful Years*, p. 28.

22 Diary of Kate S. Carney, April 21, 1859, UNC-SHC; O. G. Murrell to John Murrell, April 25, 1843, Murrell Family Papers, UVA; Trefousse, *Andrew*

Johnson, p. 21; Edwards, *People and Their Peace*, pp. 100–101; Diary of Anita Dwyer Withers, August 13, 1860, UNC-SHC.

23 Silver, *New Face on the Countryside*, pp. 14–17, 25; Lillard, *Great Forest*, p. 153; Kemble, *Journal of a Residence*, pp. 181, 206; Green, *Wood*, p. 386; Avirett, *Old Plantation*, p. 25.

24 Livermore, *Story of My Life*, pp. 176–177, 154, 360; Venet, *Strong-Minded Woman*, pp. 27–31; L. C. Norwood to Julia P. Howe, March 12, 1839, Israel Pickens Family Papers, ALA; Robertson, *Red Hills and Cotton*, pp. 60–61; Stewart, "*What Nature Suffers to Groe*," pp. 180–181.

25 Williams, *Americans and Their Forests*, p. 7; Green, *Wood*, pp. xxii, xxv; John C. Cook to John T. Coit, February 2, 1858, John T. Coit Family Papers, Dallas Historical Society (DHS); List of Property at Walton's Bend, n.d. [1830s to 1850s] belonging to Richard Archer, Richard T. Archer Family Papers, UTA; Frobel, *Civil War Diary of Anne S. Frobel*, p. 53.

26 Williams, *Americans and Their Forests*, pp. 71–72; Lillard, *Great Forest*, pp. 77–79; Silver, *New Face on the Countryside*, p. 132; Rosengarten, ed., *Tombee*, pp. 126–127.

27 Hickman, *Mississippi Harvest*, p. 101; Williams, *Americans and Their Forests*, pp. 77, 355; Diary of Francis McFarland, April 13, 1859, McFarland Family Papers, VSP; Diary of Joseph Waddell, February 22, 1857, VSP; William Nugent to Eleanor Smith, July 2, 1860, Somerville and Howorth Family Papers, Radcliffe College; Durrill, *War of Another Kind*, p. 14.

28 Fett, *Working Cures*, p. 68; Mrs. John W. Wade, Recollections of an Octogenarian, p. 13, UTA; Simons, *Planter's Guide and Family Book of Medicine*, p. 91; Smedes, *Memorials of a Southern Planter*, p. 87; P. Barry to William Gaston, December 28, 1831, William Gaston Papers, UNC-SHC.

29 Durrill, *War of Another Kind*, p. 9; Outland, *Tapping the Pines*, pp. 35–61; "Valuable Land on York River," *Richmond Whig*, July 2, 1850, p. 4; Gudmestad, *Steamboats and the Rise of the Cotton Kingdom*, pp. 148–150; J. D. Imboden to John McCue, December 3, 1860, McCue Family Papers, VSP.

30 "Improvements at the South," *DeBow's Review*, November 1855, p. 724; Outland, *Tapping the Pines*, pp. 98–99; Stoll, *Larding the Lean Earth*, pp. 129, 8, 121–124; Duncan McKenzie to Duncan McLaurin, July 6 [1846], Duncan McLaurin Papers, DU.

31 Berry, *Unsettling of America*, p. 182; Diary of Samuel Wells Leland, February 16, 1856, Samuel Wells Leland Papers, USC; Sally Jane Hibberd to Jane H. Keefer, Jane Hibberd Keefer Papers, Ohio History Connection (OHC); Eugenia Bitting to Cade Gillespie, n.d. 1928, Mrs. Cade Drew Gillespie Papers, UMIS.

32 Plake, *Southern Husband Outwitted*, p. 11; Lizzie Jackson Mann, Recollections of the Civil War, 1861 to '65, p. 7, VHS; Hickman, *Mississippi Harvest*, p. 2; Green, *Wood*, p. 386; Williams, *Americans and Their Forests*, pp. 10, 14–15.

33 Rosengarten, ed., *Tombee*, p. 126; Green, ed., *Memoirs of Mary A. Maverick*, p. 18; Schlesinger, ed., *Cotton Kingdom*, pp. 150–151; Carter, Kellison, and Wallinger, *Forestry in the U.S. South*, p. 5; Lillard, *Great Forest*, pp. 157–159;

"Trespasses on Public Lands," [Little Rock] *Arkansas Weekly Gazette*, August 16, 1850, n.p.; "The District Court," *Dallas Herald*, October 20, 1858, p. 2.

34 Garrett, *At Home*, p. 15; Bollnow, *Human Space*, pp. 124–128; Felton, *Country Life in Georgia*, p. 40; Albert Blue to his sister, July 24, 1855, Matthew P. Blue Family Papers, ALA; Cecil-Fronsman, *Common Whites*, p. 152; Sarah H. Brown to Caroline Gordon, August 5, 1848, James Gordon Hackett Papers, DU.

35 Schlesinger, ed., *Cotton Kingdom*, pp. 382, 430, 60; D. G. Rencher to William Merritt, September 5, 1851, Abraham Rencher Papers, UNC-SHC; Martineau, *Retrospect of Western Travel*, 2: 51–52; Wade, *Recollections of an Octogenarian*, p. 8.

36 Walker and Detro, eds., *Cultural Diffusion and Landscapes*, pp. 53–54; Burke, *On Slavery's Border*, pp. 71–72; Bishir, *Southern Built*, pp. 1, 11–49, 20; Fry, *Memories of Old Cahaba*, p. 37; Mary E. Starnes to Sarah J. Thompson, September 20, 1860, William H. Kilpatrick Letters, DHS.

37 Mary E. Starnes to Sarah J. Thompson, September 20, 1860, William H. Kilpatrick Letters, DHS; Taulbert, *Once Upon a Time*, p. 20; Mead Carr to Bernard Carr, December 3, 1831, Carr Family Papers, UVA; Green, ed., *The Lides Go South*, p. 24; Civil War Tennessee Veterans Questionnaires, interview with Leander K. Baker, http://tn-roots.com/tncrockett/military/quest/quest-index.html; Williams, *Americans and Their Forests*, pp. 72–73; Crofts, *Old Southampton*, p. 57; Smedes, *Memorials of a Southern Planter*, p. 67.

38 National Historic Landmarks Program, National Park Service, Berkeley, tps. cr.nps.gov/nhl/detail.cfm; Burke, *Emily Donelson of Tennessee*, 1: 43; Ierley, *Open House*, p. 238; Wyeth, *With Sabre and Scalpel*, p. 8a; Duncan Blue to Dear Cousin, October 13, 1858, Matthew P. Blue Family Papers, ALA.

39 Vlach, *Back of the Big House*, pp. 6, 8; Fry, *Memories of Old Cahaba*, pp. 53–54; Civil War Tennessee Veterans Questionnaire, Interview with Lee T. Billingsley, www.tngenweb.org/bledsoe/bdocs/htm; Roth, *American Architecture*, pp. 162–163; "For Sale," *Mobile Register*, April 11, 1860, p. 2; Bishir, *Southern Built*, pp. 44–46.

40 Martineau, *Retrospect of Western Travel*, 2: 56; Harriet Vann, Case 17229, Summary Report, S. C., Box 239, Settled Case Files, Southern Claims Commission (SCC), RG 217, National Archives and Records Administration – II, College Park, Maryland (NARA-II); Mary Ann Cobb to Howell Cobb, January 8, 1850, Howell Cobb Family Papers, University of Georgia, Hargrett Rare Book and Manuscript Library (UGA); Auction of Israel Pickens's Property, October 1827, Israel Pickens Family Papers, ALA; Anderson, *Mahogany*, pp. 13–15; Martin, *Buying into the World of Goods*, pp. 43–44, 196–197.

41 Akhtar, *Objects of Our Desire*, pp. 17–21, 49–50, 67–68; Will of Jordan Flournoy, written June 21, 1833, Will Book 9, Powhatan County, Virginia, Virginia State Library; Will of Littlebury Clark, written January 6, 1840, Will Book 8, Prince Edward County, Virginia, Virginia State Library; Marianne Gaillard to John S. Palmer, May 29, 1846, Palmer Family

Papers, USC; Felton, *Country Life in Georgia*, p. 16; Pringle, *Chronicles of Chicora Wood*, pp. 44–45; Journal of Ellen K. M. Wallace, March 6, 1855, Wallace-Starling Family Diaries, Kentucky Historical Society, Frankfort (KHS).

42 Woodward, *Understanding Material Culture*, pp. 174–175; A. E. Harris to Sarah P. Hamilton, April 29, 1838, Benjamin C. Yancey Papers, UNC-SHC; Recollections of Letitia Dabney Miller, pp. 1–2, Mrs. Cade Drew Gillespie Papers, UMIS; Diary of Hardy V. Wooten, 2: 3, Hardy Vickers Wooten Papers, ALA.

43 John L. Graydon to Lou Madden, February 7, 1858, Mabra Madden Papers, USC; Will of Hugh McLaurin, January 1846 term of court, Richmond County, North Carolina, Wills and Estates Records, 1842–1848, vol. 3, pp. 32–34, North Carolina State Archives; Federal Census of 1860, Free Schedule, Tennessee, Hardeman County, pp. 27, 28, 33.

44 Harris, *Plain Folk and Gentry*, pp. 94–95, 108–111; Crofts, *Old Southampton*, pp. 50–51, 75, 101–102; Diary of Charles Henry Shriner, December 5, 1843, UTK; William Kinney to Alexander H. H. Stuart, October 24, 1857, Alexander H. H. Stuart Letters, VSP.

45 Harris, *Plain Folk and Gentry*, pp. 130–131; Private Journal of Robert Houston Armstrong, p. 3, n.d. December [1850s], UTK; Hansen, *A Very Social Time*, pp. 13–14, 52–136; Altschuler and Blumin, *Rude Republic*, pp. 9–10, 79; Williams, *Food in the United States*, pp. 105–107; Strasser, *Waste and Want*, p. 12; Stilgoe, *Landscape and Images*, pp. 91–92, 94; Stoll, *Larding the Lean Earth*, pp. 8, 19–20, 36; Glassie, *Vernacular Architecture*, pp. 138–146; Jaffee, *New Nation of Goods*, pp. 213, 270–271, 318–319.

46 Fuller, "Last True Whig," pp. 103, 131; Storey, *Loyalty and Loss*, p. 28; Foner, *Fiery Trial*, p. 143.

47 Aughey, *Tupelo*, pp. 46–47; Tatum, *Disloyalty in the Confederacy*, p. 4; Baggett, *Scalawags*, pp. 42–65; McCaslin, *Tainted Breeze*, p. 32; Williams, Williams, and Carlson, *Plain Folk*, pp. 13, 1, 194; Ash, *When the Yankees Came*, pp. 109–110; Degler, *Other South*, pp. 129, 132–133, 145–148, 154–155, 160–163; Andrews, *War-Time Journal*, p. 191; Civil War Diary of Dora Richards Miller, December 1, 1860, April 25, 1861, Old Courthouse Museum, Vicksburg (OCM); Storey, *Loyalty and Loss*, pp. 28–32. Modern societies debate secession with the same rigor; see Doyle, ed., *Secession as an International Phenomenon*.

48 Nash, *Unknown American Revolution*, pp. xiv, xxi; Chamberlaine, *Memoirs of the Civil War*, p. 92; Strother, "Personal Recollections," p. 409; Graham, ed., *Under Both Flags*, p. 299.

49 Diary of Jason Niles, January 2, 1862, Jason Niles Papers, UNC-SHC; Crofts, *Reluctant Confederates*, p. 345; Trowbridge, *The South*, p. 250; Murrell Taylor, *Divided Family*, pp. 13–17, 31, 39; Saxon, *A Southern Woman's War*, pp. 15–16.

50 "Later from the South," *Philadelphia Inquirer*, July 30, 1861, p. 4; "Late from Charleston, SC," *Philadelphia Inquirer*, October 1, 1861, p. 2; "Items from Rebeldom," *San Francisco Bulletin*, November 20, 1861, p. 1; Escott, *Military Necessity*, p. 87; OR, Ser. 1, Vol. 4, p. 393.

CHAPTER 2: PEOPLE

1 Graham, ed., *Under Both Flags*, p. 522; Proctor, *Civilians in a World at War*, pp. 5, 11; Schrijvers, *Crash of Ruin*, pp. 109, 124–126, 200–201.

2 This estimate is based on the fact that 40 percent of white men in the slave states, including the Border States and the future Confederacy, voted against immediate secession in 1860. An unknown number in the Confederacy acquiesced in secession in 1861 and remained at home, but not all; white women, who could not vote in 1860, could express their unionism after 1861, which probably made up for the loss of some white men to the rebel cause. Only a few scholars have hazarded a guess at the numbers, and they define Unionists more narrowly than I do: Myers, *Rebels against the Confederacy*, pp. 11–12, estimates 6 percent of white North Carolinian men were unconditional Unionists, and Storey, *Loyalty and Loss*, p. 16, estimates 10 to 15 percent of white men and women in Alabama were the same.

3 Bray, *Court-Martial*, pp. 121–124, 129, 131–142; *Revised United States Army Regulations of 1861, with an Appendix*, p. 494; *Army Regulations, Adopted for the Use of the Confederate States*, pp. 171–189; *Regulations for the Army of the Confederate States*, pp. 407–420.

4 Degler, *Other South*, pp. 147–148; "Late War News," [Keene] *New Hampshire Sentinel*, April 3, 1862, p. 2; Becker and Thomas, eds., *Hearth and Knapsack*, p. 7; Charles Denby to his wife, April 4, 1862, Denby Family Papers, LC.

5 Davis, ed., *Requiem for a Lost City*, pp. 42–45; Dayton, ed., *Diary of a Confederate Soldier, James E. Hall*, pp. 6, 11; "From Macon County," *Georgia Weekly Telegraph*, May 24, 1861, p. 8.

6 Kent, ed., *Three Years with Company K*, pp. 85–86; Charles Denby to his wife, June 24, 1862, Denby Family Papers, LC; "Interesting Letter from Col. Revere, of New Jersey," *Philadelphia Inquirer*, August 8, 1862, p. 3.

7 *OR*, Ser. 1, Vol. 4, pp. 545–548; Gordon, *Reminiscences*, p. 27; Moore, *Story of a Cannoneer*, p. 27.

8 Moore, *Story of a Cannoneer*, pp. 22, 42; Cox, *Military Reminiscences of the Civil War*, 1: 7–8, 85; J. M. Godown to Dear Fannie, March 3, 1862, Diaries of J. M. Godown, Vol. 2, Allen County-Fort Wayne Historical Society.

9 "A Female's Account of the Entrance into Charlestown of the Federal Troops," *Philadelphia Inquirer*, August 13, 1861, n.p.; Henry C. Marsh to his father, May 23, 1862, Henry C. Marsh Letters and Diaries, Indiana State Library (ISL); Milan W. Serl, Residence and Adventures in the South, 1860 to 1862, n.p., Arkansas Studies Institute, Center for Arkansas History and Culture (ASI); *OR*, Ser. 1, Vol. 7, pp. 719–720; McFadden, comp., *Aunt and Soldier Boys*, p. 26.

10 Clinton Hatcher to Mary Anna Sibert, May 18, 1861, Evans-Sibert Family Papers, VSP; [Joseph Ives] to his mother, October 17, 1862, Joseph Christmas Ives Papers, LC; "Smuggling," *Chicago Tribune*, August 21, 1861, p. 3.

11 Van Tuyll, *The Netherlands and World War I*, pp. 136–138; "The Week's Review of Trade," *Richmond Examiner*, December 21, 1861, p. 2; Dick to Ned, October 29, 1862, Joseph Christmas Ives Papers, LC; Lizzie Jackson Mann, Recollections of the Civil War, 1861 to '65, p. 12, VHS; *OR*, Ser. 1, Vol. 4, p. 51.

12 Hajdinjak, *Smuggling in Southeast Europe*, pp. 22–31; "Smuggling," *Chicago Tribune*, August 21, 1861, p. 3; *OR*, Ser. 2, Vol. 2, p. 1023; "From Cairo and Below," *Chicago Tribune*, July 18, 1862, p. 1; Barber, *Army Memoirs*, pp. 104–105; *OR*, Ser. 2, Vol. 2, pp. 183–184, 192.

13 Rable, *Civil Wars*, pp. 1–2, 15–17, 30; "Smuggling along the Lower Ohio," *Chicago Tribune*, February 8, 1862, p. 1; "A Heroine," *Macon* [GA] *Daily Telegraph*, January 7, 1862, p. 2; Moore, *Story of a Cannoneer*, p. 142.

14 *OR*, Ser. 1, Vol. 17, Part 2, pp. 15, 187; "Our Cairo Correspondence," *New York Times*, January 12, 1862, p. 1; "From Cairo and Below," *Chicago Tribune*, July 18, 1862, p. 1; "Local Matters," [Baltimore] *Sun*, September 9, 1861, p. 1; Sarna, *When General Grant Expelled the Jews*, pp. 5–7, 21–22, 29–30.

15 Fishel, *Secret War*, pp. 73–74; *OR*, Ser. 2, Vol. 2, p. 192; "Later from the South," *Philadelphia Inquirer*, July 30, 1861, p. 4; "Contraband Trade in the West," *Philadelphia Inquirer*, April 11, 1863, n.p.; Harrison and Klotter, *New History of Kentucky*, pp. 207–208.

16 *OR*, Ser. 2, Vol. 2, p. 192; Ash, *When the Yankees Came*, p. 87; Myer Lusky, Folder KK 195, Records of the Office of the Judge Advocate General, Court Martial Files, RG 153, National Archives and Records Administration (NARA); Federal Census of 1860, Free Schedule, Tennessee, Davidson County, pp. 71–72; *OR*, Ser. 2, Vol. 1, p. 662. At the National Archives, I read court-martial files for the surnames A through K, although the files were not in strict alphabetical order and sometimes included more than one case per file.

17 Hickey, *War of 1812*, pp. 170, 225–227, 252; Risch, *Quartermaster Support*, p. 345; "Affairs on the Tennessee and Mississippi Border" [San Francisco] *Daily Evening Bulletin*, October 17, 1862, p. 3; Towne, *Surveillance and Spies*, p. 66; *OR*, Ser. 1, Vol. 17, Part 2, p. 187.

18 Hassler, ed., *General to His Lady*, p. 51; *OR*, Ser. 1, Vol. 26, Part 2, pp. 153–154; Diaz, *Border Contraband*, pp. 32–33; French, *Two Wars*, p. 155.

19 "Running the Blockade," *Augusta* [GA] *Chronicle*, April 4, 1862, p. 2; "Miscellaneous Southern News," *New York Times*, July 11, 1862, n.p.; Pryor, *Clara Barton*, pp. 36–37, 65–67, 130–131.

20 Cashin, *First Lady of the Confederacy*, p. 114; Bevie Cain to James M. Davis, October 24, 1861, Bevie Cain Letters, Western Kentucky University; Murrell Taylor, *Divided Family*, p. 108.

21 Whites, "Corresponding with the Enemy," pp. 103–106; Fishel, *Secret War*, p. 56; Sallie McDowell to Tom Moffett, June 23, 1862, Sallie McDowell Moffett Papers, East Tennessee Historical Society (ETHS); Samuel T. Brekenbrige to My Dear Wife, postscript by S. C. Means, June 6, 1862, Miscellaneous Records, Intercepted Letters, 1861–1865, Entry 189, War Department Collection of Confederate Records, RG 109, NARA.

22 M. to My dearest Mother [Mrs. Pringle], August 13 [1861 or 1862], Miscellaneous Records, Intercepted Letters, 1861–1865, Entry 189, War Department Collection of Confederate Records, RG 109, NARA; Thomas Dibboe, Folder NN 195, Records of the Office of the Judge Advocate General, Court Martial Files, RG 153, NARA; *OR*, Ser. 2, Vol. 2, pp. 1361–1362; *OR*, Ser. 2, Vol. 2, p. 1431; Joseph Ives to his mother, October 6, 1862, Joseph Christmas Ives Papers, LC.

23 Matthews, *Statutes at Large, 1861–1862*, p. 284; *OR*, Ser. 2, Vol. 2, pp. 1361–1362; *OR*, Ser. 1, Vol. 13, pp. 524–525; Sheridan, *Personal Memoirs*, p. 93.

24 Fishel, *Secret War*, p. 2; Shackley with Finney, *Spymaster*, p. 1; *OR*, Ser. 1, Vol. 17, Part 2, pp. 14–15; Diary of Johanna L. Underwood Nazro, May 8, 1861, Western Kentucky University; Diary of Thirza Finch, April 27, 1862, Thirza Finch Diary and Letter Transcriptions, University of Michigan, William L. Clements Library (UM).

25 *OR*, Ser. 1, Vol. 2, p. 992; Storey, *Loyalty and Loss*, pp. 151–152; *OR*, Ser. 1, Vol. 10, Part 1, pp. 35–36.

26 Gallagher, ed., *Fighting for the Confederacy*, pp. 69–70; Gordon, *Reminiscences*, pp. 41–42; Wills, *Army Life of an Illinois Soldier*, pp. 90–91.

27 *OR*, Ser. 1, Vol. 17, Part 2, pp. 14–15; Feis, *Grant's Secret Service*, pp. 16, 31, 128; Blackford, *War Years with Jeb Stuart*, p. 18; *OR*, Ser. 1, Vol. 4, p. 320.

28 *OR*, Ser. 1, Vol. 8, pp. 47–48; *OR*, Ser. 1, Vol. 4, p. 242; Schrijvers, *Crash of Ruin*, pp. 192–193; Cox, *Military Reminiscences of the Civil War*, 1: 251.

29 Fishel, *Secret War*, pp. 8, 58–68, 175–177; *OR*, Ser. 1, Vol. 1, p. 433; Gallagher, ed., *Fighting for the Confederacy*, p. 140; Bonds, *Stealing the General*; Shackley with Finney, *Spymaster*, p. 12.

30 Joseph E. Johnston to Robert E. Lee, May 28, 1861, Miscellaneous Mss., LC; "Further Outrages at Hampton," *Macon [GA] Daily Telegraph*, June 8, 1861, p. 3; "Captures of Rebel Smugglers on the Upper Potomac," *New York Herald*, February 26, 1863, p. 1.

31 Memoirs of A. G. Brown, pp. 16–17, J. F. H. Claiborne Papers, UNC-SHC; "Home Department," *Daily [New Orleans] True Delta*, January 12, 1862, p. 3; Cox, *Military Reminiscences of the Civil War*, 1: 86–87.

32 Blanton and Cook, *They Fought Like Demons*, p. 58; *OR*, Ser. 2, Vol. 5, pp. 121–122.

33 P. M. Burkhardt, Folder NN 200, Records of the Office of the Judge Advocate General, Court Martial Files, RG 153, NARA; *OR*, Ser. 2, Vol. 2, p. 1363; Dyer, *Secret Yankees*, pp. 102–120; Fishel, *Secret War*, pp. 148–149.

34 Proctor, *Civilians in a World at War*, p. 6; McKenzie, *Lincolnites and Rebels*, pp. 137–138; Mohr, *On the Threshold of Freedom*, pp. 121–128; Escott, *Military Necessity*, p. 46; *OR*, Ser. 2, Vol. 2, pp. 1424–1425.

35 Ford and Ford, *Life in the Confederate Army*, p. 12; Eugenia Bitting to Cade Gillespie, n.d. 1928, Mrs. Cade Drew Gillespie Papers, UMIS; Rable, *Civil Wars*, pp. 121–128, 131–132; *OR*, Ser. 1, Vol. 7, p. 753.

36 Hickey, *War of 1812*, p. 228; Eugenia Bitting to Cade Gillespie, n.d. 1928, Mrs. Cade Drew Gillespie Papers, UMIS; *Regulations for the Army of the Confederate States*, p. 96; Quiroz, *Corrupt Circles*, pp. 426–427; Messrs. Dunlop, Moncure, & Co., to G. W. Randolph, November 7, 1862, Papers Relating to an Investigation of Fraud Committed by Flour Merchants, 1862–1863, Miscellaneous Confederate Records, Entry 190, RG 109, NARA.

37 Claim 961, James F. Brown, Chap. V, Vol. 43, Register of Claims, Office of the Quartermaster General, War Department Collection of Confederate Records, RG 109, NARA; Blackford, *War Years with Jeb Stuart*, pp. 64–68; *OR*, Ser. 1, Vol. 18, pp. 396–397.

38 O'Brien and Parsons, *Home-Front War;* Interview with Mr. Rosewater, 1898, p. 1, Ida Tarbell Papers, Allegheny College; *OR*, Ser. 1, Vol. 5, p. 621; *OR*, CS Navy, Ser. 2, Vol. 1, p. 756; *Regulations for the Army of the Confederate States*, pp. 12, 239.

39 Huston, *Sinews of War*, p. 170; Rusling, *Men and Things*, p. 189; Ash, *When the Yankees Came*, p. 79; Capers, *Occupied City*, pp. 81–82; "Affairs in New Orleans," *Harper's Weekly*, March 7, 1863, p. 157; Livermore, *My Story of the War*, p. 357; Sheridan, *Personal Memoirs*, pp. 137–138.

40 Federal Census of 1860, Free Schedule, Tennessee, Sullivan County, n.p.; Brief, Relative to Coal, Wood, Log and Lumber Contracts, Chattanooga and vicinity made in 1863–4, Box 301, Entry 225, Consolidated Correspondence File, 1794–1915, Records of the Office of the Quartermaster General, RG 92, NARA.

41 Merridale, *Ivan's War*, p. 237; Venet, ed., *Sam Richards's Civil War*, pp. 125–128; Civil War Stories, Interview with Reba Campbell, n.d. 1976, Maury County, Tennessee, Archives; Statement by Citizens of Mississippi County, Arkansas, September 27, 1862, ASI.

42 Murrell Taylor, *Divided Family*, p. 93; Sternhell, *Routes of War*, pp. 129–133; Neely, *Southern Rights*, pp. 2–6.

43 Pass for R. Kenner, Bethel, November 10, 1861, Samuel Downing Papers, Miscellaneous Mss., LC; Berlin, ed., *Confederate Nurse*, pp. 62–63; *OR*, Ser. 1, Vol. 11, Part 3, p. 659; *OR*, Ser. 1, Vol. 4, p. 397; "Local Intelligence," *Philadelphia Inquirer*, September 2, 1861, p. 8; Mitchel, *Reminiscences of the Civil War*, pp. 18–20; Neely, *Southern Rights*, pp. 2–4. On the ineffective passport systems in modern nation-states, see Torpey, *Invention of the Passport*, pp. 3, 22–52, 93–94.

44 Ash, *When the Yankees Came*, p. 84; Murrell Taylor, *Divided Family*, p. 93; Milan W. Serl, Residence and Adventures in the South, 1860 to 1862, n.p., ASI; *OR*, Ser. 1, Vol. 25, p. 1115; *OR*, Ser. 2, Vol. 2 pp. 1413–1414.

45 *OR*, Ser. 1, Vol. 17, Part 2, p. 158; *OR*, Ser. 1, Vol. 5, pp. 514–515; Frobel, *Civil War Diary of Anne S. Frobel*, pp. 34–36.

46 Murrell Taylor, *Divided Family*, pp. 93–98; Dick to Ned, October 29, 1862, Joseph Christmas Ives Papers, LC; "Miscellaneous Items," *Philadelphia Inquirer*, March 17, 1863, n.p.; *OR*, Ser. 2, Vol. 5, pp. 620–624; Lonn, *Foreigners in the Confederacy*, pp. 89, 178–180, 251.

47 Proctor, *Civilians in a World at War*, pp. 24, 127–128; Carnahan, *Lincoln on Trial*, pp. 140–141, n. 72; Small, "The Giving of Hostages," pp. 80–84. Fisher, *War at Every Door*, p. 149, calls hostage-taking immoral, but scholars most have neglected the ethics of the practice.

48 *OR*, Ser. 2, Vol. 1, pp. 866–867; "Dr. Smith's Death," Byron Family Papers, University of Maryland–College Park, Hornbake Library (UMCP); *OR*, Ser. 1, Vol. 19, Part 2, p. 55.

49 "Further Outrages at Hampton," *Macon* [GA] *Telegraph*, June 8, 1861, p. 3; "News From Nashville," *New York Times*, February 19, 1863, n.p.; *OR*, Ser. 1, Vol. 15, pp. 554–555.

50 "Further Outrages at Hampton," *Macon* [GA] *Telegraph*, June 8, 1861, p. 3; "Rebel Hostages and Deserters," *Chicago Tribune*, July 15, 1861, p. 1; *OR*, Ser. 2, Vol. 4, p. 855; *OR*, Ser. 2, Vol. 3, p. 156; "Dr. Smith's Death,"

Byron Family Papers, UMCP; *OR*, Ser. 1, Vol. 15, pp. 554–555; "News from Nashville," *New York Times*, February 19, 1863, n.p.

51 *OR*, Ser. 1, Vol. 21, p. 1079; *OR*, Ser. 2, Vol. 4, p. 855; *OR*, Ser. 2, Vol. 3 p. 808; *OR*, Ser. 1, Vol. 22, Part 1, p. 166.

52 *OR*, Ser. 1, Vol. 19, p. 55; "Preparations for the Murder of Southern Citizens," *Macon* [GA] *Daily Telegraph*, August 4, 1862, p. 4; *OR*, Ser. 2, Vol. 4, pp. 351, 869–870; "Dr. Smith's Death," Byron Family Papers, UMCP.

53 Griffith and Rowe, "Fredericksburg's Political Hostages," pp. 395–429.

54 Freidel, *Francis Lieber*, pp. 2–62, 115–170, 225, 235–242, 292–306, 317–320; Witt, *Lincoln's Code*, pp. 177–178.

55 Freidel, *Francis Lieber*, pp. 317–334; Witt, *Lincoln's Code*, pp. 233–234; Articles 23, 22, 24, 25, 21, 15, 16, in Witt, *Lincoln's Code*, pp. 377–378; Grimsley, *Hard Hand of War*, pp. 149–151.

56 Articles 54, 55, 56, 59, in Witt, *Lincoln's Code*, p. 383; Freidel, *Francis Lieber*, pp. 337–338; Witt, *Lincoln's Code*, pp. 283, 342–365, 245–246.

57 Neely, *Fate of Liberty*, p. 153; "The Yankee Prisoners," *Richmond Daily Dispatch*, May 5, 1863, p. 1; *OR*, Ser. 1, Vol. 31, Part 3, p. 366; *OR*, Ser. 2, Vol. 6, p. 777; *OR*, Ser. 1, Vol. 26, pp. 40–41.

58 *OR*, Ser. 1, Vol. 22, p. 267; *OR*, Ser. 1, Vol. 15, p. 312; *OR*, Ser. 1, Vol. 31, pp. 506–507; "To Be Held as Hostages," *Macon* [GA] *Weekly Telegraph*, June 5, 1863, n.p.

CHAPTER 3: SUSTENANCE

1 Bloodgood, *Personal Reminiscences*, pp. 76–77; Ritchie, *Food in Civilization*, p. 141; McNeill, *Pursuit of Power*, pp. 7, 2, 159, 183, 328, 354; Eby, *Hungary at War*, pp. 25, 39, 43, 62; Lair, *Armed with Abundance*, pp. 74–80.

2 Simpson and Weiner, eds., *Oxford English Dictionary*, 11:1104, 832; Articles of War, Chapter 20, Article 52, Article 54, www.freepages.military.rootsweb.com; *Regulations for the Army of the Confederate States*, pp. 413–414; *Revised United States Army Regulations of 1861, with an Appendix*, p. 73.

3 Johnson, *Winfield Scott*, pp. 175, 278, n. 14; *OR*, Ser. 1, Vol. 1, p. 236; *OR*, Ser. 2, Vol. 2, p. 48; Scott, *Military Dictionary*, pp. 21–22, 305–308, 478, 586–588; *OR*, Ser. 1, Vol. 2, p. 682; *OR*, Ser. 1, Vol. 7, pp. 785–786; Klingberg, *Southern Claims Commission*, pp. 21–22.

4 *Revised United States Army Regulations of 1861, with an Appendix*, p. 244; Fisher and Fisher, *Food in the American Military*, pp. 52–53, 73; Huston, *Sinews of War*, pp. 174, 239; Stillwell, *Story of a Common Soldier*, pp. 122–125; Meier, *Nature's Civil War*, p. 112; McKim, *Soldier's Recollections*, p. 63; Donald, ed., *Gone for a Soldier*, p. 120; Goodloe, *Confederate Echoes*, p. 207.

5 Weigley, *Quartermaster General*, pp. 162, 165, 219–222, 260; Wiley, *Johnny Reb*, pp. 96–97; Goff, *Confederate Supply*, pp. 53, 243–245; Hughes, ed., *Memoir of Stephenson*, pp. 23, 48; Robson, *How a One-Legged Rebel Lives*, p. 11; Michael G. Harman to H. R. Jackson, October 10, 1861, Michael

G. Harman Civil War Papers, Collection Description, Virginia Military Institute (VMI).

6 Billings, *Hardtack and Coffee*, pp. 110, 115; Wiley, *Billy Yank*, pp. 225–226; Towne, *Surveillance and Spies*, pp. 67–68; Taylor, *Supply for Tomorrow*, p. 17; Leib, *Nine Months in the Quartermaster's Department*, pp. 17–19, 28–29.

7 OR, Ser. 1, Vol. 11, Part 1, p. 1028; J. H. Hamilton to Mary Pearre, January 10, 1862, Diary of Mary L. Pearre, UTK; Diary of Correl Smith, February 18, 1862, Western Reserve Historical Society (WRHS); Taylor, *Supply for Tomorrow*, pp. 31, 111–112; Huston, *Sinews of War*, pp. 174, 230; Watkins, *Company Aytch*, p. 14; Bonner, *The Soldier's Pen*, p. 103; Herman Burhaus to Dear Sister, October 9, 1862, Burhaus Family Papers, UMCP.

8 Dayton, ed., *Diary of a Confederate Soldier, James E. Hall*, pp. 12–13; Gordon, *Reminiscences*, p. 110; Graham, ed., *Under Both Flags*, p. 467; Bloodgood, *Personal Reminiscences*, p. 26; Fisher and Fisher, *Food in the American Military*, pp. 60–61; Goodloe, *Confederate Echoes*, pp. 207–208; Kent, ed., *Three Years with Company K*, p. 141; Henry H. Aplin to Elvira Aplin, n.d. May 1862, Aplin Family Papers, UM.

9 Lizzie Jackson Mann, Recollections of the Civil War 1861 to '65, p. 5, VHS; OR, Ser. 1, Vol. 8, p. 473.

10 OR, Ser. 1, Vol. 3, p. 542; Klingberg, *Southern Claims Commission*, p. 20; Billings, *Hardtack and Coffee*, pp. 231–232; Goff, *Confederate Supply*, p. 246; OR, Ser. 1, Vol. 17, Part 2, pp. 53–54; Leib, *Nine Months in the Quartermaster's Department*, p. 20; *Revised United States Army Regulations of 1861, with an Appendix*, pp. 19, 30, 241, 254, 259, 273, 286.

11 Charles Denby to his wife, February 28, 1862, Denby Family Papers, LC; Ramold, *Baring the Iron Hand*, pp. 302–343, 344–384; Graham, ed., *Under Both Flags*, p. 384; Diary of Fannie Page Hume, July 17, 1862, LC; Cleveland Houser to Dear Sister, July 8, 1862, Houser Manuscripts, Lilly Library, Indiana University.

12 King, *From School to Battle-Field*, p. 191; Meier, *Nature's Civil War*, pp. 124–126; W. A. Pomeroy to Dear Sister, June 22, 1861, Willis A. Pomeroy Papers, UMCP; Marshall, ed., *War of the People*, p. 65; "Woes of the Border," *Macon [GA] Weekly Telegraph*, January 18, 1862, p. 2; Engs and Brooks, eds., *Patriotic Duty*, p. 50; Diary of James Pusard, August 4, 1862, FHS; Diary of Fannie Page Hume, July 17, 1862, LC; Born in Slavery, Oklahoma, Interview with Eliza Evans, p. 95, www.loc.gov.

13 "From the Connecticut Regiments," *Norwich [CT] Morning Bulletin*, June 24, 1861, p. 2; Huston, *Sinews of War*, p. 185; Diary of James Pusard, November 1, 1861, FHS; S. H. Eells to My dear Friends, July 11, 1862, Samuel Henry Eells Papers, LC; Foroughi, ed., *Go If You Think It Your Duty*, p. 106.

14 Lewis Oglevie to Dear Father and Mother, July 24, 1862, Oglevie Correspondence, OHC; OR, Ser. 1, Vol. 12, Part 3, p. 80; OR, Ser. 1, Vol. 8, p. 560.

15 Mitchell, *Civil War Soldiers*, p. 164; Civil War Diary and Memoir of Thomas Evans, May 31, 1862, June 4, 1862, Miscellaneous Mss., LC; Ansel Bement to Dear Father and Mother, September 24, 1861, Ansel Bement Letter, FHS; Marshall, ed., *War of the People*, p. 80.

16 Ansel Bement to Dear Father and Mother, September 24, 1861, Bement Letter, FHS; Charles Denby to his wife, April 13, 1862, Denby Family Papers, LC; Hassler, ed., *General to His Lady*, pp. 22, 27; Berlin, Favreau, and Miller, eds., *Remembering Slavery*, p. 251; Stillwell, *Story of a Common Soldier*, pp. 125–128.

17 *OR*, Ser. 4, Vol. 1, pp. 878–879; "Is This Starvation?" *Macon* [GA] *Daily Telegraph*, July 19, 1861, p. 4; Enoch Colby, Jr., to his father, n.d. February 1862, Reminiscences of Francelia Colby, Chicago History Museum Research Center (CHMRC); Hain, *Confederate Chronicle*, p. 29.

18 Goff, *Confederate Supply*, pp. 41–42; *OR*, Ser. 1, Vol. 4, p. 202; Form, Isabella Harrison, April 26, 1862, Abstracts and Vouchers (No. 12), 2nd Quarter 1862, Charles D. Hill Collection, Confederate Memorial Literary Society, under the management of the Virginia Historical Society (CMLS-VHS); Quitman Rifle Company, Receipts for Provisions, July 12, 1861, Heiskell Civil War Collection, ASI; "Miscellaneous," *Richmond Examiner*, September 26, 1861, p. 1; Claim 1203, A. M. Glassell, Chap. V, Vol. 43, Register of Claims, Office of the Quartermaster General, War Department Collection of Confederate Records, RG 109, NARA.

19 Becker and Thomas, eds., *Hearth and Knapsack*, p. 7; Geer, *Beyond the Lines*, pp. 22–23; M. A. McAdoo to Dear Son, December 15, 1861, William G. McAdoo to Dear Mother, December 18, 1861, William McAdoo Papers, LC; Born in Slavery, Oklahoma, Interview with Katie Rowe, p. 279, www.loc.gov.

20 Leon, *Diary of a Tar Heel*, p. 3; *OR*, Ser. 1, Vol. 4, p. 546; Worsham, *Jackson's Foot Cavalry*, pp. 72–73.

21 Storey, *Loyalty and Loss*, p. 90; *OR*, Ser. 1, Vol. 4, p. 546; *OR*, Ser. 1, Vol. 9, p. 402; Jane Pettitt, Case 20446, Tenn., Box 256, Settled Case Files, SCC, RG 217, NARA-II.

22 Smith, *Leaves from a Soldier's Diary*, pp. 10–11; Kent, ed., *Three Years with Company K*, pp. 159, 47; George Van Horn to his brother, November 13, 1863, Gray Family Papers, VHS; MacClancy, *Consuming Culture*, pp. 17–18; Moore, *Story of a Cannoneer*, p. 188; Stillwell, *Story of a Common Soldier*, p. 163.

23 Moore, *Story of a Cannoneer*, p. 110; Willett, *Union Soldier Returns South*, p. 26; Warwick, comp., *Williamson County*, p. 172; Diary of Silas S. Huntley, April 1, 1862, CHMRC; Mennell, *All Manners of Food*, pp. 62, 304; MacClancy, *Consuming Culture*, p. 146; Kent, ed., *Three Years with Company K*, pp. 61–62; Donald, ed., *Gone for a Soldier*, p. 122.

24 Sherman, *Memoirs*, p. 786; Stillwell, *Story of a Common Soldier*, pp. 267, 263; Goodloe, *Confederate Echoes*, p. 210; Fletcher, *Charlemagne's Tablecloth*, p. 64; USDA Blog, January 28, 2013, www.blogs.usda.gov/2013/01/28; *OR*, Ser. 1, Vol. 2, pp. 303–305; *OR*, Ser. 1, Vol. 10, Part 2, pp. 17–18; Taylor, *Destruction and Reconstruction*, p. 38.

25 *OR*, Ser. 1, Vol. 2, p. 107; *OR*, Ser. 1, Vol. 3, p. 614; Donald, ed., *Gone for a Soldier*, p. 131; McCarthy, *Detailed Minutiae*, pp. 63–64; Coffin, *Four Years of Fighting*, pp. 123, 126.

26 Donald, ed., *Gone for a Soldier*, pp. 97–98; Born in Slavery, North Carolina, Interview with Parker Pool, p. 190, www.loc.gov; Isaac Bevier to Dear

Parents, March 12, 1862, Correspondence of Isaac Bevier, Lincoln Museum Research Library, Fort Wayne, Indiana (LMRL).

27 *OR*, Ser. 1, Vol. 3, p. 738; Gordon, *Reminiscences*, pp. 48–49; Eckert, *John Brown Gordon*, pp. 17–21.

28 Lonn, *Desertion during the Civil War*, pp. 12–13; Gordon, *Reminiscences*, p. 48; Parrish, *Richard Taylor*, pp. 24–26, 33–39; Taylor, *Destruction and Reconstruction*, p. 60; McCarthy, *Detailed Minutiae*, pp. 61–62.

29 Gates, *Agriculture and the Civil War*, p. 15; Diary of Fannie Page Hume, July 18, 1862, LC; Elizabeth Parham, Case 8056, Tenn., Box 261, Settled Case Files, SCC, RG 217, NARA-II; Escott, *After Secession*, p. 112; McKim, *Soldier's Recollections*, pp. 28–29.

30 Leib, *Nine Months in the Quartermaster's Department*, pp. 38, 33–35, 50–51; O. H. Anderson to General Meigs, October 19, 1864, Box 33, Entry 225, Consolidated Correspondence File, Records of the Office of the Quartermaster General, RG 92, NARA; Diary of Kate S. Carney, June 18, 1862, UNC-SHC; "The Woes of the Border," *Macon* [GA] *Daily Telegraph*, January 18, 1862, p. 2; Armstrong, *Old Massa's People*, pp. 309–310.

31 Barber, *Army Memoirs*, p. 64; E.A.J. [*sic*] to no name, n.d. [1862], Miscellaneous Records, Intercepted Letters, 1861–1865, Entry 189, War Department Collection of Confederate Records, RG 109, NARA; Federal Census of 1860, Free Schedule, Virginia, Loudoun County, p. 56; Stillwell, *Story of a Common Soldier*, pp. 73–74.

32 Diary of Thomas D. Phillip, February 25, 1862, FHS; Loughborough, *My Cave Life*, pp. 155–157; United Confederate Veterans of Arkansas, *Confederate Women*, p. 56.

33 Goodloe, *Some Rebel Relics*, p. 40; William Craig to Levica Craig, March 13, 1862, Civil War Letters of William Samuel Craig, Ohio State University, Department of History, eHistory (OSU); McKim, *Soldier's Recollections*, p. 63; Moore, *Story of a Cannoneer*, p. 42; "The Woes of the Border," *Macon* [GA] *Daily Telegraph*, January 18, 1862, p. 2; Margaret Hildebrand, Case 8156, Missi., Box 196, Settled Case Files, SCC, RG 217, NARA-II.

34 Spence, *Diary of the Civil War*, p. 21; Memoir of Fanny W. Gaines Tinsley, p. 10, VHS; Davis, ed., *Diary of a Confederate Soldier*, p. 54; Margaret Hildebrand, Case 8156, Missi., Box 196, Settled Case Files, SCC, RG 217, NARA-II.

35 *OR*, Ser. 1, Vol. 8, pp. 68–69; Kent, ed., *Three Years with Company K*, pp. 35–36; Born in Slavery, South Carolina, Interview with Thomas Jefferson, p. 20, www.loc.gov; Civil War Diary of Franklin Eldredge, May 31, 1862, OSU; *OR*, Ser. 1, Vol. 13, p. 369; Winn, ed., *Civil War Diary of Mrs. Henrietta Fitzhugh Barr*, p. 8.

36 Enoch Colby, Jr., to his father, n.d. February 1862, Reminiscences of Francelia Colby, CHMRC; Born in Slavery, Texas, Interview with Ellen Betts, p. 82, www.loc.gov; McCarthy, *Detailed Minutiae*, p. 61.

37 Fletcher, *Charlemagne's Tablecloth*, p. 147; "Farmers Beware," *Richmond Whig*, November 8, 1861, p. 2; *OR*, Ser. 1, Vol. 52, Part 2, p. 283; Memoir of Roger Hannaford, Box 1, Folder 1, Section 1, n.p., Roger Hannaford Papers, Cincinnati Historical Society Library (CHSL).

38 Robertson, ed., *Lucy Breckinridge*, pp. 34, 38; Louise Clack, My Experience, p. 7, Robert Livingston Papers, LC; Diary of Ann Webster Christian, November 1, 1861, VHS; Civil War Diary of Dora Richards Miller, July 8, 1862, OCM; Charles Denby to his wife, June 21, 1862, Denby Family Papers, LC.

39 Davis, *Jefferson Davis*, p. 438; F. A. Polk to Leonidas Polk, December 17, 1861, Leonidas Polk Papers, University of the South-Sewanee; Mary A. Houston to her sister, January 5, n.d. [1866], Mary A. Houston Letter, Western Illinois University (WIU); Massey, *Ersatz in the Confederacy*, pp. 72–74; B.M.K. [*sic*]to My Dear Sis, June 8, 1862, John Kimberly Papers, UNC-SHC; Mary Boykin Williams Harrison Ames, Childhood Recollections, pp. 21–22, USC.

40 Cozzens, *General John Pope*, pp. 3–14, 21–28, 64, 88; Townsend, *Rustics in Rebellion*, pp. 191–192; Grimsley, *Hard Hand of War*, p. 87.

41 OR, Ser. 1, Vol. 12, Part 2, p. 50; Donald, *Lincoln*, p. 361; Grimsley, *Hard Hand of War*, pp. 86–87; Gienapp, ed., *Civil War and Reconstruction*, pp. 99–100.

42 Billings, *Hardtack and Coffee*, p. 37; OR, Ser. 1, Vol. 12, Part 3, p. 573; Cozzens, *General John Pope*, pp. 198–201; McClellan, *McClellan's Own Story*, pp. 463–464; Linderman, *Embattled Courage*, p. 205; Grant, *Memoirs*; Sherman, *Memoirs*; Nelson, *Ruin Nation*, p. 74.

43 Cyrus H. Stockwell to his parents, November 3, 1862, Cyrus H. Stockwell Papers, WRHS; Small, *Road to Richmond*, pp. 51, 53; Diary of Melville Cox Follett, February 8, 1863, OSU.

44 Billings, *Hardtack and Coffee*, p. 234; Henry Haviland to My Dear Sue, November 3, 1862, Scrogin and Haviland Letters, KHS; Daniel B. Allen to his wife, November 4, 1862, Civil War Letters of Daniel Burchard Allen, Bradley University, Peoria, Illinois (BU).

45 OR, Ser. 1, Vol. 30, Part 4, pp. 366–368; Taylor, *Supply for Tomorrow*, p. 83; OR, Ser. 1, Vol. 30, Part 4, pp. 366–368; S. H. Eells to Dear Friends, September 3, 1863, Samuel Henry Eells Papers, LC.

46 S. H. Eells to Dear Friends, September 3, 1863, Samuel Henry Eells Papers, LC; Looby, ed., *Journal and Letters of Higginson*, p. 112; Lizzie Jackson Mann, Recollections of the Civil War, 1861 to '65, p. 5, VHS.

47 Willett, *Union Soldier Returns South*, p. 22; Oliver Oglevie to Dear Brother and Sister, February 12, 1863, Oglevie Correspondence, OHC; Barber, *Army Memoirs*, p. 91. Oliver Oglevie was Lewis Oglevie's brother.

48 OR, Ser. 1, Vol. 16, Part 1, pp. 870–871; Hiram Strong to his wife, December 4–6, 1862, Colonel Hiram Strong Papers, Dayton, Ohio, Metro Library (DML); Diary of James Pusard, September 22, 1862, FHS; "From Gen. Burnside's Army," *Brooklyn Eagle*, November 26, 1862, p. 3.

49 Diary of Mary L. Pearre, February 9, 1863, February 13, 1863, UTK; Kent, ed., *Three Years with Company K*, pp. 141–142; Gwin, ed., *Cornelia Peake McDonald*, p. 104.

50 Barber, *Army Memoirs*, pp. 10–11, 48–57, 81–85, 91–92, 218–219, 221.

51 Pryor, *Reading the Man*, pp. 325–326; Longstreet, *From Manassas to Appomattox*, pp. 154–155; James L. Clements to his wife, August 13, 1862, James L. Clements Papers, Arkansas History Commission; Taylor, *Destruction and Reconstruction*, pp. 95, 111–112, 149; Gordon, *Reminiscences*, p. 123.

52 J. W. McLure to Kate McLure, October 8, 1862, McLure Family Papers, USC; Worsham, *Jackson's Foot Cavalry*, p. 138; Neese, *Three Years in the Confederate Horse Artillery*, pp. 92, 54; Henry Haviland to My Dear Sue, November 3, 1862, Scrogin and Haviland Letters, KHS; Hassler, ed., *General to His Lady*, p. 175.

53 Watkins, *Company Aytch*, p. 41; "Curious Incident in the War," *Daily* [New Orleans] *Delta*, December 20, 1862, p. 1; *OR*, Ser. 1, Vol. 22, Part 2, p. 825.

54 Mary Houston to her sister, January 5, n.d. [1866], Mary A. Houston Letter, WIU; Goff, *Confederate Supply*, p. 54; Loughborough, *My Cave Life*, pp. 76–77; Russell, *Hunger*, pp. 137–138; Civil War Diary of Dora Richards Miller, November 20, 1862, OCM; Warwick, comp., *Williamson County*, p. 169; *OR*, Ser. 1, Vol. 8, p. 25; S. H. Eells to Dear Uncle, October 12, 1862, Samuel Henry Eells Papers, LC.

55 *Regulations for the Army of the Confederate States*, pp. 407–420.

56 To Jesse Payne, July 18, 1863, Charles D. Hill, Charles D. Hill Collection, CMLS-VHS; Diary of Joseph Waddell, March 15, 1863, VSP; Goff, *Confederate Supply*, pp. 75–89; Diary of W. C. Brown, October 19, 1863, CPL; Driskell, ed., History of the 25th Alabama Infantry Regiment 1861–1865, n.p. [June–July] 1863, https://sites.google.com/site/25thalabama/ Home.

57 Recollections of Maria Southgate Hawes, p. 26, OCM; Reyburn and Wilson, eds., *"Jottings from Dixie,"* pp. 72–73; Diary of Mary L. Pearre, February 18, 1863, UTK; *Confederate Receipt Book*, pp. 3, 7, 17.

58 Excerpts of Diary and Letter by Franklin P. Waggoner, July 25, 1863, ISL; Botkin, ed., *Lay My Burden Down*, p. 253; Percival, *Great Famine*, pp. 71–72; "News from Washington," *New York Herald*, March 22, 1863, p. 4; Schrijvers, *Crash of Ruin*, pp. 174–176, 188; Asa W. Marine to Ann Marine, July 13, 1863, Asa W. Marine Letters, Indiana State University at Terre Haute.

59 "The Poor and Their Necessities," *Macon* [GA] *Daily Telegraph*, November 6, 1861, p. 1; Rable, *Civil Wars*, pp. 104–105; Henry C. Lay to his wife, January 28–February 15, 1863, Henry C. Lay Collection, ASI; Davis, ed., *Diary of a Confederate Soldier*, p. 24; *OR*, Ser. 1, Vol. 15, pp. 204–205; *OR*, Ser. 1, Vol. 7, pp. 663–664.

60 Thomas, *Confederate Nation*, p. 196; An Act to Regulation Impressments, March 25, 1863, Matthews, *Public Laws of the Confederate States, 1862–1864*, pp. 102–104; *OR*, Ser. 1, Vol. 1, p. 353; *OR*, Ser. 1, Vol. 9, p. 144.

61 Rable, *Confederate Republic*, p. 193; "Congress," *Chattanooga Daily Rebel*, March 31, 1863, p. 2; "The Courts," *Richmond Examiner*, November 13, 1863, p. 1; "Impressment – the Right Way – the Wrong Way," *Macon* [GA] *Daily Telegraph*, December 18, 1863, p. 2. Cf. Thomas, *Confederate Nation*, p. 196, who argues that most civilians submitted to the measure.

62 McWilliams, *Revolution in Eating*, pp. 291–293; Your Mother to My Dear Child, April 3, 1863, Bread Riot Letter, National Civil War Museum, Harrisburg, PA; Escott, *After Secession*, p. 128; "A Bold Experiment," *Macon* [GA] *Weekly Telegraph*, April 10, 1863, p. 1; *OR*, Ser. 1, Vol. 25, Part 2, pp. 196–197; Rable, *Civil Wars*, p. 110. When Alexander Lawton replaced Abraham Myers as quartermaster general in August 1863, he too failed

to provide adequate supplies for the military; Goff, *Confederate Supply*, pp. 142–144, 158.

63 Articles 17, 15, 38, 22, 156, in Witt, *Lincoln's Code*, pp. 377–378, 380, 393–394.

64 *OR*, Ser. 1, Vol. 24, Part 3, pp. 524–525; Civil War Diary of Robert Sample Dilworth, June 24, 1863, Allen County, Ohio, Historical Society; Charles E. Bates to Dear Parents, April 16, 1863, Charles Bates Papers, VHS; John Nevin Sketchbook, pp. 16–18, Lieutenant Colonel John I. Nevin Papers, Historical Society of Western Pennsylvania (HSWP); Margaret Hildebrand, Case 8156, Missi., Box 196, Settled Case Files, SCC, RG 217, NARA-II. The *Revised United States Army Regulations, with an Appendix*, p. 512, emphasized anew in June 1863 the importance of issuing paperwork to civilians and the officer's responsibility to manage foraging parties properly.

65 John K. Clark, Folder NN1795, Records of the Office of the Judge Advocate General, Court Martial Files, RG 153, NARA.

66 *OR*, Ser. 1, Vol. 31, Part 3, p. 446; Recollections of Anna Clayton Logan, p. 43, VHS; Henry C. Lay to his wife, January 28–February 15, 1863, Henry C. Lay Collection, ASI; "The South Neither," *New York Herald*, May 31, 1863, p. 8; Russell, *Hunger*, pp. 3, 120, 126, 154–155; Becker, *Hungry Ghosts*, pp. 198–199.

67 Diary of Thomas D. Phillip, February 25, 1862, FHS; Warwick, comp., *Williamson County*, p. 171; Mohr and Winslow, eds., *Cormany Diaries*, pp. 333–334, 337; Doubleday, *Campaigns of the Civil War*, p. 96; Graham, ed., *Under Both Flags*, p. 374.

68 Gordon, *Reminiscences*, p. 188; Watkins, *Company Aytch*, pp. 75–76; *OR*, Ser. 1, Vol. 22, Part 2, pp. 1032–1033.

CHAPTER 4: TIMBER

1 Fickle, *Green Gold*, p. 39; Matthews, *Statutes at Large, 1861–1862*, pp. 94–95; Hickman, *Mississippi Harvest*, pp. 72–73, 89, 93, 99–100; Doubleday, *Campaigns of the Civil War*, p. 15; Latimer, *1812: War with America*, pp. 259–260; Tucker, "World Wars and the Globalization of Timber Cutting," in Tucker and Russell, eds., *Natural Enemy, Natural Ally*, pp. 110–114.

2 Articles of War, Chapter 20, Article 52, Article 54, www.freepages.military.rootsweb.com; *Regulations for the Army of the Confederate States*, pp. 413–414.

3 Scott, *Military Dictionary*, pp. 534, 147–150, 504, 451, 606, 9–10, 160, 673, 283.

4 Stoll, *Larding the Lean Earth*, pp. 37–40, 150–160; Scott, *Military Dictionary*, pp. 132, 534, 477, 147–150, 139, 545–546, 118, 148.

5 Scott, *Military Dictionary*, p. 463; *Regulations for the Army of the Confederate States*, p. 74.

6 Rusling, *Men and Things*, pp. 161–162; Edgar Ely to Mrs. Theodore Fowler, September 3, 1862, Ely Family Letters, NYPL; James Doak to Dear Sister, April 30, 1862, July 12, 1862, Doak Family Correspondence, gift from

Dominica Leeds to the author; *OR*, Ser. 1, Vol. 24, p. 494; McCarthy, *Detailed Minutiae*, p. 57; *OR*, Ser. 1, Vol. 11, Part 2, pp. 158–159.

7   Sherman, *Memoirs*, p. 448; *OR*, Ser. 1, Vol. 24, p. 177; *OR*, Ser. 3, Vol. 5, p. 121; Storey, *Loyalty and Loss*, p. 117; *OR*, Ser. 1, Vol. 24, Part 2, p. 580; *OR*, Ser. 1, Vol. 7, pp. 736–737.

8   Edgar Ely to Mrs. Theodore Fowler, September 3, 1862, Ely Family Papers, NYPL; *OR*, Ser. 1, Vol. 29, p. 248; Diary of Thomas D. Phillip, January 4, 1862, FHS; Billings, *Hardtack and Coffee*, pp. 378, 100–101; McDonald, ed., *Make Me a Map*, p. 35; McKim, *Soldier's Recollections*, p. 43; Diary of John C. Tidball, April 24, 1861, John C. Tidball Papers, Gettysburg College, Special Collections and College Archives (GC); Sherman, *Memoirs*, pp. 292–293; McCarthy, *Detailed Minutiae*, p. 82. Soldiers also worked for the construction corps building railroads; Huston, *Sinews of War*, p. 170.

9   McGuire, *Southern Refugee*, pp. 35, 51, 66; Livermore, *My Story of the War*, p. 637; Hess, *Field Armies and Fortifications*, p. 24; *OR*, Ser. 1, Vol. 3, p. 626.

10 Petition by Ellen Tompkins, November 26, 1869, to the Secretary of War, Tompkins Family Papers, VHS; Billings, *Hardtack and Coffee*, pp. 154–155; Kent, ed., *Three Years with Company K*, p. 60.

11 *OR*, Ser. 1, Vol. 2, pp. 103–104; Adam W. Kersh to George P. Kersh, October 20, 1861, Kersh Family Papers, VSP; Cash and Howorth, eds., *My Dear Nellie*, p. 49.

12 Worsham, *Jackson's Foot Cavalry*, p. 51; Blackford, *War Years with Jeb Stuart*, pp. 60–61; Leon, *Diary of a Tar Heel*, p. 5.

13 "New Orleans," [NY] *Evening Post*, June 26, 1862, p. 3; Andrew J. Richardson to Martha Richardson, October 27, 1861, Civil War Collection, Lawrence County, Tennessee, Archives (LCTA); Worsham, *Jackson's Foot Cavalry*, p. 52; Edward Bagby to Virginia B. Pollard, June 30, 1862, Clarke Family Papers, VHS.

14 Claim 2909, Willis J. Bunkley, Chap. V, Vol. 44, Register of Claims, Office of the Quartermaster General, War Department Collection of Confederate Records, RG 109, NARA; *OR*, Ser. 1, Vol. 16, Part 2, pp. 155–156; Frobel, *Civil War Diary of Anne S. Frobel*, pp. 53, 77.

15 Wills, *Army Life of an Illinois Soldier*, pp. 48–49; Granville W. Belcher to Mary Caroline Belcher, May 4, 1862, Belcher Letters, University of Southern Miss.; Scott, *Military Dictionary*, p. 139; Billings, *Hardtack and Coffee*, pp. 73–75; Radigan, ed., *Desolating This Fair Country*, pp. 68, 59.

16 Williams, *Americans and Their Forests*, p. 193; Davis, ed., *Diary of a Confederate Soldier*, p. 4; Winther, ed., *With Sherman to the Sea*, p. 44; Simpson and Weiner, eds., *Oxford English Dictionary*, 15:142; Kent, ed., *Three Years with Company K*, pp. 65–67; Leon, *Diary of a Tar Heel*, pp. 1–2; McKim, *Soldier's Recollections*, pp. 50–51; Memoir of Archibald Atkinson, Jr., p. 33, Virginia Polytechnic Institute and State University; Rusling, *Men and Things*, p. 160.

17 Longstreet, *From Manassas to Appomattox*, p. 235; Diary of Correl Smith, February 18, 1862, WRHS; McDonald, ed., *Make Me a Map*, p. 102; Hiram Strong to Dear Wife, November 10, 1862, Colonel Hiram Strong Papers, DML; Anderson, ed., *When War Becomes Personal*, p. 44; A. J. Richardson

to his wife, June 18, 1862, Civil War Collection, LCTA; Diary of John Newton Ferguson, August 15, 1862, LC.

18 H. Harper Bill to his father, March 15, 1862, Horace Harper Bill Letters, Sandusky, Ohio, Library, Archives Research Center; Hughes, ed., *Memoir of Stephenson*, p. 93; Graham, ed., *Under Both Flags*, p. 198; Baumgartner, ed., *Blood and Sacrifice*, p. 12; Memoir of Roger Hannaford, section 59, n.p., Roger Hannaford Papers, CHSL.

19 Kricher, *Field Guide to Eastern Forests*, pp. 13, 94; Rutkow, *American Canopy*, pp. 1–4; Silver, *New Face on the Countryside*, pp. 17, 21; Hickman, *Mississippi Harvest*, pp. 2–3; "Live Oak," *Brooklyn Eagle*, May 17, 1861, p. 2.

20 McCarthy, *Detailed Minutiae*, pp. 83–84; Billings, *Hardtack and Coffee*, p. 87; *OR*, Ser. 1, Vol. 2, p. 641; *OR*, Ser. 1, Vol. 11, Part 3, p. 235; *OR*, Ser. 1, Vol. 2, p. 641; *OR*, Ser. 1, Vol. 11, Part 1, p. 590; *OR*, Ser. 1, Vol. 51, Part 1, p. 6.

21 Davis, ed., *Diary of a Confederate Soldier*, p. 102; Sherman, *Memoirs*, p. 787; United States Department of Agriculture, Natural Resources Conservation Service, Plant Guide, http://usdasearch.usda.gov/search; McCarthy, *Detailed Minutiae*, p. 81; Craigie and Halbert, *Dictionary of American English*, 3: 1745; Moore, *Story of a Cannoneer*, p. 169; Porcher, *Resources of the Southern Fields and Forests*, p. 495.

22 Berger, *Forests Forever*, p. 119; *Merriam-Webster's Collegiate Dictionary*, 11th edn, p. 230; *OR*, Ser. 1, Vol. 5, p. 136; Donald, ed., *Gone for a Soldier*, pp. 52–53, 45.

23 Diary of Samuel A. Murray, March 8, 1862, Pennsylvania State Archives; Donald, ed., *Gone for a Soldier*, p. 66; McKim, *Soldier's Recollections*, p. 54.

24 John Wesley Stipe, Reluctant Rebel, p. 2, Reverend John Wesley Stipe Papers, Atlanta History Center; Goodloe, *Confederate Echoes*, pp. 183–184; McCarthy, *Detailed Minutiae*, p. 80.

25 Ford and Ford, *Life in the Confederate Army*, p. 42; *OR*, Ser. 1, Vol. 9, pp. 327–330; Worsham, *Jackson's Foot Cavalry*, p. 74.

26 Billings, *Hardtack and Coffee*, pp. 178–180; Kent, ed., *Three Years with Company K*, pp. 54–55; Worsham, *Jackson's Foot Cavalry*, p. 73; Frobel, *Civil War Diary of Anne S. Frobel*, p. 82.

27 Davis, ed., *Diary of Confederate Soldier*, p. 33; G. W. Davison to Dear Uncle, May 2, 1862, G. W. Davison Letters, GC; Donald, ed., *Gone for a Soldier*, pp. 66, 55; Radigan, ed., *Desolating This Fair Country*, p. 88; James Whiting, Plantation and Farm Instruction, Regulation, Record, February 20, 1862, March 24, 1862, F. Brooke Whiting House, Cumberland, MD.

28 *OR*, Ser. 1, Vol. 12, Part 1, pp. 76–79; Journal of George L. Wood, April 22, 1862, OHC; Soldier's Life of Philo Pearce, p. 6, Ottawa County, Ohio, History Museum.

29 Chapman, *Georgia Soldier in the Civil War*, p. 7; Radigan, ed., *Desolating This Fair Country*, pp. 87, 94; Samuel T. Wells to My Dear Lizzie, April 21, 1862, Samuel T. Wells Papers, FHS; Moore, *Story of a Cannoneer*, p. 52; Looby, ed., *Journal and Letters of Higginson*, p. 127; Seneca Thrall to his

wife, February 14, 1863, Letters of Seneca Thrall, Civil War Archive, www.civilwararchive.com/LETTERS/thrall1.htm.

30 Memoir of Roger Hannaford, section 61, n.p., Roger Hannaford Papers, CHSL; *OR*, Ser. 1, Vol. 15, pp. 19–20; W.H.A. [*sic*] to Josie Cooper, January 14, 1863, Confederate Correspondence, GC.

31 Le Duc, *This Business of War*, pp. 6, 20, 13–15, 31, 65–67, 72–74.

32 Diary of Thomas D. Phillip, January 18, 1862, FHS; S. H. Eells to Dear Uncle and Aunt, April 28, 1862, Samuel Henry Eells Papers, LC; William Parkinson to his brother, June 13, 1862, William M. Parkinson Papers, OHC; Diary of Samuel A. Murray, March 8, 1862, Pennsylvania State Archives; Moore, *Story of a Cannoneer*, pp. 128–129.

33 Loyd, *My War Gone By*, pp. 244–245; Nelson, *Ruin Nation*, p. 147; Graham, ed., *Under Both Flags*, p. 354; Barber, *Army Memoirs*, p. 56.

34 Pyne, *Fire in America*, pp. xii, 393; *OR*, Ser. 1, Vol. 51, Part 2, pp. 570–571; McPhee, *Pine Barrens*, p. 112; Samuel T. Wells to Sarah E. Wells, March 12, 1862, Samuel T. Wells Papers, FHS.

35 Billings, *Hardtack and Coffee*, pp. 232–234; *OR*, Ser. 1, Vol. 11, Part 3, p. 161; Denby, A Southern War Episode, pp. 4–6, Denby Family Papers, LC.

36 *OR*, Ser. 1, Vol. 12, Part 1, pp. 88–89; Abstracts and Vouchers (no. 12) 2nd Quarter 1862, John M. Shivers, Henry Tynes, Charles D. Hill Papers, CMLS-VHS; "To Contractors," *Charleston Mercury*, September 16, 1861, p. 2.

37 Weiner, *Mistresses and Slaves*, p. 163; Lupold and French, Jr., *Bridging Deep South Rivers*, pp. 167, 233; J. T. Hanlow, p. 6, J. C. C. Cox and R. Otis, p. 12, R. T. Higginbotham, p. 34, Eli S. and Thomas H. Tutwiler, p. 39, Chap. V, Vol. 113, Register of Contracts, 1861–1864, Miscellaneous Records, Office of the Quartermaster General, War Department Collection of Confederate Records, RG 109, NARA; *OR*, Ser. 1, Vol. 3, Part 3, p. 575; Townsend, *Rustics in Rebellion*, p. 37.

38 Goodloe, *Confederate Echoes*, p. 184; Statement for Col. J. H. Cleaugh, August 14, 1861, Arkadelphia, Arkansas, Heiskell Civil War Collection, ASI; *OR*, Ser. 1, Vol. 5, p. 40; *OR*, Ser. 1, Vol. 24, p. 424.

39 "Woes of the Border," *Macon* [GA] *Daily Telegraph*, January 18, 1862, p. 2; Diary of Samuel A. Murray, March 20, 1862, Pennsylvania State Archives; Diary of Fannie Page Hume, April 12, 1862, LC.

40 Rice and Campbell, eds., *A Woman's War*, pp. 83–84; "The Poor and Their Necessities," *Macon* [GA] *Daily Telegraph*, November 6, 1861, p. 1; Citizens' Claims for Damages, pp. 15, 30, 32, 43, 48, 68, Fredericksburg and Spotsylvania National Military Park; Maria Collins to My Dear Brother, October 2, 1861, Collins Family Papers, UKL.

41 Frobel, *Civil War Diary of Anne S. Frobel*, p. 53; Diary of Fannie Page Hume, April 7, 1862, LC; "The Woes of the Border," *Macon* [GA] *Daily Telegraph*, January 18, 1862, p. 2.

42 Claims 130, 293, 501, 660, 846, Chap. V, Vol. 43, Register of Claims; Claims 1766, 2909, 3010, 4484, Chap. V, Vol. 44, Register of Claims, Office of the Quartermaster General, War Department Collection of Confederate Records, RG 109, NARA.

43 Mary Dedrick to Henry Dedrick, February 1, 1862, Henry H. Dedrick Civil War Letters, VMI; Diary of Fannie Page Hume, November 9, 1862, November 16, 1862, LC; Civil War Diary of Daniel Burchard Allen, December 20, 1862, BU.

44 Spence, *Diary of the Civil War*, pp. 85–86; East, ed., *Civil War Diary of Sarah Morgan*, pp. 164–165; McGuire, *Southern Refugee*, p. 67. Cf. Nelson, *Ruin Nation*, pp. 104, 118, 157, who argues that most civilians and soldiers accepted or admired the way that war altered the landscape.

45 Klingberg, *Southern Claims Commission*, p. 128; *OR*, Ser. 1, Vol. 12, Part 3, p. 573.

46 Taylor, *Supply for Tomorrow*, pp. 165, 103; *OR*, Ser. 1, Vol. 31, Part 3, p. 198.

47 Sherman, *Memoirs*, p. 266.

48 Thomas, *Confederate Nation*, p. 155; Gwin, ed., *Cornelia Peake McDonald*, pp. 101–102; Civil War Diary of Daniel Burchard Allen, October 18, 1862, BU; Donald, ed., *Gone for a Soldier*, p. 167.

49 Gienapp, ed., *Civil War and Reconstruction*, p. 241; Diary of Silas S. Huntley, March 4, 1862, CHMRC; Small, *Road to Richmond*, pp. 200–201.

50 Soldier's Life of Philo Pearce, pp. 18–19, Ottawa County, Ohio, History Museum; Anthony W. Ross to Sarah E. Ross, November 9, 1862, Sarah Emily Ross Papers, OHC; Entry for Anthony W. Ross, National Park Service, www.nps.gov/civilwar/search; Hiram Strong to Dear Wife, November 10, 1862, Colonel Hiram Strong Papers, DML.

51 Diary of Cyrus Hussey, January 5, 1863, January 6, 1863, January 19, 1863, January 20, 1863, University of Toledo; W. G. Kendrick to Dearest Wife, February 20, 1863, William G. Kendrick Letters, Lancaster County, PA, Historical Society; Hiram Strong to Dear Wife, April 17, 1863, Colonel Hiram Strong Papers, DML.

52 Kent, ed., *Three Years with Company K*, pp. 225, 142; Mohr and Winslow, eds., *Cormany Diaries*, p. 317.

53 Soldier's Life of Philo Pearce, p. 15, Ottawa County, Ohio, History Museum; Gallagher, ed., *Fighting for the Confederacy*, p. 172; Paxton, *Memoir and Memorials*, p. 74; *OR*, Ser. 1, Vol. 15, pp. 874–876.

54 *Regulations for the Army of the Confederate States*, pp. 413–414, 290, 77–78.

55 Abstract F (No. 28) + Voucher (No. 29) 2nd Qtr. 1863, by Colonel William J. Hoke, Charles D. Hill Collection, CMLS-VHS; Lieutenant General Ewell to Brigadier General George Steuart, September 14–15, 1863, by A. S. Pendleton, CMLS-VHS; *OR*, Ser. 1, Vol. 31, Part 3, pp. 575–576.

56 Cunningham, *Doctors in Gray*, p. 97; Leon, *Diary of a Tar Heel*, p. 15; Cash and Howorth, eds., *My Dear Nellie*, p. 107; Memoir of Archibald Atkinson, Jr., pp. 20–21, Virginia Polytechnic Institute and State University.

57 W.H.A. [*sic*] to Josie Cooper, January 14, 1863, Confederate Correspondence, GC; Paxton, *Memoir and Memorials*, p. 90; Davis, ed., *Diary of a Confederate Soldier*, p. 83; Diary of William R. Townsend, July 11, 1863, Southern Illinois University–Edwardsville; Engs and Brooks, eds., *Patriotic Duty*, p. 225; Gallagher, ed., *Fighting for the Confederacy*, p. 269.

58 Warwick, comp., *Williamson County*, p. 42; Marshall, ed., *War of the People*, pp. 157–158; Diary of Samuel A. Agnew, December 4, 1863, UNC-SHC.

59 *OR*, Ser. 1, Vol. 17, Part 2, p. 836; Gallagher, ed., *Fighting for the Confederacy*, p. 313; W. A. Wainright to no name, September 12, 1866, Box 673, Entry 225, Records of the Office of the Quartermaster General, Consolidated Correspondence File, 1794–1915, RG 92, NARA.

60 Looby, ed., *Journal and Letters of Higginson*, p. 109; "The Yankees in Stafford," *Richmond Examiner*, June 26, 1863, p. 1; Kent, ed., *Three Years with Company K*, p. 170; "The War in Virginia," *Fayetteville* [NC] *Observer*, June 22, 1863, n.p.; Russell and Tucker, "Introduction," in Russell and Tucker, eds., *Natural Enemy, Natural Ally*, p. 4.

61 Berger, *Forests Forever*, pp. 33–34, 121; "A Blockade [sic] Correspondence," October 3, 1863, *Southern Illustrated News*, 2 (13): 101; Jordan, *Trees and People*, p. 116; Timothy C. Cheney, Impressions of Chattanooga, pp. 3, Timothy C. Cheney Papers, CPL; Grant, *Memoirs*, pp. 410–411.

62 Tree Facts, www.americanforests.org; Livermore, *My Story of the War*, pp. 659, 341–342; *OR*, Ser. 1, Vol. 11, Part 2, p. 629; Neese, *Three Years in the Confederate Horse Artillery*, p. 51.

63 Stiles, *Four Years under Marse Robert*, p. 83; J. Godown to My Dear Fannie, April 9, 1862, Diaries of J. M. Godown, Vol. 2, Allen County-Fort Wayne, Indiana, Historical Society; Wood, *Mud: A Military History*, pp. 77–95; Rusling, *Men and Things*, p. 296; Neese, *Three Years in the Confederate Horse Artillery*, p. 51; Marvel, *Burnside*, pp. 212–213.

64 Bearss, "Fortress Rosecrans Research Report," 1960, www.nps.gov/stri/historyculture/foro.htm; Hiram Strong to Dear Wife, April 17, 1863, Colonel Hiram Strong Papers, DML; Richard H. Collins to My dear Wife, December 13, 1863, Collins Family Papers, UKL.

65 L. McLawrence, A Narrative of the War, p. 2, Confederate Miscellaneous Letters, South Carolina Historical Society, Charleston (SCHS); "Substitute for Quinine," *Weekly* [Jackson] *Mississippian*, December 18, 1861, n.p.; "Dogwood Bark vs. Quinine," *Daily Columbus* [GA] *Enquirer*, September 20, 1861, pp. 2–3.

66 Sutherland, *Seasons of War*, p. 287; Spence, *Diary of the Civil War*, pp. 85–86; Murfree, *Where the Battle Was Fought*, pp. 1–2.

67 Porcher, *Resources of the Southern Fields and Forests*, pp. vii, 22, 26, 56, 60–61, 130, 141, 204–205, 320, 8; "Notice – Barks Wanted," [Atlanta] *Southern Confederacy*, August 1, 1862, p. 4; "From Cairo and Below," *Chicago Tribune*, July 18, 1862, p. 1.

68 Diary of Myra Adelaide Inman Carter, October 13, 1863, CPL; Deaderick, Diary or Register, pp. 31–36, David Anderson Deaderick Collection, LC; Diary of Josephine Forney Roedil, November 5, 1863, Miscellaneous Mss., LC.

69 M. M. Champion to My dear Husband, April 6, 1863, Champion Family Papers, OCM; "Extortion," *Hillsborough* [NC] *Recorder*, December 3, 1862, p. 3; Diary of Josephine H. Hooke, September 9, 1863, September 28, 1863, UTK.

CHAPTER 5: HABITAT

1 Ward, *War for Independence*, pp. 85–86, 95; Schrijvers, *Crash of Ruin*, pp. 104–105; Articles of War, Chapter 20, Article 52, Article 54, www.freepages.military.rootsweb.com.

2 Journal of George L. Wood, April 21, 1862, OHC; Civil War Reminiscences of James Mitchell, pp. 23, 29–30, OHC; Mitchell, *Civil War Soldiers*, pp. 113–115; Seneca Thrall to his wife, March 8, 1862, Seneca Thrall Letters, Civil War Archive, www.civilwararchive.com/LETTERS/thrall1.htm; Stephen Allen Osborn Manuscript, p. 28, GC; Kent, ed., *Three Years with Company K*, pp. 159–162; John Nevin Sketchbook, pp. 14–15, Lieutenant Colonel John I. Nevin Papers, HSWP.

3 Neese, *Three Years in the Confederate Horse Artillery*, p. 128; Chamberlaine, *Memoirs of the Civil War*, p. 28; Blackford, *War Years with Jeb Stuart*, pp. 20, 94; Moore, *Story of a Cannoneer*, p. 59; Everson and Simpson, eds., *Far, Far from Home*, p. 56.

4 Townsend, *Rustics in Rebellion*, pp. 180, 161, 14; OR, Ser. 1, Vol. 11, Part 1, p. 239; OR, Ser. 1, Vol. 16, Part 2, p. 229; H. Pernot to Dear Wife, January 26, 1862, Miscellaneous Letter Collection, ASI; Scott, *Military Dictionary*, pp. 122–123.

5 Ries and Leighton, *History of the Clay-Working Industry*, p. 12; Campbell and Pryce, *Brick: A World History*, pp. 13–14, 202; National Historic Landmarks Program, National Park Service, Berkeley, tps.cr.nps.gov/nhl/detail.cfm.

6 Neese, *Three Years in the Confederate Horse Artillery*, pp. 225–226; Blackford, *War Years with Jeb Stuart*, p. 45; OR, Ser. 1, Vol. 5, pp. 244–245; OR, Ser. 1, Vol. 12, Part 1, pp. 451–453; Edward P. Bridgman to Sidney E. Bridgman, February 24, 1895, James B. Pond Papers, UM.

7 OR, Ser. 1, Vol. 2, p. 38; Lynch, *Civil War Diary*, p. 32; OR, Ser. 1, Vol. 10, Part 1, pp. 46–47.

8 "Woes of the Border," *Macon [GA] Daily Telegraph*, January 18, 1862, p. 2; OR, Ser. 1, Vol. 51, Part 1, p. 63; Pryor, *Reading the Man*, pp. 301–308; OR, Ser. 1, Vol. 2, p. 664.

9 Gwin, ed., *Cornelia Peake McDonald*, pp. 12, 28, 277, n. 12; Rable, *Fredericksburg!*, p. 150; OR, Ser. 1, Vol. 12, Part 1, pp. 84–86; Townsend, *Rustics in Rebellion*, pp. 107–108.

10 Enoch Colby, Jr., to Enoch Colby, June 19, 1862, Reminiscences of Francelia Colby, CHMRC; Taylor, *Destruction and Reconstruction*, p. 111; Cashin, "Trophies of War," pp. 342–346, 349–352; Diary of James Pusard, November 30, 1861, FHS; OR, Ser. 1, Vol. 15, pp. 22–23; Livermore, *My Story of the War*, pp. 659–660.

11 OR, Ser. 1, Vol. 11, Part 1, p. 1017; OR, Ser. 1, Vol. 10, Part 1, p. 899; OR, Ser. 1, Vol. 6, pp. 143–144.

12 OR, Ser. 1, Vol. 5, pp. 404–405; James L. Clements to Dear Mollie, October 26, 1861, James L. Clements Papers, Arkansas History Commission; Ellen Buchanan Screven Reminiscences, pp. 3, 12, UGA.

13 OR, Ser. 1, Vol. 12, pp. 463–464; OR, Ser. 1, Vol. 11, Part 1, p. 160; OR, Ser. 1, Vol. 5, pp. 404–405.

14 F. A. Polk to Leonidas Polk, December 17, 1861, Leonidas Polk Papers, University of the South-Sewanee; Autobiography of Philip Sartorius, pp. 21, 24, American Jewish Archives; Martha Read to Thomas G. Read, February 16–17, 1862, Read Family Correspondence, Notre Dame University; Diary of Mary Elizabeth Shrewsbury Van Meter, n.d. February–March, 1862, FHS; Grant, *Memoirs*, p. 261.

15 Diary of Fannie Page Hume, March 16, 1862, LC; "Bivouac of Brooklyn Fourteenth," *Brooklyn Eagle*, March 21, 1862, p. 2; McFadden, comp., *Aunt and Soldier Boys*, p. 26; Samuel V. Fulkerson to his mother, March 9, 1862, Fulkerson Family Papers, VMI.

16 Federal Census of 1860, Slave Schedule, Virginia, Fairfax County, p. 2; *OR*, Ser. 1, Vol. 5, pp. 29–30, 21.

17 Townsend, *Rustics in Rebellion*, pp. 211–212; Harrison, *Rhetoric of Rebel Women*, pp. 25–29; Jacob D. Cox to Ellen Tompkins, December 7, 1870, Tompkins Family Papers, VHS; "Woes of the Border," *Macon* [GA] *Daily Telegraph*, January 18, 1862, p. 2; S. Henry Eells to Dear Friends, June 25, 1862, Samuel Henry Eells Papers, LC.

18 *OR*, Ser. 1, Vol. 51, Part 1, p. 468; John Nevin Sketchbook, pp. 14–15, 17, Lieutenant Colonel John I. Nevin Papers, HSWP; Townsend, *Rustics in Rebellion*, pp. 37–38.

19 Abstract B (No. 13) and Vouchers (No. 15), 4th Quarter, 1862, Charles D. Hill Collection, CMLS-VHS; *OR*, Ser. 2, Vol. 3, p. 803; Indenture, December 3, 1861, between Messrs. Ward and Southmayde and Algernon D. Cabell, Heiskell Civil War Collection, ASI.

20 *OR*, Ser. 1, Vol. 11, Part 3, p. 454; Casdorph, *Prince John Magruder*, pp. 9, 29–30, 101–102.

21 Frobel, *Civil War Diary* of Anne S. Frobel, pp. 52–53; "The Latest News," *Providence* [RI] *Evening Press*, September 24, 1861, p. 3; *OR*, Ser. 1, Vol. 4, pp. 248–249; Cashin, "Trophies of War," p. 346; "Occupation of Nashville by Federal Troops," [Madison] *Wisconsin Patriot*, March 15, 1862, p. 5.

22 "Late from Charleston, SC," *Philadelphia Inquirer*, October 1, 1861, p. 2; *OR*, Ser. 1, Vol. 8, pp. 771–772; Davis, ed., *Diary of a Confederate Soldier*, p. 67.

23 Worsham, *Jackson's Foot Cavalry*, p. 55; Diary of John M. Porter, p. 48, n.d. [1861], Octagon Hall and Kentucky Confederate Archives, Franklin, Kentucky.

24 *OR*, Ser. 1, Vol. 8, pp. 796–797; *OR*, Ser. 1, Vol. 17, Part 2, pp. 729–730.

25 James H. Gardner to Anna Reynolds, July 29, 1861, James H. Gardner Papers, VHS; Chamberlaine, *Memoirs of the Civil War*, p. 30; Moore, *Story of a Cannoneer*, pp. 68–69.

26 "Meeting of Virginians in Washington," *Alexandria [VA] Gazette*, February 3, 1854, p. 2; Federal Census of 1860, Slave Schedule, Virginia, Prince William County, p. 23; *OR*, Ser. 1, Vol. 5, pp. 998–999.

27 Calhoun, ed., *Witness to Sorrow*, pp. 227–228; "Near Yorktown," *Philadelphia Inquirer*, April 17, 1862, p. 2.

28 John S. Mosby to F. W. Powell et al., February 4, 1863, John Singleton Mosby Papers, LC; Sutherland, *Savage Conflict*, p. 165.

29 *OR*, Ser. 1, Vol. 12, Part 2, pp. 51–52; *OR*, Ser. 1, Vol. 12, Part 3, p. 509.

30 Sherman, *Memoirs*, p. 277; Donald, ed., *Gone for a Soldier*, p. 146; Fremantle, *Three Months*, pp. 116–117.

31 S. Henry Eells to Dear Aunty, April 22, 1863, Samuel Henry Eells Papers, LC; Albert Gibonney to Sallie Gibonney, December 15, 1862, Gibonney Letters, gift from Mark Baldwin to the author; *OR*, Ser. 1, Vol. 24, p. 642.

32 Gelernter, *History of American Architecture*, p. 157; Looby, ed., *Journal and Letters of Higginson*, p. 93; Diary or Register, pp. 32, 36, David Anderson Deaderick Collection, LC; Albert Gibonney to Sallie Gibonney, July 25, 1863, Gibonney Letters, gift from Mark Baldwin to the author; James Stillwell to his wife, March 31, 1863, James Stillwell Papers, OHC.

33 Civil War Reminiscences of James Mitchell, p. 23, OHC; Diary of Van Bennett, January 8, 1863, January 9, 1863, Van Bennett Papers, Wisconsin Historical Society; Looby, ed., *Journal and Letters of Higginson*, pp. 282, 289; Seneca Thrall to his wife, November 6, 1862, December 3, 1862, Civil War Archive, www.civilwararchive.com.LETTERS/thrall1.htm. Cf. Grimsley, *Hard Hand of War*, p. 104, who believes that US troops rarely burned homes, and Royster, *Destructive War*, p. 342, who argues that most occupied houses were spared.

34 Diary of Oliver H. Protsman, March 14, 1863, Wright State University; Captain Owen, Folder MM 1395, Records of the Office of the Judge Advocate General, Court Martial Case Files, RG 153, NARA; *OR*, Ser. 1, Vol. 25, p. 314.

35 Sutherland, *Savage Conflict*, p. 134; Myers, ed., *Children of Pride*, p. 312; Diary of Franklin A. Wise, December 23, 1862, Franklin A. Wise Papers, WRHS; Newton Scott to Miss Cone, April 9, 1863, Letters of Private Newton Robert Scott, Civil War Letters, www.civilwarletters.com/letters_toc.html.

36 Warwick, comp., *Williamson County*, p. 301; McCurry, *Confederate Reckoning*, pp. 114–115; J. T. Swayne, on behalf of Mrs. Mattie C. Porter, n.d. 1863, to A. N. Eddy, notation by A. N. Eddy, Porter-Rice Family Papers, UMS; Knox, *Camp-Fire and Cotton-Field*, p. 340.

37 Kent, ed., *Three Years with Company K*, pp. 157–158; *OR*, Ser. 2, Vol. 6, pp. 602–603; Hiram Root to Mary Root, October 19, 1862, Hiram Root Collection, Toledo-Lucas County Public Library; *OR*, Ser. 1, Vol. 24, pp. 492–493; James Stillwell to his wife, September 25, 1862, James Stillwell Papers, OHC; *OR*, Ser. 1, Vol. 25, Part 1, p. 1115; George Bingham, Folder LL 1234, Records of the Office of the Judge Advocate General, Court Martial Case Files, RG 153, NARA; *OR*, Ser. 1, Vol. 12, p. 23. Scholars disagree on wartime looting; Cashin, "Trophies of War," pp. 339–367; Rable, *Fredericksburg!*, pp. 177–184, 271; and Royster, *Destructive War*, emphasize its severity and frequency, while Grimsley, *Hard Hand of War*, pp. 2–6, 104–105, 142–170, 204, and Neely, *Civil War and the Limits of Destruction*, pp. 2–5, 19, 29, 34–37, 108, 219, portray it as relatively restrained.

38 Rhodes, ed., *All for the Union*, p. 133; Marshall, ed., *War of the People*, p. 140; R. L. Symington et al. to Brigadier General Ewing, August 12, 1863, Box 1, Entry 182, Papers Relating to Confederate Sympathizers, Deserters, Guerillas, and Prisoners, Miscellaneous Confederate Records, RG 109, NARA.

39 Finding Aid, John Perkins Papers, UNC-SHC; Diary of John E. Wilkins, April 26, 1863, LMRL; Matthews, *Public Laws of the Confederate States, 1862*, p. 2.

40 Nelson, *Ruin Nation*, pp. 77–78, 81–82; Diary of Sarah Lois Wadley, June 19, 1861, Sarah Lois Wadley Papers, UNC-SHC; Diary of Mrs. W. W. Lord, p. 11, LC; Citizens' Claims for Damages, p. 42, Fredericksburg and Spotsylvania National Military Park; Diary of Mary L. Pearre, January 29, 1863, May 3, 1863, UTK.

41 OR, Ser. 1, Vol. 24, Part 1, pp. 513–514; Anna M. Farrar to Jefferson Davis, June 20, 1863, Jefferson Davis Papers, DU; Federal Census of 1860, Free Schedule, Louisiana, Tensas Parish, p. 32; Warwick, comp., *Williamson County*, p. 193; Federal Census of 1850, Free Schedule, Tennessee, Montgomery County, p. 455.

42 Spence, *Diary of the Civil War*, p. 86; "Chattanooga in War Time," *Chattanooga Star*, November 23, 1907, n.p., Clipping File, CPL; Edward P. Bridgman to Sidney E. Bridgman, February 24, 1895, James B. Pond Papers, UM.

43 Gordon, *Reminiscences*, pp. 302–303; Born in Slavery, Arkansas, Interview with Mose King, p. 208, www.loc.gov; James Stillwell to his wife, March 31, 1863, James Stillwell Papers, OHC; Warwick, comp., *Williamson County*, p. 169; Federal Census of 1860, Free Schedule, Tennessee, Williamson County, p. 129.

44 Eugenia Bitting to Cade Gillespie, n.d. 1928, Mrs. Cade Drew Gillespie Papers, UMIS; James P. Doughtery to Zeralda Hood, December 13, 1863, Letters to Zeralda Hood, ISL; Coffin, *Four Years of Fighting*, p. 98; M. J. French to Colonel J. P. Lowe, May 30, 1868, Box 661, Entry 225, Consolidated Correspondence File, 1794–1915, Records of the Office of the Quartermaster General, RG 92, NARA; Iserson, *Death to Dust*, pp. 49–52; Tobias C. Miller to My Dear Brother, April 20, 1863, Tobias C. Miller Diary and Letters, CHMRC.

45 James Stillwell to his wife, July 4, 1863, James Stillwell Papers, OHC; S. Henry Eells to no name, June 9, 1863, Samuel Henry Eells Papers, LC; J. M. Hawks to My Dear Wife, June 15, 1862, Papers of Doctors J. M. and Esther H. Hawks, LC; Miss Walker's Journal, Entry of March 12, 1862, Susan Walker Papers, CHSL; Simon, ed., *Personal Memoirs of Julia Dent Grant*, p. 105.

46 *Regulations for the Army of the Confederate States*, pp. 413–414, 77–78.

47 Major William Barnewall, Jr., p. 33, Chap. V, Vol. 113, Register of Contracts, 1861–1864, Miscellaneous Records, Office of the Quartermaster General, War Department Collection of Confederate Records, RG 109, NARA; Claim 2287, Martin Tutwiler, Chap. V, Vol. 44, Register of Claims, Office of the Quartermaster General, War Department Collection of Confederate Records, RG 109, NARA; Mrs. Loeb to General Johnston, November 22, 1863, Department of Tennessee, Letters Received, Endorsements on, Chap. 2, Vol. 1581/4, CSA Military Commands, War Department Collection of Confederate Records, RG 109, NARA.

48 McDonald, ed., *Make Me a Map*, pp. 187, 308, n. 31; *OR*, Ser. 1, Vol. 25, p. 314; Phillips, *Story of My Life*, p. 40.

49 Neese, *Three Years in the Confederate Horse Artillery*, p. 232; Rhodes, ed., *All for the Union*, p. 133; Federal Census of 1850, Slave Schedule, Virginia, Henrico County, p. 395; *OR*, Ser. 1, Vol. 32, Part 2, p. 29; *OR*, Ser. 1, Vol. 24, p. 494; *Regulations for the Army of the Confederate States*, p. 92. On Bott's contradictory political views, see Sutherland, *Seasons of War*, pp. 380–381.

50 Bridges, *Lee's Maverick General*, pp. 6, 18, 20–22, 26–27, 163–172, 149, 178; Durrill, *War of Another Kind*, pp. 137–139; *OR*, Ser. 2, Vol. 5, pp. 389–390.

51 Escott, *Military Necessity*, pp. 17, 93–94; Knight, *Standard History of Georgia and Georgians*, 5: 2780; "Important Decision," *Macon [GA] Daily Telegraph*, November 9, 1863, p. 2; "Correspondence of the Telegraph," *Macon [GA] Daily Telegraph* November 11, 1863, p. 1.

52 "Louisiana Getting Her 'Rights'," *Chicago Tribune*, March 26, 1863, p. 2; Mitt [Bond] to her mother, September 2, 1863, Priscilla Munnikhuysen Bond Papers, Collection Inventory, LSU.

53 Allmendinger, *Ruffin*, pp. 162–164; Deaderick, Diary or Register, pp. 31–38, David Anderson Deaderick Collection, LC; Federal Census of 1860, Free Schedule, Mississippi, Hinds County, pp. 60–61; Federal Census of 1860, Slave Schedule, Mississippi, Hinds County, n.p.; Davis, ed., *Diary of a Confederate Soldier*, pp. 79–80.

54 Interview with Addie Patterson, p. 2, SC, Folkways, American Life Histories, LC, http://rs6.loc.gov; Recollections of Letitia Dabney Miller, p. 12, Mrs. Cade Drew Gillespie Papers, UMIS; Diary of Sarah Lois Wadley, May 16, 1863, Collection Description, Sarah Lois Wadley Papers, UNC-SHC.

55 Neese, *Three Years in the Confederate Horse Artillery*, p. 61; Cashin, "Into the Trackless Wilderness," pp. 45, 51; C. M. Stacy to James Hamner, August 2, 1863, Hamner–Stacy Correspondence, UMS; Deaderick, Diary or Register, pp. 37–38, David Anderson Deaderick Collection, LC.

56 Townsend, *Rustics in Rebellion*, p. 35; Engs and Brooks, eds., *Patriotic Duty*, p. 114; Rhodes, ed., *All for the Union*, pp. 113–114; "A Sample of Pope's Handiwork," [Macon] *Georgia Weekly Telegraph*, September 12, 1862, p. 2.

CHAPTER 6: BREAKDOWN

1 Klingberg, *Southern Claims Commission*, p. 99; Beattie, Cole, and Waugh, eds., *A Distant War Comes Home*, pp. 219–220.

2 *OR*, Ser. 1, Vol. 34, Part 1, p. 125; *OR*, Ser. 1, Vol. 26, pp. 276–277; "From Memphis and Below," *Chicago Tribune*, July 23, 1864, p. 3; "A Female Smuggler," [Baltimore] *Sun*, August 6, 1864, p. 1; "Affairs in the Southwest," *Philadelphia Inquirer*, May 3, 1864, p. 4.

3 Branch, *Memoirs of a Southern Woman*, pp. 9–23, 39–40.

4 Diary of Joseph Waddell, June 13, 1864, VSP; Ada Thornburg to Carrie Stakely, December 8, 1864, Hall–Stakely Papers, ETHS; Deaderick, Diary or Register, p. 39, David Anderson Deaderick Collection, LC; Murrell Taylor,

Divided Family, p. 111; Joseph Leddy, Folder NN 1453, Records of the Office of the Judge Advocate General, Court Martial Case Files, RG 153, NARA.

5 OR, Ser. 1, Vol. 32, Part 1, p. 155; OR, Ser. 1, Vol. 52, Part 2, p. 767; Record Book, August 23, 1864, James Fowler Chapman Papers, Sandusky, Ohio, Library, Archives Research Center; OR, Ser. 1, Vol. 36, Part 2, p. 390.

6 Charles H. Lake to My dear Brother, January 14, 1864, Heiskell Civil War Collection, ASI; Moneyhon, "David O. Dodd," pp. 203–205; Diary of Frances Woolfolk Wallace, June 17, 1864, UNC-SHC; OR, Ser. 2, Vol. 7, pp. 18–19.

7 Rusling, *Men and Things*, p. 322; Putnam, *Richmond during the War*, pp. 173–175, 288; Hitt, *Charged with Treason*.

8 Richard H. Collins to My Dearest Mary, January 20, 1864, Collins Family Papers, UKL; Diary of Lucy Rebecca Buck, August 18, n.d. [1864], Johns Hopkins University; OR, Ser. 1, Vol. 35, Part 2, p. 243; Diary of Mary A. Dickinson, April 20, 1864, ETHS; Charles H. Lake to My dear Brother, January 14, 1864, Heiskell Civil War Collection, ASI.

9 OR, Ser. 1, Vol. 32, Part 1, pp. 659–660; OR, Ser. 1, Vol. 39, Part 1, p. 876; OR, Ser. 2, Vol. 7, p. 70.

10 OR, Ser. 1, Vol. 33, p. 400; OR, Ser. 1, Vol. 32, Part 3, pp. 745–748; Federal Census of 1860, Free Schedule, Alabama, Marion County, p. 12.

11 Wilkeson, *Recollections of a Private Soldier*, p. 40; Clark, ed., *Alexander G. Downing's Civil War*, p. 192; Hurt, *Agriculture and the Confederacy*, pp. 191, 222; Mohr and Winslow, eds., *Cormany Diaries*, pp. 425, 427; Kent, ed., *Three Years with Company K*, p. 277, 281.

12 Richard Gwathmey to My dear children, January 4, 1864, Gwathmey Family Papers, VHS; Huston, *Sinews of War*, pp. 224, 234; Civil War History of John Ritland, chapter 2, n.p., OSU; Mohr and Winslow, eds., *Cormany Diaries*, p. 427.

13 OR, Ser. 1, Vol. 34, Part 2, pp. 752–753; Civil War Diaries of John Merrilies, September 11, 1864, October 5, 1864, CHMRC; Reuben Wickham to My Dear Wife, November 11, 1864, gift from Kristen Fuller to the author.

14 Diary of Theodore Allen, October 17, 1864, FHS; Civil War History of John Ritland, chapter 5, n.p., OSU; Fletcher, *Rebel Private*, p. 140.

15 Menge and Shimrak, eds., *Civil War Notebook of Daniel Chisholm*, p. 23; James Stepter to My Dear Wife, January 15, 1864, James F. Stepter Papers, UMCP; Mohr and Winslow, eds., *Cormany Diaries*, p. 426.

16 Engs and Brooks, eds., *Patriotic Duty*, p. 279; C. M. Stacy to My Dearest boys, M[arch] 11, 1864, Hamner–Stacy Correspondence, UMS; Diary of Jason Niles, March 1, 1864, Jason Niles Papers, UNC-SHC; Graham, ed., *Under Both Flags*, pp. 318–319; Federal Census of 1860, Free Schedule, Georgia, Walker County, p. 693.

17 Fellman, *Citizen Sherman*, pp. 213–222; Kennett, *Sherman*, pp. 262–276, 343–344, 352; Frank, *Civilian War*, pp. 1–18, 148–164; Hess, *Civil War in the West*, pp. 220, 270; Sherman, *Memoirs*, p. 602.

18 Goff, *Confederate Supply*, pp. 138, 212; Warfield, *Confederate Soldier's Memoirs*, p. 171; OR, Ser. 4, Vol. 3, pp. 2–3; "To the Farmers of Augusta, Rockingham, and Shenandoah," *Staunton* [VA] *Spectator*, March 8, 1864, p. 1.

19 Wiley, ed., *Fourteen Hundred and Ninety-One Days*, p. 223. Diary of Joseph Belknap Smith, June 17, 1864, Joseph Belknap Smith Papers, DU; Tunnard, *Southern Record*, pp. 342–343, 288–291.

20 *OR*, Ser. 1, Vol. 34, Part 2, pp. 989–990; Felton, *Country Life in Georgia*, pp. 86–87, 89; *OR*, Ser. 1, Vol. 34, Part 2, p. 903; Escott, *After Secession*, p. 111.

21 Diary of Mary L. Pearre, December 16–17, 1864, UTK; Fletcher, *Rebel Private*, pp. 111–112; *OR*, Ser. 1, Vol. 35, Part 2, p. 544.

22 Mame to My dear little auntie, February 4, 1864, Lenoir Family Papers, UNC-SHC; Goff, *Confederate Supply*, p. 219; *OR*, Ser. 1, Vol. 34, Part 4, p. 690; Major General Churchill, Circular, December 30, 1864, Camp Lee, Arkansas, Order Book, pp. 68–69, Churchill's Division, CSA, General Order Book, FHS.

23 Rhodes, ed., *All for the Union*, p. 178; Billings, *Hardtack and Coffee*, p. 234; Drucilla Cameron, Case 19404, Missi., Box 202, Settled Case Files, SCC, RG 217, NARA-II; Botts, *Great Rebellion*, p. 296.

24 O'Grada, *Famine*, pp. 48–52; Billings, *Hardtack and Coffee*, p. 246; Hughes, ed., *Memoir of Stephenson*, p. 276; Autobiography of J. D. Goldman, p. 9, American Jewish Archives.

25 Cashin, "Hungry People in the Wartime South," pp. 167, 160; Massey, *Ersatz in the Confederacy*, pp. 62–63, 71.

26 E. F. Grabill to Anna Jenney, January 23, 1864, Elliott F. Grabill Papers, Oberlin College Archives; Hughes, ed., *Memoir of Stephenson*, pp. 350–351; Ford and Ford, *Life in the Confederate Army*, p. 31.

27 *OR*, Ser. 1, Vol. 41 Part 4, p. 943; *OR*, Ser. 1, Vol. 42, Part 2, p. 763; Williams, Williams, and Carlson, *Plain Folk*, p. 61; Ritchie, *Food in Civilization*, p. 175; *OR*, Ser. 1, Vol. 52, Part 2, p. 667.

28 "From the Front," *Tri-weekly* [Houston] *Telegraph*, January 6, 1864, n.p.; No name to My Dear Wife, October 11, 1864, Johnson Family Papers, VMI; Worsham, *Jackson's Foot Cavalry*, p. 208; *OR*, Ser. 1, Vol. 36, Part 1, p. 218; Sherman, *Memoirs*, p. 447; *OR*, Ser. 1, Vol. 41, Part 1, p. 645.

29 *OR*, Ser. 1, Vol. 35, Part 2, p. 66; Mohr and Winslow, eds., *Cormany Diaries*, p. 488; Winther, ed., *With Sherman to the Sea*, p. 140; Jaquette, ed., *Letters of a Civil War Nurse*, pp. 49–51; William and A. W. Ross to Sarah Ross, April 26, 1864, Sarah Emily Ross Papers, OHC; Wittenberg, ed., *One of Custer's Wolverines*, p. 88; *OR*, Ser. 1, Vol. 32, Part 1, p. 278; Hopkins, *The Seventh Regiment*, p. 154.

30 Rhodes, ed., *All for the Union*, p. 179; *OR*, Ser. 1, Vol. 38, Part 2, p. 907; Stillwell, *Story of a Common Soldier*, p. 236.

31 *OR*, Ser. 1, Vol. 33, pp. 377–379; Smith and Baker, eds., *"Burning Rails as We Please,"* p. 85; Winther, ed., *With Sherman to the Sea*, p. 131.

32 A Friend of the Union to Montgomery Meigs, October 20, 1864, Box 637, Entry 225, Consolidated Correspondence File, 1794–1915, Records of the Office of the Quartermaster General, RG 92, NARA; *OR*, Ser. 1, Vol. 33, pp. 377–379; *OR*, Ser. 1, Vol. 34, Part 2, pp. 577–578.

33 *OR*, Ser. 1, Vol. 34, Part 2, p. 497; Memoir of Roger Hannaford, section 244–245, n.p., Roger Hannaford Papers, CHSL; Eicher and Eicher, *Civil*

War High Commands, p. 425; Dallas Brewster, Folder NN 1795, Records of the Office of the Judge Advocate General, Court Martial Case Files, RG 153, NARA.

34 Anderson, *Memoirs Historical and Personal*, p. 392; Neese, *Three Years in the Confederate Horse Artillery*, p. 271; McDonald, ed., *Make Me a Map*, p. 236; Craig, ed., *Upcountry South Carolina Goes to War*, pp. 152, 154; *OR*, Ser. 1, Vol. 37, Part 1, p. 292; Memoir of Roger Hannaford, section 61, n.p., Roger Hannaford Papers, CHSL.

35 *OR*, Ser. 1, Vol. 34, Part 1, p. 590; Hughes, ed., *Memoir of Stephenson*, p. 204; *OR*, Ser. 1, Vol. 39, Part 1, pp. 545–547.

36 General Order No. 4, April 12, 1864, Headquarters, Near Mansfield, La., Churchill's Division, CSA, General Order Book, FHS; Stiles, *Four Years under Marse Robert*, pp. 314–315; The Confederate States to Oliver Hamilton, June 30, 1864, December 31, 1864, The Confederate States to Mrs. O. Hamilton, October 14, 1864, Virginia Harrold Collection, UMCP.

37 Warwick, comp., *Williamson County*, pp. 61, 230; Jane Garrett and Edward Sevier to John B. Palmer, April 4, 1864, Special Order No. 98, May 8, 1864, Undescribed 43, Papers Relating to Depredations by Confederate Cavalry in Western North Carolina, May 1864, Office of the Quartermaster General, War Department Collection of Confederate Records, RG 109, NARA.

38 Diary of Samuel A. Agnew, June 29, 1864, UNC-SHC; Louisa Lovell to Joseph Lovell, February 7, 1864, Quitman Family Papers, UNC-SHC; Diary of Margaret L. L. Ramsey, December 3, 1864, December 6, 1864, Margaret Lawrence (Lindsley) Ramsey Papers, LC; Federal Census of 1850, Free Schedule, Tennessee, Davidson County, p. 593.

39 B. H. Haxall to Paulus Powell, February 7, 1865, Paulus Powell Papers, VHS; Claim 4419, Samuel Goode, Chap. V, Vol. 44, Register of Claims, Office of the Quartermaster General, War Department Collection of Confederate Records, RG 109, NARA; Diary of William King, September 6, 1864, William King Papers, UNC-SHC. I found no references by civilians or soldiers to George P. Marsh's classic work on the environment, *Man and Nature*, published in 1864; see Lowenthal, *George Perkins Marsh*.

40 Charles E. Bates to Dear Parents, July 19, 1864, Charles Bates Papers, VHS; Howe, ed., *Marching with Sherman*, p. 20; "Continuation of the Work of Destruction," *New York Times*, December 25, 1864, p. 1; Diary of Mary Rawson, September 6, 1864, Rawson–Collier–Harris Family Collection, Atlanta History Center; Watkins, *Company Aytch*, p. 123.

41 Rhodes, ed., *All for the Union*, p. 190; George B. Caldwell to A. B. Caldwell, July 1, 1864, George B. Caldwell Ms., Washington and Jefferson College; Fountain, ed., *Sisters, Seeds, and Cedars*, p. 157; James Stillwell to his wife, July 28, 1864, James Stillwell Papers, OHC; "Fernandina, Florida," *Fayetteville* [NC] *Observer*, January 4, 1864, n.p.; Sherman, *Memoirs*, p. 469.

42 Warwick, comp., *Williamson County*, pp. 155, 183; Anonymous [Orloff Dorman], Memoranda of Events that Transpired at Jacksonville, Florida, & in its Vicinity, 2: 246, passim, Orloff M. Dorman Papers, LC.

43 *OR*, Ser. 1, Vol. 34, Part 2, pp. 106–108; Mrs. Joseph Barrett, Memories of the Civil War, p. 9, Rutherford B. Hayes Presidential Center; *OR*, Ser. 1, Vol. 37, Part 1, pp. 556–557.

44 Royster, *Destructive War*, pp. 344–346; Born in Slavery, South Carolina, Interview with Daphney Wright, p. 267, www.loc.gov; *OR*, Ser. 1, Vol. 26, p. 305; Sherman, *Memoirs*, p. 538.

45 Stillwell, *Story of a Common Soldier*, p. 206; Rhodes, ed., *All for the Union*, pp. 166, 187.

46 John S. Timberlake to Thomas W. Bartlett, December 1, 1864, Blanton Family Papers, VHS; Alexander, *Stratford Hall and the Lees*, pp. 284–287, 331–332; Federal Census of 1850, Slave Schedule, Virginia, Jefferson County, p. 917; Mrs. Edmund Jennings Lee to David Hunter, July 20, 1864, Custis-Lee Family Papers, LC.

47 Smith and Baker, eds., *"Burning Rails as We Please,"* p. 124; Charles Kingsley to Frank Kingsley, August 6, 1864, Charles Kingsley Letter, VHS; Chauncey E. Barton to Dear Sister, April 14, 1864, Chauncey E. Barton Letter, LC.

48 Hughes, ed., *Memoir of Stephenson*, pp. 284, 261, 341, 217, 353; Wynne and Taylor, eds., *This War So Horrible*, p. 105; William D. Gale to no name, January 19, 1865, Leonidas Polk Papers, University of the South-Sewanee; Civil War Memories of Robert C. Carden, chapter 10, n.p., http://sunsite.utk.edu/civil-war.

49 *OR*, Ser. 1, Vol. 32, pp. 849–850; Wynne and Taylor, eds., *This War So Horrible*, pp. 105–106; Statements by Rachel Lanning, May 10, 1864, Elizabeth Youngblood, May 10, 1864, Undescribed 43, Papers Relating to Depredations by Confederate Cavalry in Western North Carolina, May 1864, Office of the Quartermaster General, War Department Collection of Confederate Records, RG 109, NARA; Federal Census of 1860, Free Schedule, North Carolina, Henderson County, p. 60.

50 Caroline Muirhead, Folder LL 3336, Records of the Office of the Judge Advocate General, Court Martial Case Files, RG 153, NARA.

51 Warwick, comp., *Williamson County*, p. 35; Diary of Margaret L. L. Ramsey, December 13, 1864, Margaret Lawrence (Lindsley) Ramsey Papers, LC; Diary of John Breese, May 17, 1864, Breese Family Letters, Allen County, Ohio, Historical Society, Lima; Emerson and Stokes, eds., *Confederate Englishman*, p. 56.

52 Entry for Lawrence J. Messerry, 1843–1874, Colleton District, SC, www.carolana.com/SC/Towns/All.htm; *OR*, Ser. 1, Vol. 35, Part 1, pp. 637–639.

53 *OR*, Ser. 1, Vol. 45, Part 1, pp. 1246–1248; Adams, *Living Hell*, pp. 166–172; John B. Palmer to J. Harris, May 16, 1864, Statement by David Morrell, May 9, 1864, Undescribed 43, Papers Relating to Depredations by Confederate Cavalry in Western North Carolina, May 1864, Office of the Quartermaster General, War Department Collection of Confederate Records, RG 109, NARA.

54 Hughes, ed., *Memoir of Stephenson*, p. 229; Neese, *Three Years in the Confederate Horse Artillery*, p. 294; Allmendinger, *Ruffin*, p. 164; Chamberlaine, *Memoirs of the Civil War*, p. 92.

55 General Order No. 17, April 17, 1864, Headquarters, Churchill's Division, CSA, General Order Book, FHS; *OR*, Ser. 1, Vol. 32, Part 3, pp. 849–850; *OR*, Ser. 1, Vol. 43, Part 1, pp. 7–8; Pauley, *Unreconstructed Rebel*, pp. 53–64.

56 Recollections of Anna Clayton Logan, p. 48, VHS; Driskell, ed., History of the 25th Alabama Infantry Regiment, n.p. (spring–summer 1864), https://sites.google.com/site/25thalabamaHome; Statement by Captain M. E. Carter, May 12, 1864, Undescribed 43, Papers Relating to Depredations by Confederate Cavalry in Western North Carolina, May 1864, Office of the Quartermaster General, War Department Collection of Confederate Records, RG 109, NARA.

57 Baumgartner, ed., *Blood and Sacrifice*, pp. 130–131; Fountain, ed., *Sisters, Seeds, and Cedars*, p. 174; Circular by Secretary Seddon, February 10, 1864, Joseph Cloyd Collection, CMLS-VHS.

58 McCarthy, *Detailed Minutiae*, pp. 108–109; Watkins, *Company Aytch*, pp. 168–169; Douglas, *I Rode with Stonewall*, pp. 315–316. On the scholarly debate over the extent of the war's damage to the Shenandoah Valley, see Brady, *War upon the Land*, pp. 90–92.

59 Diary of John E. Wilkins, May 13, 1864, LMRL; Marshall, ed., *War of the People*, p. 265; Harriet E. Johnson, Written for my Grandchildren, vol. 40, n.p., in Rutherford, comp., Historical Records of the United Daughters of the Confederacy: Women of the Confederacy, CMLS-VHS.

60 Willett, *Union Soldier Returns South*, p. 49; Graham, ed., *Under Both Flags*, p. 160; Hughes, ed., *Memoir of Stephenson*, p. 215; Gallagher, ed., *Fighting for the Confederacy*, p. 379.

61 Gordon, *Reminiscences*, p. 71; Diary of Albert M. Cook, October 18, 1862, Syracuse University; Richardson, *Death, Dissection, and the Destitute*, p. 19; Ash, *Year in the South*, pp. 12–16; Diary of Samuel A. Agnew, June 16, 1864, UNC-SHC.

CHAPTER 7: 1865 AND AFTER

1 Hughes, *A Boy's Experience*, p. 41; Browning and Smith, eds., *Letters from a North Carolina Unionist*, pp. 256–257; *OR*, Ser. 1, Vol. 46, Part 2, p. 1154; *OR*, Ser. 1, Vol. 47, Part 1, p. 933; Ledger Book, Record of Persons and Articles Employed for Transportation by the US Army Quartermaster, Little Rock, p. 63, March 1865, ASI; Property Returns, Box 1, Entry 27, Confederate Engineering Dept., Miscellaneous Papers, 1862–1865, RG 109, NARA; *OR*, Ser. 1, Vol. 5, p. 499.

2 *OR*, Ser. 2, Vol. 8, p. 425; *OR*, Ser. 1, Vol. 48, Part 2, pp. 77–78; Watkins, *Company Aytch*, p. 209.

3 *OR*, Ser. 1, Vol. 16, p. 165; Edwin Finch to [Richmond Finch?], March 23, 1865, Thirza Finch Diary and Letter Transcriptions, UM; General Order No. 27, April 18, 1865, Churchill's Division, CSA, General Order Book, FHS.

4 Sarah Jane Sams to Randolph Sams, February 3–March 25, 1865, Sarah Jane Sams Letter, USC; *OR*, Ser. 1, Vol. 49, Part 1, p. 43; *OR*, Ser. 4, Vol. 3, pp. 1050–1053.

5 Pryor, *Reminiscences of Peace and War*, p. 333; Wills, *Army Life of an Illinois Soldier*, p. 357; Diary of James A. Congleton, April 11, 1865, LC; McKim, *Soldier's Recollections*, p. 250; Mollie T. Mallay to her aunt, January 8, 1865, Mollie T. Mallay Letter, FHS; Federal Census of 1860, Free Schedule, Kentucky, Davies County, p. 111.

6 Eliza Cleveland, Case 20032, Tenn., Box 258, Settled Case Files, SCC, RG 217, NARA-II; Federal Census of 1860, Free Schedule, Tennessee, Claiborne County, p. 195; Memoir of Roger Hannaford, section 275, n.p., March 6, 1865, Roger Hannaford Papers, CHSL; Brady, *War upon the Land*, pp. 112–113; Wills, *Army Life of an Illinois Soldier*, p. 341.

7 Diary of James A. Congleton, February 18, 1865, LC; Gates, *Agriculture and the Civil War*, p. 124; Robert Winn to Martha Winn, March 13, 1865, Winn–Cook Family Papers, FHS; Wills, *Army Life of an Illinois Soldier*, p. 361; Trowbridge, *The South*, p. 563.

8 Anonymous [Orloff Dorman], Memoranda of Events that Transpired at Jacksonville, Florida, & in its Vicinity, 3: 112–115, Orloff M. Dorman Papers, LC; Laurentiza to Dear Brother, January 24, 30, 31, 1865, Christian D. Koch and Family Papers, LSU; Baumgartner, ed., *Blood and Sacrifice*, p. 202; *OR*, Ser. 1, Vol. 46, Part 1, p. 520; *OR*, Ser. 1, Vol. 48, Part 1, p. 1008.

9 Lyon and Lyon, *Reminiscences of the Civil War*, p. 201; James Stillwell to his wife, March 29, 1865, James Stillwell Papers, OHC; Gallagher, ed., *Fighting for the Confederacy*, p. 519; Longstreet, *From Manassas to Appomattox*, p. 620.

10 Varon, *Appomattox*, pp. 53–54; Authority File, Registrar, Item 1920.750, Wilmer McLean Table, CHMRC; Gallagher, ed., *Fighting for the Confederacy*, pp. 46–47, 544.

11 "From Charleston," *New York Daily Tribune*, April 18, 1865, p. 5; "From Salisbury, North Carolina," *Sacramento Daily Union*, April 26, 1865, p. 4; Kosto, *Hostages in the Middle Ages*, p. 200; Panayi, *Prisoners of Britain*, pp. 284–285; "Dr. Smith's Death," n.p., Bryon Family Papers, UMCP.

12 Recollections of Maria Southgate Hawes, p. 51, OCM; Margaret to Sister, April 10, 1865, Hall–Stakely Papers, ETHS; Litwack, *Been in the Storm So Long*, pp. 171–172; Anderson, ed., *Brokenburn*, pp. 342–344; no name to My Dear Kinsman, October 31, 1865, Carnot Bellinger Papers, ALA.

13 Houghton and Houghton, *Two Boys in the Civil War*, p. 54; Diaries of John Hemphill Simpson, April 30, 1865, May 3, 1865, May 24, 1865, SCHS; *OR*, Ser. 1, Vol. 48, Part 2, pp. 966–967.

14 Baumgartner, ed., *Blood and Sacrifice*, p. 225; McCarthy, *Detailed Minutiae*, p. 164; Burge, *Woman's Wartime Journal*, p. 49; Dana, *Recollections of the Civil War*, p. 266; Mohr and Winslow, eds., *Cormany Diaries*, p. 554; Ramold, *Baring the Iron Hand*, pp. 386–390.

15 Memoir of Margaret Stanly Beckwith, p. 31, VHS; James R. Slack to Ann Slack, April 19, 1865, James R. Slack Letters, ISL; Davis, ed., *Requiem for a Lost City*, pp. 4, 155; Andrews, *War-Time Journal*, pp. 258, 199.

16 Wright, *Southern Girl in '61*, pp. 244–245; H. Thompson to Anne, July 26, 1865, gift from Barbara Joyce to the author; Diaries of John Hemphill Simpson, May 8, 1865, SCHS; Susan C. Williams to Dear sister, May 30, 1866, Hackworth Collection, OSU.

17 OR, Ser. 1, Vol. 49, Part 2, p. 1002; Trowbridge, *The South*, p. 445; Giesberg, "Fortieth Congress," pp. 185–193; McKenzie, "'Oh! Ours Is a Deplorable Condition'," pp. 206–210, 214; Hurt, *Agriculture and the Confederacy*, p. 287.

18 Rhodes, ed., *All for the Union*, p. 235; Henry M. Bullitt to My Dear Sallie, July 3, 1865, Bullitt Family Papers–Oxmoor Collection, FHS; Andrews, *War-Time Journal*, p. 258; Smith, Smith, and Childs, eds., *Mason Smith Family Letters*, p. 195; Eugenia Bitting to Cade Gillespie, n.d. 1928, Mrs. Cade Drew Gillespie Papers, UMIS.

19 "Awful Condition of North Carolina," *Cincinnati Daily Enquirer*, May 31, 1865, n.p.; Myers, ed., *Children of Pride*, p. 603; Harvey Moorehead to Lavinia Newton, February 6, 1866, Lavinia Murdoch (Graham) Newton Letters, CHSL.

20 "A Trip to Culpeper," *Alexandria* [VA] *Gazette*, June 8, 1866, p. 4; Berger, *Forests Forever*, pp. 123–124, 128, 161; Lillard, *Great Forest*, p. 184; Muir, *Story of My Boyhood and Youth*, p. 313; Williams, *Americans and Their Forests*, pp. 240, 81, 238–239, 272–273.

21 "The South as It Is," *New York Times*, August 30, 1865, n.p.; Reid, *After the War*, p. 292; Diary of Edwin Knox, May 14, 1865, WIU; "The Fortifications around Richmond," *Richmond Dispatch*, July 11, 1866, n.p.

22 Diary of John M. Porter, p. 66, Octagon Hall and Kentucky Confederate Archives, Franklin, Kentucky; Anonymous [Orloff Dorman], Memoranda of Events that Transpired at Jacksonville, Florida, & in its Vicinity, 3: 504–505, Orloff M. Dorman Papers, LC; Frobel, *Civil War Diary of Anne S. Frobel*, p. 227; Brown, ed., *Reminiscences of Newton Cannon*, p. 73. Cf. Paskoff, "Measures of War," pp. 35–62, who argues that the war's damage to the region's cities has been exaggerated.

23 Engs and Brooks, eds., *Patriotic Duty*, pp. 380–381; Interview with John Franklin Smith, Bates County, Missouri, p. 10, American Life Histories, LC, http://rs6.loc.gov; Journal of Margaret Barton Crozier Ramsey, pp. 8, 16, UTK; Diary of Elvira Ascenith Scott, pp. 228–233, Western Historical Manuscript Collection, University of Missouri–Columbia.

24 Harvey Moorehead to Lavinia Newton, February 2, 1866, Lavinia Murdoch (Graham) Newton Letters, CHSL; Diary of John M. Porter, p. 66, Octagon Hall and Kentucky Confederate Archives, Franklin, Kentucky; Janney, *Remembering the Civil War*, p. 92; Neff, *Honoring the Civil War Dead*, pp. 126–130, 134; M. J. French to Colonel J. P. Lowe, May 30, 1868, Box 661, Entry 225, Consolidated Correspondence File, 1794–1915, Union Quartermaster Records, Records of the Office of the Quartermaster General, RG 92, NARA; Pryor, *Reminiscences of Peace and War*, pp. 385, 39, 131, 373.

25 Diary of John Houston Bills, August 26, 1865, UNC-SHC; Smith, Smith, and Childs, eds., *Mason Smith Family Letters*, p. 200; Burge, *Woman's Wartime Journal*, pp. 47–48; Trowbridge, *The South*, pp. 157–158.

26 "Condition of the South," *New York Herald*, July 14, 1865, p. 5; Diary of Anna Hasell Thomas, pp. 18–19, SCHS; "Condition of the South," *New York Herald*, July 14, 1865, p. 5. The reporter gave the wrong title for the poem, calling it "Ode to Liberty."

27 Dolan, *Commemorating the Irish Civil War*, p. 3; Botts, *Great Rebellion*, pp. viii, ix, 70, 114–116; Link, *Atlanta, Cradle of the New South*, pp. 87–89; Eliza Cleveland, Case 20032, Tenn., Box 258, Settled Case Files, SCC, RG 217, NARA-II.

28 Bodnar, *"Good War" in American Memory*, pp. 235–242; Lair, *Armed with Abundance*, pp. 4–5, 8–9; Faber, *Memory Battles of the Spanish Civil War*; Tunnard, *Southern Record*, pp. 125, 342–343; Taylor, *Destruction and Reconstruction*, pp. 60, 208–209; Watkins, *Company Aytch*, p. 41.

29 French, *Two Wars*, p. 320; Rable, *Damn Yankees!* pp. 131–141; Campbell, *When Sherman Marched North*, p. 103; Janney, *Remembering the Civil War*, pp. 84, 147; Ott, *Confederate Daughters*, pp. 131–137, 141.

30 Capt. Charles H. Deane to Brigadier Major General J. S. Donaldson, July 21, 1865, Box 14, Entry 225, Consolidated Correspondence File, 1794–1915, Records of the Office of the Quartermaster General, RG 92, NARA; Nell Key to My Dear Sallie, n.d. 1865, Bullitt Family Papers–Oxmoor Collection, FHS; *OR*, Ser. 1, Vol. 48, Part 2, pp. 966–967.

31 Wilson, *Business of Civil War*, pp. 196–197; R. J. Atkinson to Edwin Stanton, July 9, 1867, Box 324, Entry 225, Consolidated Correspondence File, 1794–1915, Records of the Office of the Quartermaster General, RG 92, NARA; Finding Aid, Tennessee General Claims Commission, 1868, TSLA; Rebel Claims, 1860–1869, LCTA.

32 Klingberg, *Southern Claims Commission*, pp. 55, 77, 157, 25, 89, 73, 77, 84–85, 92, 17, 102–103.

33 Klingberg, *Southern Claims Commission*, pp. 157–159, 76, 18; Lee, *Claiming the Union*, pp. 67–89, 90–112. When the states of Missouri and Kentucky submitted claims to the US government for war damages and expenses, the process was just as unpredictable; Sinisi, *Sacred Debts*, pp. 34–85, 86–131.

34 Klingberg, *Southern Claims Commission*, p. 185; 55th Congress, Second Session, Senate Report No. 435, Ravensworth Estate, January 12, 1898, Mary Custis Lee Papers, VHS; Gaughan, *Last Battle of the Civil War*, p. 190; Bynum, *Long Shadow of the Civil War*, p. 148; Storey, *Loyalty and Loss*, p. 235; Current, *Lincoln's Loyalists*, p. 195; Marshall, *Creating a Confederate Kentucky*, pp. 20, 94, 117. On the Lee family's lawsuit over Arlington plantation, see Gaughan, *Last Battle of the Civil War*.

35 Gordon, *Broken Regiment*, pp. 206–219, 228; Billings, *Hardtack and Coffee*, p. 380; Cozzens and Girardi, eds., *Military Memoirs of General John Pope*, pp. 132–133; Eugenia Bitting to Cade Gillespie, n.d. 1928, Mrs. Cade Drew Gillespie Papers, UMIS; Federal Census of 1860, Free Schedule, Georgia, Whitfield County, p. 69.

36 Worcester, *Passion for Nature*, pp. 13, 35, 68, 81–103, 121; Muir, *Story of My Boyhood and Youth*, p. 313; William D. Gale to William Polk, August 25, 1865, Leonidas Polk Papers, University of the South–Sewanee; Mary A. Houston to her sister, January 5, n.d. [1866], Mary A. Houston Letter, WIU; Campbell, *When Sherman Marched North*, pp. 103, 106.

37 Aldrich, *Building Resilience*, pp. 2, 150.

Works Cited

Primary Sources

Archives and Manuscripts Collections

Alabama Department of Archives and History
Carnot Bellinger Papers
Matthew P. Blue Family Papers
Israel Pickens Family Papers
Hardy Vickers Wooten Papers

Allegheny College, Meadville, Pennsylvania
Ida Tarbell Papers

Allen County, Indiana-Fort Wayne Historical Society
Diaries of J. M. Godown

Allen County, Ohio, Historical Society
Breese Family Letters
Civil War Diary of Lieutenant Robert Sample Dilworth, Edited by Carol Radebaugh

American Jewish Archives, Hebrew Union College
Autobiography of Philip Sartorius
Autobiography of J. D. Goldman

Arkansas History Commission
James L. Clements Papers

Arkansas Studies Institute, Center for Arkansas History and Culture
J. N. Heiskell Civil War Collection
Henry C. Lay Collection
Ledger Book, Record of Persons and Articles Employed for Transportation by the
    US Army Quartermaster, Little Rock

Miscellaneous Letter Collection
Milan W. Serl, Residence and Adventures in the South, 1860 to 1862
Statement by Citizens of Mississippi County, Arkansas, September 27, 1862

Atlanta History Center
Rawson-Collier-Harris Family Collection
Reverend John Wesley Stipe Papers

Bradley University, Peoria, Illinois
Civil War Diary of Daniel Burchard Allen
Civil War Letters of Daniel Burchard Allen

Chattanooga Public Library, Local History Section
Diary of W. C. Brown
Diary of Myra Adelaide Inman Carter
Timothy C. Cheney Papers
Clipping File

Chicago History Museum Research Center
Authority File, Registrar, Item 1920–750, Wilmer McLean Table
Reminiscences of Francelia Colby
Diary of Silas S. Huntley
Civil War Diaries of John Merrilies
Tobias C. Miller Diary and Letters

Cincinnati Historical Society Library
Roger Hannaford Papers
Lavinia Murdoch (Graham) Newton Letters
Susan Walker Papers

**Confederate Memorial Literary Society, under the management of the Virginia
   Historical Society**
Joseph Cloyd Collection
Lieutenant General Ewell to Brigadier General George Steuart, September 14–15,
   1863, by A. S. Pendleton
Charles D. Hill Collection
Harriet E. Johnson, Written for My Grandchildren, Vol. 40: n.p., in Historical
   Records of the United Daughters of the Confederacy, Women of the Confederacy,
   Compiled by Mildred Lewis Rutherford

Dallas Historical Society
John T. Coit Family Papers
William H. Kilpatrick Letters

Dayton, Ohio, Metro Library
Colonel Hiram Strong Papers

Dinsmore Homestead Foundation, Burlington, Kentucky
Recipe Book of Martha M. Dinsmore, 1829–1857

Duke University, David M. Rubenstein Rare Book and Manuscript Library
Jefferson Davis Papers
James Gordon Hackett Papers
Duncan McLaurin Papers
Person Family Papers
Joseph Belknap Smith Papers

East Tennessee Historical Society, Knoxville
Diary of Mary A. Dickinson
Hall-Stakely Papers
Sallie McDowell Moffett Papers

F. Brooke Whiting House, Cumberland, Maryland
James Whiting Plantation and Farm Instruction, Regulation, Record

Filson Historical Society, Louisville
Diary of Theodore Allen
Ansel Bement Letter
Bullitt Family Papers-Oxmoor Collection
Churchill's Division, CSA, General Order Book
Grigsby Collection
Mollie T. Mallay Letter
Diary of Thomas D. Phillip
Diary of James Pusard
Diary of Mary Elizabeth Shrewsbury Van Meter
Samuel T. Wells Papers
Winn-Cook Family Papers

Fredericksburg and Spotsylvania National Military Park
Citizens' Claims for Damages, Originals at Historic Court Records, Fredericksburg,
    Virginia

Gettysburg College, Special Collections and College Archives
Confederate Correspondence
G. W. Davison Letters
Stephen Allen Osborn Manuscript
John C. Tidball Papers

Rutherford B. Hayes Presidential Center, Fremont, Ohio
Mrs. Joseph Barrett, Memories of the Civil War

Historical Society of Western Pennsylvania
Lieutenant Colonel John I. Nevin Papers

Indiana State Library, Indianapolis
Letters to Zeralda Hood
Henry C. Marsh Letters and Diaries
James R. Slack Letters
Excerpts of Diary and Letter by Franklin P. Waggoner

Indiana State University at Terre Haute
Asa W. Marine Letters

Indiana University, Lilly Library
Houser Manuscripts

Johns Hopkins University, Milton S. Eisenhower Library
Diary of Lucy Rebecca Buck

Kentucky Historical Society, Frankfort
Scrogin and Haviland Letters
Journal of Ellen Kenton McGaughey Wallace, Wallace-Starling Family Diaries

Lancaster County, Pennsylvania, Historical Society
William G. Kendrick Letters, Compiled by David W. Bash

Lawrence County, Tennessee, Archives, Leoma
Civil War Collection
Rebel Claims, 1860–1869

Library of Congress, Manuscript Division
Chauncey E. Barton Letter, Miscellaneous Manuscripts
Diary of James A. Congleton
Custis-Lee Family Papers
David Anderson Deaderick Collection
Denby Family Papers
Orloff M. Dorman Papers
Samuel Downing Papers, Miscellaneous Manuscripts
Samuel Henry Eells Papers
Civil War Diary and Memoirs of Thomas Evans, Miscellaneous Manuscripts
Diary of John Newton Ferguson
Papers of Doctors J. M. and Esther H. Hawks
Diary of Fannie Page Hume
Joseph Christmas Ives Papers
Joseph E. Johnston to Robert E. Lee, May 28, 1861, Miscellaneous Manuscripts
Robert Livingston Papers
Diary of Mrs. W. W. Lord
William McAdoo Papers
John Singleton Mosby Papers
Margaret Lawrence (Lindsley) Ramsey Papers
Diary of Josephine Forney Roedil, Miscellaneous Manuscripts

Lincoln Museum Research Library, Fort Wayne, Indiana (now closed)
Correspondence of Isaac Bevier
Civil War Diary of John E. Wilkins

Louisiana State University, Hill Memorial Library
Priscilla Munnikhuysen Bond Papers
Christian D. Koch and Family Papers

Maury County, Tennessee, Archives
Civil War Stories, Oral History Project, 1976

National Archives and Records Administration, Washington, DC
Records of the Office of the Quartermaster General, Record Group 92
War Department Collection of Confederate Records, Record Group 109
Records of the Office of the Judge Advocate General, Court Martial Files, Record
    Group 153

National Archives and Records Administration-II, College Park, Maryland
Southern Claims Commission, Record Group 217

National Civil War Museum, Harrisburg, Pennsylvania
Bread Riot Letter

New York Public Library
Ely Family Letters

North Carolina State Archives
Wills and Estates Records, 1842–1848, Richmond County, North Carolina

**Notre Dame University, Hesburgh Libraries, Rare Books and Special
    Collections**
Read Family Correspondence

Oberlin College Archives
Elliott F. Grabill Papers

Octagon Hall and Kentucky Confederate Archives, Franklin, Kentucky
Diary of John M. Porter

Ohio History Connection, Columbus
Jane Hibberd Keefer Papers
Civil War Reminiscences of James Mitchell
William Oglevie Correspondence
William M. Parkinson Papers
Sarah Emily Ross Papers
James Stillwell Papers
Journal of George L. Wood

Old Courthouse Museum, Vicksburg, Mississippi
Champion Family Papers
Recollections of Maria Southgate Hawes
Civil War Diary of Dora Richards Miller

Ottawa County, Ohio, History Museum
Soldier's Life of Philo Pearce

Pennsylvania State Archives
Diary of Samuel A. Murray

Radcliffe College
Somerville and Howorth Family Papers

Sandusky, Ohio, Library, Archives Research Center
Horace Harper Bill Letters
James Fowler Chapman Papers

South Carolina Historical Society, Charleston
Confederate Miscellaneous Letters
Diaries of John Hemphill Simpson
Diary of Anna Hasell Thomas

Southern Illinois University–Edwardsville
Diary of William R. Townsend

Syracuse University, Manuscript Room
Diary of Albert M. Cook

Tennessee State Library and Archives
Douglass-Maney Family Papers
Finding Aid, Tennessee General Claims Commission, 1868

Texas State Library and Archives Commission
Records of the Methodist Episcopal Church, Quarterly Conference, Montgomery
   Circuit

Toledo-Lucas County Public Library, Local History Section
Hiram Root Collection

University of Georgia, Hargrett Rare Book and Manuscript Library
Howell Cobb Family Papers
Ellen Buchanan Screven Reminiscences

University of Kentucky-Lexington
Collins Family Papers

University of Maryland–College Park, Hornbake Library
Burhaus Family Papers
Byron Family Papers
Virginia Harrold Collection
Willis A. Pomeroy Papers
James F. Stepter Papers

University of Memphis, Special Collections
Hamner-Stacy Correspondence
Porter-Rice Family Papers

University of Michigan, William L. Clements Library
Aplin Family Papers
Thirza Finch Diary and Letter Transcriptions
James B. Pond Papers

University of Mississippi, Special Collections
Mrs. Cade Drew Gillespie Papers

University of Missouri-Columbia, Western Historical Manuscript Collection
Diary of Elvira Ascenith Scott

University of North Carolina-Chapel Hill, Southern Historical Collection, Louis Round Wilson Library
Diary of Samuel A. Agnew
John Houston Bills Papers
Diary of Kate S. Carney
J. F. H. Claiborne Papers
Gale and Polk Family Papers
William Gaston Papers
William H. Holcombe Diary and Autobiography
John Kimberly Papers
William King Papers
Lea Family Papers
Lenoir Family Papers
Jason Niles Papers
John Perkins Papers
Quitman Family Papers
Abraham Rencher Papers
Eliza Ann Marsh Robertson Papers
Sarah Lois Wadley Papers
Diary of Anita Dwyer Withers
Diary of Frances Woolfolk Wallace
Benjamin C. Yancey Papers

University of the South, Sewanee, Tennessee, Jessie Ball duPont Library
Leonidas Polk Papers

University of South Carolina, South Caroliniana Library
Mary Boykin Williams Harrison Ames, Childhood Recollections
Journal of Micajah Adolphus Clark
Cox and Chesnut Families Papers
Maxcy Gregg Papers
Samuel Wells Leland Papers
McLure Family Papers
Mabra Madden Papers
Palmer Family Papers
Sarah Jane Sams Letter

University of Southern Mississippi
Belcher Letters

University of Tennessee at Knoxville
Private Journal of Robert Houston Armstrong
Diary of Josephine H. Hooke
Diary of Mary L. Pearre
Journal of Margaret Barton Crozier Ramsey
Diary of Charles Henry Shriner

University of Texas at Austin, Dolph Briscoe Center for American History
Richard T. Archer Family Papers, Natchez Trace Collection
Mrs. John W. Wade, Recollections of an Octogenarian

University of Toledo, Ohio, Canaday Center
Diary of Cyrus Hussey

University of Virginia, Albert and Shirley Small Special Collections Library
Carr Family Papers
Murrell Family Papers

Virginia Historical Society
Charles Bates Papers
Memoir of Margaret Stanly Beckwith
Blanton Family Papers
Diary of Ann Webster Christian
Clarke Family Papers
James H. Gardner Papers
Gray Family Papers
Gwathmey Family Papers
Charles Kingsley Letter
Mary Custis Lee Papers
Recollections of Anna Clayton Logan

Lizzie Jackson Mann, Recollections of the Civil War, 1861 to '65
Munford Family Papers
Paulus Powell Papers
Memoir of Fanny W. Gaines Tinsley
Tompkins Family Papers

Virginia Military Institute
Henry H. Dedrick Civil War Letters
Fulkerson Family Papers
Michael G. Harman Civil War Papers
Johnson Family Papers

Virginia Polytechnic Institute and State University
Memoir of Archibald Atkinson, Jr.

Virginia State Library
Will Books, Powhatan County
Will Books, Prince Edward County

Washington and Jefferson College, Washington, Pennsylvania
George B. Caldwell Manuscript

Western Illinois University, Macomb, Illinois, Archives and Special Collections
Mary A. Houston Letter
Diary of Edwin Knox

Western Kentucky University, Bowling Green
Bevie Cain Letters
Diary of Johanna Louisa Underwood Nazro

Western Reserve Historical Society
Diary of Correl Smith
Cyrus H. Stockwell Papers
Franklin A. Wise Papers

Wisconsin Historical Society
Diary of Van Bennett, Van Bennett Papers

Wright State University, Dayton, Ohio
Diary of Oliver H. Protsman

Manuscripts Given to the Author
Doak Family Correspondence, gift from Dominica Leeds
Gibonney Letters, gift from Mark Baldwin
H. Thompson to Anne, July 26, 1865, gift from Barbara Joyce
Reuben Wickham to My Dear Wife, November 11, 1864, gift from Kristen
    Fuller

Primary Sources Online

American Civil War Homepage, Civil War Memories of Robert C. Carden, Company B, Sixteenth Tennessee Infantry, http://sunsite.utk.edu/civil-war

American Life Histories: Manuscripts from the Federal Writer's Project, 1936–1940, Library of Congress, http://rs6.loc.gov

Born in Slavery: Slave Narratives from the Federal Writers' Project, 1936 to 1938, Library of Congress, www.loc.gov

Letters of Private Newton Robert Scott, Civil War Letters, www.civilwarletters.com/letters_toc.html.

Letters of Seneca Thrall, Civil War Archive, www.civilwararchive.com/LETTERS/thrall1.htm

Ohio State University, Department of History, eHistory, ehistory.osu.edu
Civil War Letters of William Samuel Craig
Civil War Diary of Franklin Eldredge
Diary of Melville Cox Follett
Hackworth Collection
Civil War History of John Ritland

Tennessee Civil War Veterans Questionnaires
www.tngenweb.org/bledsoe/bdocs/htm
http://tn-roots.com/tncrockett/mililtary/quest/quest-index.html

United States Articles of War
www.freepages.military.rootsweb.com

Valley of the Shadow Project, University of Virginia, valley.lib.virginia.edu
Evans-Sibert Family Papers
Kersh Family Papers
Alexander H. H. Stuart Letters
McCue Family Papers
McFarland Family Papers
Diary of Joseph Waddell

Newspapers

Alexandria [VA] *Gazette*
[Little Rock] *Arkansas Weekly Gazette*
[Atlanta] *Southern Confederacy*
Augusta [GA] *Chronicle*
[Baltimore] *Sun*
Brooklyn Eagle
Charleston Mercury
Chattanooga Daily Rebel
Chicago Tribune
Cincinnati Daily Enquirer

Daily Columbus [GA] *Enquirer*
Dallas Herald
DeBow's Review
Fayetteville [NC] *Observer*
Harper's Weekly
Hillsborough [NC] *Recorder*
[Keene] *New Hampshire Sentinel*
Macon [GA] *Daily Telegraph*
Macon [GA] *Weekly Telegraph*
[Macon] *Georgia Weekly Telegraph*
Macon [GA] *Telegraph*
[Madison] *Wisconsin Patriot*
Mobile Register
Daily [New Orleans] *Delta*
Daily [New Orleans] *True Delta*
New York Daily Tribune
[New York] *Evening Post*
New York Herald
New York Times
Norwich [CT] *Morning Bulletin*
Philadelphia Inquirer
Providence [RI] *Evening Press*
Richmond Daily Dispatch
Richmond Dispatch
Richmond Examiner
Richmond Whig
Sacramento Daily Union
San Francisco Bulletin
[San Francisco] *Daily Evening Bulletin*
Southern Illustrated News
Staunton [VA] *Spectator*
Tri-weekly [Houston] *Telegraph*
Weekly [Jackson] *Mississippian*

Primary Sources in Print

Adams, Charles Francis. *Charles Frances Adams: 1835–1915: An Autobiography, with a Memorial Address Delivered November 17, 1915, by Henry Cabot Lodge*. Boston, MA: Houghton Mifflin, 1916.

Anderson, Donald, ed. *When War Becomes Personal: Soldiers' Accounts from the Civil War to Iraq*. Iowa City, IA: University of Iowa Press, 2008.

Anderson, Ephraim McD. *Memoirs Historical and Personal; Including the Campaigns of the First Missouri Confederate Brigade*. St. Louis, MO: Times Printing Co., 1868.

Anderson, John Q., ed. *Brokenburn: The Journal of Kate Stone, 1861–1868*. With a New Introduction by Drew Gilpin Faust. Baton Rouge, LA: Louisiana State University Press, 1995.

Andrews, Eliza Frances. *The War-Time Journal of a Georgia Girl, 1864–1865.* New York, NY: D. Appleton & Company, 1908.

Armstrong, Orland Kay. *Old Massa's People: The Old Slaves Tell Their Story.* Indianapolis, IN: The Bobbs-Merrill Company, Publishers, 1931.

Aughey, John H. *Tupelo.* Chicago, IL: Rhodes & McClure, 1905.

Avirett, James Battle. *The Old Plantation: How We Lived in Great House and Cabin before the War.* New York, NY: F. Tennyson Neely Co., 1901.

Barber, Lucius W. *Army Memoirs of Lucius W. Barber, Company D, 15th Illinois Volunteer Infantry: May 24, 1861, to September 30, 1865.* Chicago, IL: J. M. W. Jones Stationery & Printing Company, 1894.

Baumgartner, Richard A., ed. *Blood and Sacrifice: The Civil War Journal of a Confederate Soldier.* Huntington, WV: Blue Acorn Press, 1994.

Beattie, Donald W., Rodney M. Cole, and Charles G. Waugh, eds. *A Distant War Comes Home: Maine in the Civil War Era.* Camden, ME: Down East Books, 1996.

Becker, Carl M., and Ritchie Thomas, eds. *Hearth and Knapsack: The Ladley Letters, 1857–1880.* Athens, OH: Ohio University Press, 1988.

Berlin, Ira, Marc Favreau, and Steven F. Miller, eds. *Remembering Slavery: African Americans Talk about Their Personal Experiences of Slavery and Freedom.* New York, NY: The New Press in Association with the Library of Congress, 1998.

Berlin, Jean V., ed. *A Confederate Nurse: The Diary of Ada W. Bacot, 1860–1863.* Columbia, SC: University of South Carolina Press, 1994.

Billings, John D. *Hardtack and Coffee: The Unwritten Story of Army Life.* Introduction by William L. Shea. Illustrated by Charles W. Reed. Lincoln, NE: University of Nebraska Press, 1993.

Blackford, W. W. *War Years with Jeb Stuart.* Baton Rouge, LA: Louisiana State University Press, 1993.

Bloodgood, J. D. *Personal Reminiscences of the War.* New York, NY: Hunt & Eaton, 1893.

Bonner, Robert E. *The Soldier's Pen: Firsthand Impressions of the Civil War.* New York, NY: Hill & Wang, 2006.

Botkin, B. A., ed. *Lay My Burden Down: A Folk History of Slavery.* Chicago, IL: University of Chicago Press, 1945.

Botts, John Minor. *The Great Rebellion: Its Secret History, Rise, Progress, and Disastrous Failure.* New York, NY: Harper & Brothers, Publishers, 1866.

Branch, Mary Polk. *Memoirs of a Southern Woman "Within the Lines," and a Genealogical Record.* Chicago, IL: Joseph G. Branch, 1912.

Brown, Campbell H., ed. *The Reminiscences of Sergeant Newton Cannon, from Holograph Material Provided by His Grandson, Samuel M. Fleming, Jr.* Introduction by Stanley F. Horn. Franklin, TN: Carter House Association, 1963.

Browning, Judkin, and Michael Thomas Smith, eds. *Letters from a North Carolina Unionist: John A. Hedrick to Benjamin S. Hedrick, 1862–1865.* Raleigh, NC: Division of Archives and History, North Carolina Department of Cultural Resources, 2001.

Burge, Mrs. Thomas [Dolly Sumner Lunt]. *A Woman's Wartime Journal: An Account of the Passage over a Georgia Plantation of Sherman's Army on the March to the Sea* ... New York, NY: The Century Company, 1918.

Burke, Pauline Wilcox. *Emily Donelson of Tennessee*. Vol. I. Richmond, VA: Garrette & Massie, Incorporated, 1941.

Calhoun, Richard J., ed. *Witness to Sorrow: The Antebellum Autobiography of William J. Grayson*. Columbia, SC: University of South Carolina Press, 1990.

Cash, William M., and Lucy Somerville Howorth, eds. *My Dear Nellie: The Civil War Letters of William L. Nugent to Eleanor Smith Nugent*. Jackson, MS: University Press of Mississippi, 1977.

Cashin, Joan E., ed. *Our Common Affairs: Texts from Women in the Old South*. Baltimore, MD: Johns Hopkins University Press, 1996.

Chamberlaine, William W. *Memoirs of the Civil War between the Northern and Southern Sections of the United States of America, 1861 to 1865*. Washington, DC: Press of Byron S. Adams, 1912.

Chapman, R. D. *A Georgia Soldier in the Civil War, 1861–1865*. Houston, TX: By the Author, 1923.

Clark, Olynthus B., ed. *Alexander G. Downing's Civil War Diary*. Des Moines, IA: The Historical Department of Iowa, 1916.

Coffin, Charles Carleton. *Four Years of Fighting: A Volume of Personal Observation with the Army and Navy*. Boston, MA: Ticknor & Fields, 1866.

Confederate Receipt Book: A Compilation of Over One Hundred Receipts Adapted to the Times. Richmond, VA: West and Johnson, 1863.

Cooper-Hopley, Catherine. *Life in the South: From the Commencement of the War by a Blockaded British Subject*. Vol. I. London: Chapman & Hall, 1863.

Cox, Jacob Dolson. *Military Reminiscences of the Civil War, Vol. I: April 1861– November 1863*. New York, NY: Charles Scribner's Sons, 1900.

Cozzens, Peter, and Robert I. Girardi, eds. *The Military Memoirs of General John Pope*. Chapel Hill, NC: University of North Carolina Press, 1998.

Craig, Tom Moore, ed. *Upcountry South Carolina Goes to War: Letters of the Anderson, Brockman, and Moore Families, 1853–1865*. Introduction by Melissa Walker and Tom Moore Craig. Columbia, SC: University of South Carolina Press, 2009.

Dana, Charles A. *Recollections of the Civil War, with the Leaders at Washington and in the Field in the Sixties*. New York, NY: D. Appleton & Company, 1898.

Davis, Robert Scott, ed. *Requiem for a Lost City: A Memoir of Civil War Atlanta and the Old South, by Sarah "Sallie" Conley Clayton*. Macon, GA: Mercer University Press, 1999.

Davis, William C. Editor and Author of the Introduction. *Diary of a Confederate Soldier: John S. Jackman of the Orphan Brigade*. Columbia, SC: University of South Carolina Press, 1990.

Dayton, Ruth Woods, ed. *The Diary of a Confederate Soldier, James E. Hall*. N.p., Mrs. Elizabeth Teter Phillips, 1961.

Donald, David Herbert, ed. *Gone for a Soldier: The Civil War Memoirs of Private Alfred Bellard, from the Alec Thomas Archives*. Boston, MA: Little, Brown & Company, 1975.

Doubleday, Abner. *Campaigns of the Civil War: Chancellorsville and Gettysburg.* With a New Introduction by Gary W. Gallagher. New York, NY: Da Capo Press, 1994.

East, Charles, ed. *The Civil War Diary of Sarah Morgan*. Athens, GA: University of Georgia Press, 1991.

Eggleston, George Cary. *A Rebel's Recollections*. New York, NY: Hurd & Houghton, 1875.

Emerson, W. Eric, and Karen Stokes, eds. *A Confederate Englishman: The Civil War Letters of Henry Wemyss Feilden*. Columbia, SC: University of South Carolina Press, 2013.

Engs, Robert F., and Corey M. Brooks, eds. *Their Patriotic Duty: The Civil War Letters of the Evans Family of Brown County, Ohio*. New York, NY: Fordham University Press, 2007.

Eppes, Susan Bradford. *Through Some Eventful Years*. With an Introduction and Index by Joseph D. Cushman, Jr. Gainesville, FL: University of Florida Press, 1968.

Everson, Guy R., and Edward H. Simpson, Jr., eds. *Far, Far from Home: The Wartime Letters of Dick and Tally Simpson, Third South Carolina Volunteers.* Oxford: Oxford University Press, 1994.

Felton, Rebecca Latimer. *Country Life in Georgia in the Days of My Youth.* Atlanta, GA: Index Printing Company, 1919.

Fletcher, William A. *Rebel Private: Front and Rear, Memoirs of a Confederate Soldier*. Introduction by Richard Wheeler. Afterword by Vallie Fletcher Taylor. New York, NY: Dutton, 1995.

Ford, Arthur P., and Marion Johnstone Ford. *Life in the Confederate Army: Being Personal Experiences of a Private Soldier in the Confederate Army, and Some Experiences and Sketches of Southern Life*. New York, NY: The Neale Publishing Company, 1905.

Foroughi, Andrea R., ed. *Go If You Think It Your Duty: A Minnesota Couple's Civil War Letters*. St. Paul, MN: Minnesota Historical Society Press, 2008.

Fountain, Sarah M., ed. *Sisters, Seeds, and Cedars: Rediscovering Nineteenth-Century Life through Correspondence from Rural Arkansas and Alabama*. Conway, AR: VCA Press, 1995.

Fremantle, Arthur James Lyon. *Three Months in the Southern States, April–June 1863*. Mobile, AL: S. H. Goetzel, 1864.

French, Samuel Gibbs. *Two Wars: An Autobiography of Gen. Samuel G. French*. Nashville, TN: Confederate Veteran, 1901.

Frobel, Anne S. *The Civil War Diary of Anne S. Frobel*. With Introduction and Appendices by Mary H. and Dallas M. Lancaster. McLean, VA: EPM Publications, 1992.

Fry, Anna M. Gayle. *Memories of Old Cahaba*. Nashville, TN: Publishing House of the ME Church, South, 1908.

Gallagher, Gary W., ed. *Fighting for the Confederacy: The Personal Recollections of General Edward Porter Alexander*. Chapel Hill, NC: University of North Carolina Press, 1989.

Geer, J. J. *Beyond the Lines; or, A Yankee Prisoner Loose in Dixie*. With an Introduction by Reverend Alexander Clark. Philadelphia, PA: J. W. Daughaday, Publishers, 1863.

Gienapp, William E., ed. *The Civil War and Reconstruction: A Documentary Collection*. New York, NY: W. W. Norton & Company, 2001.

Goodloe, Albert Theodore. *Confederate Echoes: A Voice from the South in the Days of Secession and of the Southern Confederacy*. Nashville, TN: Smith & Lamar, 1907.

Some Rebel Relics from the Seat of War. Nashville, TN: Printed for the Author, 1893.

Gordon, John B. *Reminiscences of the Civil War*. New York, NY: Charles Scribner's Sons, 1903.

Graham, C. R., ed. *Under Both Flags: A Panorama of the Great Civil War as Represented in Story, Anecdote, Adventure, and the Romance of Reality*. New York, NY: Skyhorse Publishing, 2013.

Grant, Ulysses S. *Memoirs and Selected Letters: Personal Memoirs of U. S. Grant and Selected Letters, 1839–1865*. New York, NY: The Library of America, 1990.

Green, Fletcher M., ed. *The Lides Go South ... and West: The Records of a Planter Migration in 1835*. Columbia, SC: University of South Carolina Press, 1952.

Green, Rena Maverick, ed. *Memoirs of Mary A. Maverick, Arranged by Mary A. Maverick and Her Son George Madison Maverick*. San Antonio, TX: Alamo Printing Co., 1921.

Gwin, Minrose C. Editor and Author of Introduction. *Cornelia Peake McDonald, A Woman's Civil War: A Diary, with Reminiscences of the War, from March 1862*. Madison, WI: University of Wisconsin Press, 1992.

Hassler, William W., ed. *The General to His Lady: The Civil War Letters of William Dorsey Pender to Fanny Pender*. Chapel Hill, NC: University of North Carolina Press, 1965.

Hopkins, William P. *The Seventh Regiment: Rhode Island Volunteers in the Civil War, 1862–1865*. Providence, RI: The Providence Press, 1903.

Houghton, W. R., and M. B. Houghton. *Two Boys in the Civil War and After*. Montgomery, AL: The Paragon Press, 1912.

Howe, M. A. DeWolfe, ed. *Marching with Sherman: Passages from the Letters and Campaign Diaries of Henry Hitchcock, Major and Assistant Adjutant General of Volunteers, November 1864–May 1865*. Introduction by Brooks S. Simpson. Lincoln, NE: University of Nebraska Press, 1995.

Hughes, Nathaniel Cheairs, Jr., ed. *The Civil War Memoir of Philip Daingerfield Stephenson, DD, Private, Company K, 13th Arkansas Volunteer Infantry and Loader, Piece No. 4, 5th Company, Washington Artillery, Army of the Tennessee, CSA*. Conway, AR: University of Central Arkansas Press, 1995.

Hughes, Thomas. *A Boy's Experience in the Civil War, 1860–1865*. N.p., 1904.

Ingraham, J. H. *The South-west*. Vol. 2. New York, NY: Harper & Brothers, 1835.

Jaquette, Henrietta Stratton, ed. *Letters of a Civil War Nurse: Cornelia Hancock, 1863–1865*. Introduction to the Bison Books Edition by Jean V. Berlin. Lincoln, NE: University of Nebraska Press, 1998.

Kemble, Frances Anne. *Journal of a Residence on a Georgian Plantation in 1838–1839*. New York, NY: Harper & Brothers, Publishers, 1864.

Kent, Arthur A., ed. *Three Years with Company K: Sergeant Austin C. Stearns, Company K, 13th Massachusetts Infantry (Deceased).* Rutherford, NJ: Fairleigh Dickinson University Press, 1976.

King, Charles. *From School to Battle-Field: A Story of the War Days.* Philadelphia, PA: J. B. Lippincott Company, 1899.

Knox, Thomas Wallace. *Camp-Fire and Cotton-Field: Southern Adventure in Time of War.* New York, NY: Blelock & Company, 1865.

Le Duc, William G. *This Business of War: Recollections of a Civil War Quartermaster.* Foreword by Adam E. Scher. St. Paul, MN: Minnesota Historical Society Press, 2004.

Leib, Charles. *Nine Months in the Quartermaster's Department, or, The Chances for Making a Million.* Cincinnati, OH: Moore, Wilstach, Keys, 1862.

Leon, Louis. *Diary of a Tar Heel Confederate Soldier.* Charlotte, NC: Stone Publishing Company, 1913.

Livermore, Mary A. *My Story of the War: A Woman's Narrative of Four Years Personal Experience.* Hartford, CT: A. D. Worthington & Company, 1889.

The Story of My Life, Or, The Sunshine and Shadow of Seventy Years. Hartford, CT: A. D. Worthington & Co., 1897.

Longstreet, James. *From Manassas to Appomattox: Memoirs of the Civil War in America.* New York, NY: Konecky & Konecky, 1992.

Looby, Christopher, ed. *The Complete Civil War Journal and Selected Letters of Thomas Wentworth Higginson.* Chicago, IL: University of Chicago Press, 2000.

Loughborough, Mary Webster. *My Cave Life in Vicksburg, with Letters of Trial and Travel.* Vicksburg, MS: Vicksburg and Warren County Historical Society, 1990.

Lynch, Charles H. *The Civil War Diary 1862–1865 of Charles H. Lynch, 18th Conn. Vols.* Hartford, CT: Privately Printed, 1915.

Lyon, William Penn, and Adelia C. D. Lyon. *Reminiscences of the Civil War.* San Jose, CA: Press of Muirson & Wright, 1907.

Marshall, Jeffrey D., ed. *A War of the People: Vermont Civil War Letters.* Foreword by Edwin C. Bearss. Hanover, NH: University Press of New England, 1999.

Martineau, Harriet. *Retrospect of Western Travel.* Vol. 2. London: Saunders & Otley, 1838.

McCarthy, Carlton. *Detailed Minutiae of Soldier Life in the Army of Northern Virginia, 1861–1865.* Richmond, VA: Carlton McCarthy and Company, 1882.

McClellan, George B. *McClellan's Own Story: The War for the Union, the Soldiers Who Fought It, and His Relations to It and Them.* New York, NY: Charles L. Webster & Company, 1887.

McDonald, Archie P., ed. *Make Me a Map of the Valley: The Civil War Journal of Stonewall Jackson's Topographer.* Foreword by T. Harry Williams. Dallas, TX: Southern Methodist University Press, 1973.

McFadden, Janice Bartlett Reeder, comp. *Aunt and the Soldier Boys from Cross Creek Village, Pennsylvania, 1856–1867.* Wooster, OH: By the Compiler, 1991.

McGuire, Judith White. *Diary of a Southern Refugee during the War, by a Lady of Virginia*. 2nd edn. New York, NY: E. J. Hale & Son, 1868.

McKim, Randolph H. *A Soldier's Recollections: Leaves from the Diary of a Young Confederate*. London: Longman's, Green, & Co., 1910.

Menge, W. Springer, and J. August Shimrak, eds. *The Civil War Notebook of Daniel Chisholm: A Chronicle of Daily Life in the Union Army 1864–1865*. New York, NY: Ballantine Books, 1989.

Mitchel, Cora. *Reminiscences of the Civil War*. Providence, RI: Snow & Farnham Co., 1916.

Mohr, James C., and Richard E. Winslow III, eds. *The Cormany Diaries: A Northern Family in the Civil War*. Pittsburgh, PA: University of Pittsburgh Press, 1982.

Moore, Edward A. *The Story of a Cannoneer under Stonewall Jackson, in Which Is Told the Part Taken by the Rockbridge Artillery in the Army of Northern Virginia*. With Introduction by Capt. Robert E. Lee, Jr., and Hon. Henry St. George Tucker. Lynchburg, VA: J. P. Bell Company, Inc., 1910.

Moore, John Hammond, ed. *A Plantation Mistress on the Eve of the Civil War: The Diary of Keziah Goodwyn Hopkins Brevard*. Columbia, SC: University of South Carolina Press, 1993.

Muir, John. *The Story of My Boyhood and Youth, and a Thousand-Mile Walk to the Gulf*. Boston, MA: Houghton Mifflin Company, 1916.

Murfree, Mary Noailles. *Where the Battle Was Fought: A Novel*. Boston, MA: Houghton Mifflin & Company, 1884.

Murr, Erika L., ed. *A Rebel Wife in Texas: The Diary and Letters of Elizabeth Scott Neblett, 1852–1864*. Baton Rouge, LA: Louisiana State University Press, 2001.

Myers, Robert Manson, ed. *The Children of Pride: Selected Letters of the Family of the Rev. Dr. Charles Colcock Jones from the Years 1860–1868, with the Addition of Several Previously Unpublished Letters*. New Abridged Edn. New Haven, CT: Yale University Press, 1984.

Neese, George M. *Three Years in the Confederate Horse Artillery*. New York, NY: The Neale Publishing Company, 1911.

Paxton, John Gallatin. *Memoir and Memorials: Elisha Franklin Paxton, Brigadier-General, CSA: Composed of His Letters from Camp and Field While an Officer in the Confederate Army, with an Introductory and Connecting Narrative Collected and Arranged by his Son, John Gallatin Paxton*. New York, NY: The Neale Publishing Company, 1907.

Perdue, Charles L., Jr., Thomas E. Barden, and Robert K. Phillips, eds. *Weevils in the Wheat: Interviews with Virginia Ex-Slaves*. Charlottesville, VA: University Press of Virginia, 1976.

Phillips, J. R. *The Story of My Life*. Tuscaloosa, AL: n.p., 1923.

Plake, Kate. *The Southern Husband Outwitted by His Union Wife*. Philadelphia, PA: Printed for the Authoress by Moore and Brother, 1868.

Porcher, Francis Peyre. *Resources of the Southern Fields and Forests, Medical, Economical, and Agricultural*. Charleston, SC: n.p., 1863.

Pringle, Elizabeth W. Allston. *Chronicles of Chicora Wood*. New York, NY: Charles Scribner's Sons, 1922.

Pryor, Mrs. Roger A. *Reminiscences of Peace and War*. Rev. and enlarged edn. New York, NY: The Macmillan Company, 1905.

Putnam, Sallie A. B. *Richmond During the War: Four Years of Personal Observation*. New York, NY: G. W. Carleton & Co., Publishers, 1867.

Radigan, Emily N., ed. *Desolating This Fair Country: The Civil War Diary and Letters of Lt. Henry C. Lyon, 34th New York*. Foreword by Michael Radigan. Jefferson, NC: McFarland & Company, Inc., Publishers, 1999.

Reyburn, Philip J., and Terry L. Wilson, eds. *"Jottings from Dixie": The Civil War Dispatches of Sergeant Major Stephen F. Fleharty, USA*. Baton Rouge, LA: Louisiana State University Press, 1999.

Rhodes, Robert Hunt, ed. *All for the Union: The Civil War Diary and Letters of Elisha Hunt Rhodes*. Foreword by Geoffrey C. Ward. New York, NY: Orion Books, 1991.

Robertson, Mary D., ed. *Lucy Breckinridge of Grove Hill: The Journal of a Virginia Girl, 1862–1864*. Columbia, SC: University of South Carolina Press, 1994.

Robson, John S. *How a One-Legged Rebel Lives: Reminiscences of the Civil War*. Durham, NC: Educator Company Printers and Binders, 1898.

Rosengarten, Theodore, ed. *Tombee: Portrait of a Cotton Planter, with the Journal of Thomas B. Chaplin (1822–1890)*. New York, NY: William Morrow & Company, Inc., 1986.

Saxon, Elizabeth Lyle. *A Southern Woman's War Time Reminiscences*. Memphis, TN: Pilcher Printing Co., 1905.

Schlesinger, Sr., Arthur M., ed. *The Cotton Kingdom: A Traveller's Observations on Cotton and Slavery in the American Slave States, by Frederick Law Olmsted*. Introduction by Lawrence N. Powell. New York, NY: The Modern Library, 1984.

Sheridan, P. H. *Personal Memoirs of P. H. Sheridan, General United States Army*. Introduction by Jeffry Wert. New York, NY: Da Capo Press, 1992.

Sherman, William T. *Memoirs*. Introduction by Ian M. Cuthbertson. New York, NY: Barnes & Noble, 2005.

Simon, John Y., ed. *The Personal Memoirs of Julia Dent Grant*. With an Introduction by Bruce Catton, and "The First Lady as an Author," by Ralph G. Newman. New York, NY: G. P. Putnam's Sons, 1975.

Simons, John Hume. *The Planter's Guide and Family Book of Medicine*. Charleston, SC: M'Carter and Allen, 1848.

Small, Abner R. *The Road to Richmond: The Civil War Memoirs of Major Abner R. Small of the Sixteenth Maine Volunteers, Together with the Diary Which He Kept When He Was a Prisoner of War*. With an Introduction by Earl J. Hess. New York, NY: Fordham University Press, 2000.

Smedes, Susan Dabney. *Memorials of a Southern Planter*. Baltimore, MD: Cushings & Bailey, 1887.

Smith, Barbara Bentley, and Nina Bentley Baker, eds. *"Burning Rails as We Please": The Civil War Letters of William Garrigues Bentley, 104th Ohio Volunteer Infantry*. Jefferson, NC: McFarland & Company, Inc., Publishers, 2004.

Smith, Daniel E. Huger, Alice R. Huger Smith, and Arney R. Childs, eds. *Mason Smith Family Letters, 1860–1868.* Columbia, SC: University of South Carolina Press, 1950.

Smith, George G. *Leaves from a Soldier's Diary: The Personal Record of Lieutenant George G. Smith, Co. C, 1st Louisiana [US] Regiment Infantry.* Putnam, CT: George G. Smith, 1906.

Spence, John C. *A Diary of the Civil War.* Murfreesboro, TN: The Rutherford County Historical Society, 1993.

Stiles, Robert. *Four Years under Marse Robert.* New York, NY: The Neale Publishing Company, 1904.

Stillwell, Leander. *The Story of a Common Soldier of Army Life in the Civil War, 1861–1865.* 2nd edn. N.p.: Franklin Hudson, 1920.

Strother, David H. "Personal Recollections of the War," *Harper's New Monthly Magazine* 33 (September 1866): 409–428.

"Rural Pictures," *Harper's Magazine* 20 (January 1860): 166–180.

Taulbert, Clifton T. *Once Upon a Time When We Were Colored.* New York, NY: Penguin Books, 1995.

Taylor, Richard. *Destruction and Reconstruction: Personal Experiences of the Late War.* New York, NY: D. Appleton & Company, 1879.

Townsend, George Alfred. *Rustics in Rebellion: A Yankee Reporter on the Road to Richmond, 1861–65.* With an Introduction by Lida Mayo. Chapel Hill, NC: University of North Carolina Press, 1950.

Trowbridge, J. T. *The South: A Tour of Its Battle-Fields and Ruined Cities.* New York, NY: Arno Press and The New York Times, 1969.

Tunnard, W. H. *A Southern Record: The History of the Third Regiment, Louisiana Infantry.* Baton Rouge, LA: Printed for the Author, 1866.

United Confederate Veterans of Arkansas. *Confederate Women of Arkansas in the Civil War, 1861–65, Memorial Reminiscences.* Little Rock, AR: H. G. Pugh Printing Co., 1907.

Venet, Wendy Hamand, ed. *Sam Richards's Civil War Diary: A Chronicle of the Atlanta Home Front.* Athens, GA: University of Georgia Press, 2009.

Warwick, Rick, comp. *Williamson County: The Civil War Years Revealed through Letters, Diaries, and Memoirs.* Franklin, TN: The Heritage Foundation of Franklin and Williamson County, 2006.

Watkins, Sam. *Company Aytch, or, A Side Show of the Big Show and Other Sketches.* Edited and with an Introduction by M. Thomas Inge. New York, NY: Plume, 1999.

Wiley, Bell Irvin, ed. *Fourteen Hundred and Ninety-One Days in the Confederate Army: A Journal Kept by W. W. Heartsill.* Jackson, TN: McCowat-Mercer Press, 1953.

Wilkeson, Frank. *Recollections of a Private Soldier in the Army of the Potomac.* New York, NY: G. P. Putnam's Sons, 1887.

Willett, Charles E., ed. *A Union Soldier Returns South: The Civil War Letters and Diary of Alfred C. Willett, 113th Ohio Volunteer Infantry.* Introduction and Epilogue by Mary Ann (Willett) Litton. Johnson City, TN: The Overmountain Press, 1994.

Wills, Charles W. *Army Life of an Illinois Soldier*. Washington, DC: Globe Printing Company, 1906.

Winn, Sallie Kiger, ed. *The Civil War Diary of Mrs. Henrietta Fitzhugh Barr, 1862–1863, Ravenswood, Virginia (West Virginia)*. Marietta, OH: Hyde Brothers Printing Company, n.d.

Winther, Oscar Osburn. Editor and Author of Introduction. *With Sherman to the Sea: The Civil War Letters, Diaries, and Reminiscences of Theodore F. Upson*. Edited and with an Introduction by Oscar Osburn Winther. Bloomington, IN: Indiana University Press, 1958.

Wittenberg, Eric J., ed. *One of Custer's Wolverines: The Civil War Letters of Brevet Brigadier General James H. Kidd, 6th Michigan Cavalry*. Kent, OH: Kent State University Press, 2000.

Worsham, John W. *One of Jackson's Foot Cavalry: His Experience and What He Saw during the War, 1861–1865*. New York, NY: The Neale Publishing Company, 1912.

Wright, Louise Wigfall. *A Southern Girl in '61: The War-Time Memories of a Confederate Senator's Daughter*. New York, NY: Doubleday, Page & Company, 1905.

Wyeth, John A. *With Sabre and Scalpel: The Autobiography of a Soldier and Surgeon*. New York, NY: Harper & Brothers, 1914.

Wynne, Lewis N., and Robert A. Taylor, eds. *This War So Horrible: The Civil War Diary of Hiram Smith Williams*. Tuscaloosa, AL: University of Alabama Press, 1993.

Government Documents and Publications

Army Regulations, Adopted for the Use of the Army of the Confederate States, in Accordance with Late Acts of Congress. Richmond, VA: West and Johnston, 1861.

Federal Census Returns, Free Schedules, Slave Schedules. Ancestry.com.

Kennedy, Joseph G. *Agriculture of the United States in 1860, Compiled from the Original Returns of the Eighth Census, Under the Direction of the Secretary of the Interior*. Washington, DC: Government Printing Office, 1864.

Matthews, James M. *Public Laws of the Confederate States of America, First Congress, 1862–1864*. Richmond, VA: R. M. Smith, 1862–1864.

Public Laws of the Confederate States of America, Passed at the First Session of the First Congress, 1862. Richmond, VA: R. M. Smith, 1862.

The Statutes at Large of the Confederate States of America ... February 8, 1861 to ... February 18, 1862, Inclusive. Richmond, VA: R. M. Smith, 1864.

Regulations for the Army of the Confederate States, 1863, with a Full Index. Richmond, VA: West and Johnston, 1863.

Revised United States Army Regulations of 1861, with an Appendix Containing the Changes and Laws Affecting Army Regulations and Articles of War to June 25, 1863. Washington, DC: Government Printing Office, 1863.

Scott, Henry Lee. *Military Dictionary*. New York, NY: D. Van Nostrand, 1861.

United States War Department. *The War of the Rebellion: A Compilation of the Official Records of the Union and Confederate Armies*. 128 vols. Washington, DC: U.S. Government Printing Office, 1880–1901.

Secondary Sources in Print

Adams, Michael C. C. *Living Hell: The Dark Side of the Civil War*. Baltimore, MD: Johns Hopkins University Press, 2014.

Akhtar, Salman. *Objects of Our Desire: Exploring Our Intimate Connections with the Things around Us*. New York, NY: Harmony Books, 2005.

Aldrich, Daniel P. *Building Resilience: Social Capital in Post-Disaster Recovery*. Chicago, IL: University of Chicago Press, 2012.

Alexander, Frederick Warren. *Stratford Hall and the Lees Connected with Its History*. Oak Grove, VA: By the Author, 1912.

Allmendinger, David F., *Ruffin: Family and Reform in the Old South*. Oxford: Oxford University Press, 1990.

Alotta, Robert I. *Civil War Justice: Union Army Executions under Lincoln*. Shippensburg, PA: White Mane Publishing Co., Inc., 1989.

Altschuler, Glenn C., and Stuart M. Blumin. *Rude Republic: Americans and Their Politics in the Nineteenth Century*. Princeton, NJ: Princeton University Press, 2000.

Alvesson, Mats. *Understanding Organizational Culture*. London: Sage, 2002.

Anderson, Jennifer L. *Mahogany: The Costs of Luxury in Early America*. Cambridge, MA: Harvard University Press, 2012.

Anderson, Margo. *The American Census: A Social History*. 2nd edn. New Haven, CT: Yale University Press, 2015.

Ash, Stephen V. *When the Yankees Came: Conflict and Chaos in the Occupied South, 1861–1865*. Chapel Hill, NC: University of North Carolina Press, 1995.

A Year in the South, 1865: The True Story of Four Ordinary People Who Lived through the Most Tumultuous Twelve Months in American History. New York, NY: Perennial, 2004.

Baggett, James Alex. *The Scalawags: Southern Dissenters in the Civil War and Reconstruction*. Baton Rouge, LA: Louisiana State University Press, 2003.

Barton, Michael. *Goodmen: The Character of Civil War Soldiers*. University Park, PA: Pennsylvania State University Press, 1981.

Batchelor, Jennie, and Cora Kaplan. "Introduction." In Jennie Batchelor and Cora Kaplan, eds., *Women and Material Culture, 1660–1830*, pp. 2–7. New York, NY: Palgrave Macmillan, 2007.

Becker, Jason. *Hungry Ghosts: Mao's Secret Famine*. New York, NY: Free Press, 1996.

Bensel, Richard Franklin. *Yankee Leviathan: The Origins of Central State Authority in America, 1859–1877*. Cambridge: Cambridge University Press, 1990.

Berger, John J. *Forests Forever: Their Ecology, Restoration, and Protection*. With a Foreword by Charles E. Little. San Francisco, CA: The Center for American Places at Columbia College Chicago in Association with Forests Forever Foundation, 2008.

Beringer, Richard E., Herman Hattaway, Archer Jones, and William N. Still, Jr. *Why the South Lost the Civil War*. Athens, GA: University of Georgia Press, 1986.

Berry, Wendell. *The Unsettling of America: Culture and Agriculture*. San Francisco, CA: Sierra Club Books, 1977.

Bishir, Catherine W. *Southern Built: American Architecture, Regional Practice.* Charlottesville, VA: University of Virginia Press, 2006.

Blanton, DeAnne, and Lauren M. Cook. *They Fought Like Demons: Women Soldiers in the American Civil War.* Stroud: Sutton Publishing, 2005.

Bledsoe, Andrew S. *Citizen-Officers: The Union and Confederate Volunteer Junior Officer Corps in the American Civil War.* Baton Rouge, LA: Louisiana State University Press, 2015.

Bodnar, John. *The "Good War" in American Memory.* Baltimore, MD: Johns Hopkins University Press, 2010.

Bollnow, O. F. *Human Space.* Translated by Christine Shuttleworth. Edited by Joseph Kohlmaier. London: Hyphen Press, 2011.

Bonds, Russell S. *Stealing the General: The Great Locomotive Chase and the First Medal of Honor.* Yardley, PA: Westholme Publishing, 2007.

Bonner, Michael Brem. *Confederate Political Economy: Creating and Managing a Southern Corporatist Nation.* Baton Rouge, LA: Louisiana State University Press, 2016.

Borch, Fred L., "Lore of the Corps: The First Manual for Courts-Martial," *The Army Lawyer* (June 2016): 1–3.

Brady, Lisa M. *War upon the Land: Military Strategy and the Transformation of Southern Landscapes during the American Civil War.* Athens, GA: University of Georgia Press, 2012.

Bray, Chris. *Court-Martial: How Military Justice Has Shaped America from the Revolution to 9/11 and Beyond.* New York, NY: W. W. Norton & Company, 2016.

Bridges, Hal. *Lee's Maverick General: Daniel Harvey Hill.* New York, NY: McGraw-Hill, 1961.

Brooke, John, Julia C. Strauss, and Greg Anderson, eds. *State Formations: Global Histories and Cultures of Statehood.* Cambridge: Cambridge University Press, 2018.

Burke, Diane Mutti. *On Slavery's Border: Missouri's Small-Slaveholding Households, 1815–1865.* Athens, GA: University of Georgia Press, 2010.

Burton, Orville Vernon. *In My Father's House Are Many Mansions: Family and Community in Edgefield, South Carolina.* Chapel Hill, NC: University of North Carolina Press, 1985.

Bynum, Victoria E. *The Free State of Jones: Mississippi's Longest Civil War.* Chapel Hill, NC: University of North Carolina Press, 2001.

  The Long Shadow of the Civil War: Southern Dissent and Its Legacies. Chapel Hill, NC: University of North Carolina Press, 2010.

Camp, Stephanie M. H. *Closer to Freedom: Enslaved Women and Everyday Resistance in the Plantation South.* Chapel Hill, NC: University of North Carolina Press, 2004.

Campbell, Jacqueline Glass. *When Sherman Marched North from the Sea: Resistance on the Confederate Home Front.* Chapel Hill, NC: University of North Carolina Press, 2003.

Campbell, James W. P., and Will Pryce. *Brick: A World History.* London: Thames & Hudson, 2003.

Capers, Gerald M. *Occupied City: New Orleans under the Federals, 1862–1865.* Lexington, KY: University of Kentucky Press, 1965.

Carnahan, Burrus M. *Lincoln on Trial: Southern Civilians and the Law of War.* Louisville, KY: University Press of Kentucky, 2010.

Carter, Mason C., Robert C. Kellison, and R. Scott Wallinger. *Forestry in the US South: A History.* Foreword by Steven Anderson. Baton Rouge, LA: Louisiana State University Press, 2016.

Casdorph, Paul D. *Prince John Magruder: His Life and Campaigns.* New York, NY: John Wiley & Sons, Inc., 1996.

Cashin, Joan E. "Into the Trackless Wilderness: The Refugee Experience in the Civil War." In *A Woman's War: Southern Women, Civil War, and the Confederate Legacy,* edited by Edward D. C. Campbell, Jr., and Kym S. Rice, pp. 29–53. Richmond, VA: Museum of the Confederacy and the University Press of Virginia, 1996.

First Lady of the Confederacy: Varina Davis's Civil War. Cambridge, MA: Harvard University Press, 2006.

"Hungry People in the Wartime South: Civilians, Armies, and the Food Supply." In *Weirding the War: Stories from the Civil War's Ragged Edges,* edited by Stephen Berry, pp. 160–175. Athens, GA: University of Georgia Press, 2011.

"Trophies of War: Material Culture in the Civil War Era," *Journal of the Civil War Era* 1 (September 2011): 339–367.

Cecelski, David S. *The Fire of Freedom: Abraham Galloway and the Slaves' Civil War.* Chapel Hill, NC: University of North Carolina Press, 2012.

Cecil-Fronsman, Bill. *Common Whites: Class and Culture in Antebellum North Carolina.* Lexington, KY: University Press of Kentucky, 1992.

Chetail, Vincent, and Peter Haggenmacher, eds. *Vattel's International Law in a 21st Century Perspective.* Leiden: Martinus Nijhoff Publishers, 2011.

Coffman, Edward M. *The Old Army: A Portrait of the American Army in Peacetime, 1784–1898.* Oxford: Oxford University Press, 1986.

Counihan, Carole M. "Introduction." In *Food and Gender: Identity and Power,* edited by Carole M. Counihan and Steven L. Kaplan, pp. 4–7. New York, NY: Harwood Academic Publishers, 1998.

Cozzens, Peter. *General John Pope: A Life for the Nation.* Urbana, IL: University of Illinois Press, 2000.

Craigie, William A., and James R. Halbert, eds. *A Dictionary of American English on Historical Principles.* Vol. 3. Chicago, IL: University of Chicago Press, 1968.

Crofts, Daniel W. *Old Southampton: Politics and Society in a Virginia County, 1834–1869.* Charlottesville, VA: University Press of Virginia, 1992.

Reluctant Confederates: Upper South Unionists in the Secession Crisis. Chapel Hill, NC: University of North Carolina Press, 1989.

Cunningham, H. H. *Doctors in Gray: The Confederate Medical Service.* Baton Rouge, LA: Louisiana State University Press, 1958.

Current, Richard Nelson. *Lincoln's Loyalists: Union Soldiers from the Confederacy.* Oxford: Oxford University Press, 1991.

Davis, William C. *Jefferson Davis: The Man and His Hour.* New York, NY: HarperCollins Publishers, 1991.

Degler, Carl N. *The Other South: Southern Dissenters in the Nineteenth Century.* New York, NY: Harper & Row, Publishers, 1974.

DeGruccio, Michael. "Letting the War Slip through our Hands: Material Culture and the Weakness of Words in the Civil War Era." In *Weirding the War: Stories from the War's Ragged Edges*, edited by Stephen Berry, pp. 15–35. Athens, GA: University of Georgia Press, 2011.

Diaz, George T. *Border Contraband: A History of Smuggling across the Rio Grande.* Austin, TX: University of Texas Press, 2015.

Dilbeck, D. H. *A More Civil War: How the Union Waged a Just War.* Chapel Hill, NC: University of North Carolina Press, 2016.

Dolan, Anne. *Commemorating the Irish Civil War: History and Memory, 1923–2000.* Cambridge: Cambridge University Press, 2003.

Donald, David Herbert. *Lincoln.* New York, NY: Simon & Schuster, 1995.

Downs, Jim. *Sick from Freedom: African-American Illness and Suffering during the Civil War and Reconstruction.* Oxford: Oxford University Press, 2012.

Doyle, Don H., ed. *Secession as an International Phenomenon: From America's Civil War to Contemporary Separatist Movements.* Athens, GA: University of Georgia Press, 2010.

Drake, Brian Allen, ed. *The Blue, the Gray, and the Green: Toward an Environmental History of the Civil War.* Athens, GA: University of Georgia Press, 2015.

Durrill, Wayne K. *War of Another Kind: A Southern Community in the Great Rebellion.* Oxford: Oxford University Press, 1990.

Dyer, Gwynne. *War.* New York, NY: Crown Publishers, Inc., 1985.

Dyer, Thomas G. *Secret Yankees: The Union Circle in Confederate Atlanta.* Baltimore, MD: Johns Hopkins University Press, 1999.

Eby, Cecil D. *Hungary at War: Civilians and Soldiers in World War II.* University Park, PA: Pennsylvania State University Press, 1998.

Eckert, Ralph Lowell. *John Brown Gordon: Soldier, Southerner, American.* Baton Rouge, LA: Louisiana State University Press, 1989.

Edwards, Laura F. *The People and Their Peace: Legal Culture and the Transformation of Inequality in the Post-Revolutionary South.* Chapel Hill, NC: University of North Carolina Press, 2009.

Scarlett Doesn't Live Here Anymore: Southern Women in the Civil War Era. Urbana, IL: University of Illinois Press, 2000.

Eicher, John H., and David J. Eicher. *Civil War High Commands.* Foreword by John Y. Simon. Palo Alto, CA: Stanford University Press, 2001.

Elshtain, Jean Bethke. *Women and War.* Chicago, IL: University of Chicago Press, 1995.

Escott, Paul D., *After Secession: Jefferson Davis and the Failure of Confederate Nationalism.* Baton Rouge, LA: Louisiana State University Press, 1978.

Military Necessity: Civil-Military Relations in the Confederacy. Westport, CT: Praeger Security International, 2006.

Faber, Sebastiaan. *Memory Battles of the Spanish Civil War: History, Fiction, Photography.* Nashville, TN: Vanderbilt University Press, 2017.

Faust, Drew Gilpin. *The Creation of Confederate Nationalism: Ideology and Identity in the Civil War South.* Baton Rouge, LA: Louisiana State University Press, 1988.

Mothers of Invention: Women of the Slaveholding South in the American Civil War. Chapel Hill, NC: University of North Carolina Press, 1996.

Feis, William B. *Grant's Secret Service: The Intelligence War from Belmont to Appomattox.* Lincoln, NE: University of Nebraska Press, 2002.

Fellman, Michael. *Citizen Sherman: A Life of William Tecumseh Sherman.* New York, NY: Random House, 1995.

Inside War: The Guerilla Conflict in Missouri during the American Civil War. Oxford: Oxford University Press, 1989.

Fett, Sharla M. *Working Cures: Healing, Health, and Power on Southern Slave Plantations.* Chapel Hill, NC: University of North Carolina Press, 2002.

Fickle, James E. *Green Gold: Alabama's Forests and Forest Industries.* Tuscaloosa, AL: University of Alabama Press, co-published with the Alabama Forestry Foundation, 2014.

Fiege, Mark. *The Republic of Nature: An Environmental History of the United States.* Seattle, WA: University of Washington Press, 2012.

Fishel, Edwin C. *The Secret War for the Union: The Untold Story of Military Intelligence in the Civil War.* Boston, MA: Houghton Mifflin Company, 1996.

Fisher, John C. and Carol Fisher. *Food in the American Military: A History.* Jefferson, NC: McFarland and Company, Inc., Publishers, 2011.

Fisher, Noel C. *War at Every Door: Partisan Politics and Guerrilla Violence in East Tennessee, 1860–1869.* Chapel Hill, NC: University of North Carolina Press, 1997.

Fladeland, Betty. *James Gillespie Birney: Slaveholder to Abolitionist.* Ithaca, NY: Cornell University Press, 1955.

Fletcher, Nichola, *Charlemagne's Tablecloth: A Piquant History of Feasting.* New York, NY: St. Martin's Press, 2004.

Foner, Eric. *The Fiery Trial: Abraham Lincoln and American Slavery.* New York, NY: W. W. Norton & Company, 2010.

Frank, Lisa Tendrich. *The Civilian War: Confederate Women and Union Soldiers during Sherman's March.* Baton Rouge, LA: Louisiana State University Press, 2015.

Frankel, Noralee. *Freedom's Women: Black Women and Families in Civil War Era Mississippi.* Bloomington, IN: Indiana University Press, 1999.

Freehling, William W. *The South vs. The South: How Anti-Confederate Southerners Shaped the Course of the Civil War.* Oxford: Oxford University Press, 2001.

Freidel, Frank. *Francis Lieber, Nineteenth-Century Liberal.* Baton Rouge, LA: Louisiana State University Press, 1947.

Fuller, A. James. "The Last True Whig: John Bell and the Politics of Compromise in 1860." In *The Election of 1860 Reconsidered,* edited by A. James Fuller, pp. 103–139. Kent, OH: Kent State University Press, 2012.

Gallagher, Gary W. *The Confederate War: How Popular Will, Nationalism, and Military Strategy Could Not Stave Off Defeat.* Cambridge, MA: Harvard University Press, 1997.

Gardner, Sarah E. *Blood and Irony: Southern White Women's Narratives of the Civil War, 1861–1937*. Chapel Hill, NC: University of North Carolina Press, 2004.

Garrett, Elisabeth Donaghy. *At Home: The American Family, 1750–1870*. New York, NY: Harry N. Abrams, Inc., 1990.

Gates, Paul W. *Agriculture and the Civil War*. New York, NY: Alfred A. Knopf, 1965.

Gaughan, Anthony J. *The Last Battle of the Civil War: United States versus Lee, 1861–1883*. Baton Rouge, LA: Louisiana State University Press, 2011.

Gelernter, Mark. *A History of American Architecture: Buildings in Their Cultural and Technological Context*. Manchester: Manchester University Press, 2001.

Gibson, Craig. *Behind the Front: British Soldiers and French Civilians, 1914–1918*. Cambridge: Cambridge University Press, 2014.

Giesberg, Judith. "The Fortieth Congress, Southern Women, and the Gender Politics of Postwar Occupation." In *Occupied Women: Gender, Military Occupation, and the American Civil War*, edited by LeeAnn Whites and Alecia P. Long, pp. 185–193. Baton Rouge, LA: Louisiana State University Press, 2009.

Glassie, Henry. *Vernacular Architecture*. Bloomington, IN: Indiana University Press, 2000.

Glatthaar, Joseph T. *General Lee's Army: From Victory to Collapse*. New York, NY: Free Press, 2008.

Glover, Lorri. *Southern Sons: Becoming Men in the New Nation*. Baltimore, MD: Johns Hopkins University Press, 2007.

Goff, Richard D. *Confederate Supply*. Durham, NC: Duke University Press, 1969.

Gordon, Lesley J. *A Broken Regiment: The 16th Connecticut's Civil War*. Baton Rouge, LA: Louisiana State University Press, 2014.

Green, Harvey. *Wood: Craft, Culture, History*. New York, NY: Viking, 2006.

Griffith, Lucille, and George Henry Clay Rowe, "Fredericksburg's Political Hostages: The Old Capitol Journal of George Henry Clay Rowe," *Virginia Magazine of History and Biography* 72 (October 1964): 395–429.

Grimsley, Mark. *The Hard Hand of War: Union Military Policy toward Southern Civilians, 1861–1865*. Cambridge: Cambridge University Press, 1995.

"Success and Failure in Civil War Armies: Clues from Organizational Culture." In *Warfare and Culture in World History*, edited by Wayne E. Lee, pp. 115–141. New York, NY: New York University Press, 2011.

Gudmestad, Robert H. *Steamboats and the Rise of the Cotton Kingdom*. Baton Rouge, LA: Louisiana State University Press, 2011.

Hagerman, Edward. *The American Civil War and the Origins of Modern Warfare: Ideas, Organization, and Field Command*. Bloomington, IN: Indiana University Press, 1988.

Hahn, Steven. *A Nation under Our Feet: Black Political Struggles in the Rural South from Slavery to the Great Migration*. Cambridge, MA: Harvard University Press, 2003.

Hain, Pamela Chase. *A Confederate Chronicle: The Life of a Civil War Survivor*. Columbia, MO: University of Missouri Press, 2005.

Hajdinjak, Marko. *Smuggling in Southeast Europe: The Yugoslav Wars and the Development of Regional Criminal Networks in the Balkans*. Sofia: Center for the Study of Democracy, 2002.

Hansen, Karen V. *A Very Social Time: Crafting Community in Antebellum New England*. Berkeley, CA: University of California Press, 1994.

Harris, J. William. *Plain Folk and Gentry in a Slave Society: White Liberty and Black Slavery in Augusta's Hinterlands*. Middletown, CT: Wesleyan University Press, 1985.

Harrison, Kimberly. *The Rhetoric of Rebel Women: Civil War Diaries and Confederate Persuasion*. Carbondale, IL: Southern Illinois University Press, 2013.

Harrison, Lowell H. and James C. Klotter. *A New History of Kentucky*. Lexington, KY: University Press of Kentucky, 1997.

Hazen, Margaret Hindle, and Robert M. Hazen. *Keepers of the Flame: The Role of Fire in American Culture, 1775–1925*. Princeton, NJ: Princeton University Press, 1992.

Herrera, Ricardo A. *For Liberty and the Republic: The American Citizen as Soldier, 1775–1861*. New York, NY: New York University Press, 2015.

Hess, Earl J. *The Civil War in the West: Victory and Defeat from the Appalachians to the Mississippi*. Chapel Hill, NC: University of North Carolina Press, 2012.

Field Armies and Fortifications in the Civil War: Eastern Campaigns, 1861–1864. Chapel Hill, NC: University of North Carolina Press, 2005.

Hess, Karen. *The Carolina Rice Kitchen: The African Connection*. Columbia, SC: University of South Carolina Press, 1992.

Hickey, Donald R. *The War of 1812: A Forgotten Conflict*. Urbana, IL: University of Illinois Press, 1990.

Hickman, Nollie. *Mississippi Harvest: Lumbering in the Longleaf Pine Belt, 1840–1915*. Montgomery, AL: Paragon Press, 1962.

Hilliard, Sam Bowers. *Hog Meat and Hoecake: Food Supply in the Old South, 1840–1860*. With a Foreword by James C. Cobb. Athens, GA: University of Georgia, 2014.

Hitt, Michael D. *Charged with Treason: Ordeal of Four Hundred Mill Workers during Military Operations in Roswell, Georgia, 1864–1865*. Monroe, NY: Library Research Associates, Inc., 1992.

Hoffer, Williamjames Hull. *To Enlarge the Machinery of Government: Congressional Debates and the Growth of the American State, 1858–1891*. Baltimore, MD: Johns Hopkins University Press, 2007.

Horowitz, Roger. *Putting Meat on the American Table: Taste, Technology, Transformation*. Baltimore, MD: Johns Hopkins University, 2006.

Humphreys, Margaret. *Marrow of Tragedy: The Health Crisis of the American Civil War*. Baltimore, MD: Johns Hopkins University Press, 2013.

Hurt, R. Douglas. *Agriculture and the Confederacy*. Chapel Hill, NC: University of North Carolina Press, 2015.

Huston, James A. *The Sinews of War: Army Logistics, 1775–1953*. Washington, DC: Office of the Chief of Military History, United States Army, 1966.

Ierley, Merritt. *Open House: A Guided Tour of the American Home, 1637–Present*. New York, NY: Henry Holt & Company, 1999.

Iserson, Kenneth V. *Death to Dust: What Happens to Dead Bodies*. 2nd edn. Tucson, AZ: Galen Press, Ltd., 2001.

Jabour, Anya. *Scarlett's Sisters: Young Women in the Old South*. Chapel Hill, NC: University of North Carolina Press, 2007.

Jaffee, David. *A New Nation of Goods: The Material Culture of Early America*. Philadelphia, PA: University of Pennsylvania Press, 2010.

Janney, Caroline E. *Remembering the Civil War: Reunion and the Limits of Reconciliation*. Chapel Hill, NC: University of North Carolina Press, 2013.

Jimerson, Randall C. *The Private Civil War: Popular Thought during the Sectional Conflict*. Baton Rouge, LA: Louisiana State University Press, 1988.

Johnson, Timothy D. *Winfield Scott: The Quest for Military Glory*. Lawrence, KS: University Press of Kansas, 1998.

Jordan, Richard N. *Trees and People: Forestland Ecosystem and Our Future*. Washington, DC: Regnery Publisher, 1994.

Judd, Richard W. *Second Nature: An Environmental History of New England*. Amherst, MA: University of Massachusetts Press, 2014.

Kastenberg, Joshua E. *Law in War, War as Law: Brigadier General Joseph Holt and the Judge Advocate General's Department in the Civil War and Early Reconstruction, 1861–1865*. Durham, NC: Carolina Academic Press, 2011.

Kennett, Lee. *Sherman: A Soldier's Life*. New York, NY: HarperCollins Publishers, 2001.

Klingberg, Frank W. *The Southern Claims Commission*. Berkeley, CA: University of California Press, 1955.

Knight, H. Jackson. *Confederate Invention: The Story of the Confederate States Patent Office and Its Inventors*. Baton Rouge, LA: Louisiana State University Press, 2011.

Knight, Lucian Lamar. *A Standard History of Georgia and Georgians*. Vol. 5. Chicago, IL: The Lewis Publishing Company, 1917.

Komer, Robert W. *Bureaucracy Does Its Thing: Institutional Constraints on US–GVN Performance in Vietnam, A Report Prepared for Defense Advanced Research Projects Agency*. Santa Monica, CA: Rand Corporation, 1972.

Kosto, Adam J. *Hostages in the Middle Ages*. Oxford: Oxford University Press, 2012.

Kricher, John. *A Field Guide to Eastern Forests in North America*. Boston, MA: Houghton Mifflin Company, 1988.

Lair, Meredith H. *Armed with Abundance: Consumerism and Soldiering in the Vietnam War*. Chapel Hill, NC: University of North Carolina Press, 2011.

Latimer, Jon. *1812: War with America*. Cambridge, MA: Harvard University Press, 2007.

Lee, Susanna Michele. *Claiming the Union: Citizenship in the Post-Civil War South*. Cambridge: Cambridge University Press, 2014.

Lerner, Gerda. *The Grimké Sisters from South Carolina: Rebels against Slavery*. Boston, MA: Houghton Mifflin, 1967.

Lewis, David. *Impulse: Why We Do What We Do Without Knowing Why We Do It*. Cambridge, MA: Harvard University Press, 2013.

Lillard, Richard G. *The Great Forest*. New York, NY: Alfred A. Knopf, 1947.

Linderman, Gerald F. *Embattled Courage: The Experience of Combat in the American Civil War*. New York, NY: The Free Press, 1987.

Link, William A. *Atlanta, Cradle of the New South: Race and Remembering in the Civil War's Aftermath*. Chapel Hill, NC: University of North Carolina Press, 2013.

Litwack, Leon F. *Been in the Storm So Long: The Aftermath of Slavery*. New York, NY: Alfred A. Knopf, 1980.

Lonn, Ella. *Foreigners in the Confederacy*. Chapel Hill, NC: University of North Carolina Press, 1940.

Desertion during the Civil War. New York, NY: The Century Company, 1928.

Lowenthal, David. *George Perkins Marsh, Prophet of Conservation*. Foreword by William Cronon. Seattle, WA: University of Washington Press, 2000.

Loyd, Anthony. *My War Gone By, I Miss It So*. New York, NY: Atlantic Monthly Press, 1999.

Lupold, John S. and Thomas L. French, Jr. *Bridging Deep South Rivers: The Life and Legend of Horace King*. Athens, GA: University of Georgia Press, 2004.

MacClancy, Jeremy. *Consuming Culture: Why You Eat What You Eat*. New York, NY: Henry Holt & Company, 1992.

Manning, Chandra. *What This Cruel War Was Over: Soldiers, Slavery, and the Civil War*. New York, NY: Alfred A. Knopf, 2007.

Marks, Stuart A. *Southern Hunting in Black and White: Nature, History, and Ritual in a Carolina Community*. Princeton, NJ: Princeton University Press, 1991.

Marshall, Anne E. *Creating a Confederate Kentucky: The Lost Cause and Civil War Memory in a Border State*. Chapel Hill, NC: University of North Carolina Press, 2010.

Martin, Ann Smart. *Buying into the World of Goods: Early Consumers in Backcountry Virginia*. Baltimore, MD: Johns Hopkins University Press, 2008.

Marvel, William. *Burnside*. Chapel Hill, NC: University of North Carolina Press, 1991.

Massey, Mary Elizabeth. *Bonnet Brigades*. New York, NY: Alfred A. Knopf, 1966.

Ersatz in the Confederacy: Shortages and Substitutes on the Southern Homefront. With a New Introduction by Barbara L. Bellows. Columbia, SC: University of South Carolina Press, 1993.

Refugee Life in the Confederacy. Baton Rouge, LA: Louisiana State University Press, 1964.

McCaslin, Richard B. *Tainted Breeze: The Great Hanging at Gainesville, Texas, 1862*. Baton Rouge, LA: Louisiana State University Press, 1994.

McCurry, Stephanie. *Confederate Reckoning: Power and Politics in the Civil War South*. Cambridge, MA: Harvard University Press, 2010.

McDaniel, Rick. *An Irresistible History of Southern Food: Four Centuries of Black-Eyed Peas, Collard Greens, and Whole Hog Barbecue*. Charleston, SC: The History Press, 2011.

McKenzie, Robert Tracy. *Lincolnites and Rebels: A Divided Town in the American Civil War*. Oxford: Oxford University Press, 2006.

"'Oh! Ours Is a Deplorable Condition': The Economic Impact of the Civil War in Upper East Tennessee." In *The Civil War in Appalachia: Collected Essays*, edited by Kenneth W. Noe and Shannon H. Wilson, pp. 119–226. Knoxville, TN: University of Tennessee Press, 1997.

McNeill, William H. *The Pursuit of Power: Technology, Armed Force, and Society since AD 1000*. Chicago, IL: University of Chicago Press, 1982.

McPhee, John. *The Pine Barrens*. New York, NY: Farrar, Straus, & Giroux, 1968.

McWilliams, James E. *A Revolution in Eating: How the Quest for Food Shaped America*. New York, NY: Columbia University Press, 2005.

Meier, Kathryn Shively. *Nature's Civil War: Common Soldiers and the Environment in 1862 Virginia*. Chapel Hill, NC: University of North Carolina Press, 2013.

Mennell, Stephen. *All Manners of Food: Eating and Taste in England and France from the Middle Ages to the Present*. Oxford: Basil Blackwell, 1985.

Merriam-Webster's Collegiate Dictionary. 11th edn. Springfield, MA: Merriam-Webster, Incorporated, 2003.

Merridale, Catherine. *Ivan's War: Life and Death in the Red Army, 1939–1945*. New York, NY: Metropolitan Books, 2006.

Mitchell, Reid. *Civil War Soldiers*. New York, NY: Penguin Books, 1988.

Mohr, Clarence L. *On the Threshold of Freedom: Masters and Slaves in Civil War Georgia*. Baton Rouge, LA: Louisiana State University Press, 2001.

Moneyhon, Carl H. "David O. Dodd, the 'Boy Martyr' of Arkansas: The Growth and Use of a Legend," *Arkansas Historical Quarterly* 74 (Fall 2015): 203–230.

Murrell Taylor, Amy. *The Divided Family in Civil War America*. Chapel Hill, NC: University of North Carolina Press, 2005.

Myers, Barton A. *Rebels against the Confederacy: North Carolina's Unionists*. Cambridge: Cambridge University Press, 2014.

Nash, Gary B. *The Unknown American Revolution: The Unruly Birth of Democracy and the Struggle to Create America*. New York, NY: Viking, 2005.

Neely, Mark E., Jr. *The Civil War and the Limits of Destruction*. Cambridge, MA: Harvard University Press, 2007.

The Fate of Liberty: Abraham Lincoln and Civil Liberties. Oxford: Oxford University Press, 1991.

Southern Rights: Political Prisoners and the Myth of Confederate Constitutionalism. Charlottesville, VA: University Press of Virginia, 1999.

Neff, John R. *Honoring the Civil War Dead: Commemoration and the Problem of Reconciliation*. Lawrence, KS: University Press of Kansas, 2005.

Nelson, Megan Kate. *Ruin Nation: Destruction and the American Civil War*. Athens, GA: University of Georgia, 2012.

Noe, Kenneth W. *Reluctant Rebels: The Confederates Who Joined the Army after 1861*. Chapel Hill, NC: University of North Carolina Press, 2010.

O'Brien, Paul, and Lynn Hudson Parsons, eds. *The Home-Front War: World War II and American Society*. Westport, CT: Greenwood Press, 1995.

O'Grada, Cormac. *Famine: A Short History*. Princeton, NJ: Princeton University Press, 2009.

Ott, Victoria E. *Confederate Daughters: Coming of Age during the Civil War*. Carbondale, IL: Southern Illinois University Press, 2008.

Outland, Robert B., III. *Tapping the Pines: The Naval Stores Industry in the American South*. Baton Rouge, LA: Louisiana State University Press, 2004.

Panayi, Panikos. *Prisoners of Britain: German Civilian and Combatant Internees during the First World War*. Manchester: Manchester University Press, 2012.

Parker, Geoffrey. *Global Crisis: War, Climate Change, and Catastrophe in the Seventeenth Century*. New Haven, CT: Yale University Press, 2013.

Parrish, T. Michael. *Richard Taylor, Soldier Prince of Dixie*. Chapel Hill, NC: University of North Carolina Press, 1992.

Paskoff, Paul F. "Measures of War: A Quantitative Examination of the Civil War's Destructiveness in the Confederacy," *Civil War History* 54 (March 2008): 35–62.

Pauley, Michael J. *Unreconstructed Rebel: The Life of General John McCausland, CSA*. Charleston, WV: Pictorial Histories Publishing Co., Inc., 1992.

Percival, John. *The Great Famine: Ireland's Potato Famine*. Foreword by Ian Gibson. New York, NY: Viewer Books, 1995.

Perrow, Charles. *Complex Organizations: A Critical Essay*. 3rd edn. New York, NY: Random House, 1986.

Proctor, Tammy M. *Civilians in a World at War, 1914–1918*. New York, NY: New York University Press, 2010.

Pryor, Elizabeth Brown. *Clara Barton, Professional Angel*. Philadelphia, PA: University of Pennsylvania Press, 1987.

Reading the Man: A Portrait of Robert E. Lee through His Private Letters. New York, NY: Viking Press, 2007.

Pyne, Stephen J. *America's Fires: A Historical Context for Policy and Practice*. Durham, NC: Forest History Society, 2010.

Fire in America: A Cultural History of Wildland and Rural Fire. Princeton, NJ: Princeton University Press, 1982.

Quiroz, Alfonso W. *Corrupt Circles: A History of Unbound Graft in Peru*. Baltimore, MD: Johns Hopkins University Press, 2008.

Rable, George C., *Civil Wars: Women and the Crisis of Southern Nationalism*. Urbana, IL: University of Illinois Press, 1989.

The Confederate Republic: A Revolution against Politics. Chapel Hill, NC: University of North Carolina Press, 1994.

Damn Yankees! Demonization and Defiance in the Confederate South. Baton Rouge, LA: Louisiana State University Press, 2015.

Fredericksburg! Fredericksburg! Chapel Hill, NC: University of North Carolina Press, 2002.

Ramold, Steven J. *Baring the Iron Hand: Discipline in the Union Army*. DeKalb, IL: Northern Illinois University Press, 2010.

Reardon, Carol. *With a Sword in One Hand and Jomini in the Other: The Problem of Military Thought in the Civil War North*. Chapel Hill, NC: University of North Carolina Press, 2012.

Rice, Kym S., and Edward D. C. Campbell, Jr., eds. *A Woman's War: Southern Women, Civil War, and the Confederate Legacy*. Richmond, VA: Museum of the Confederacy and the University Press of Virginia, 1996.

Richardson, Ruth. *Death, Dissection, and the Destitute*. 2nd edn. Chicago, IL: University of Chicago Press, 2000.

Ries, Heinrich, and Henry Leighton. *History of the Clay-Working Industry in the United States*. New York, NY: John Wiley & Sons, 1909.

Risch, Erna. *Quartermaster Support of the Army: A History of the Corps 1775–1939*. Washington, DC: Center of Military History, United States Army, 1989.

Ritchie, Carson I. A. *Food in Civilization: How History Has Been Affected by Human Tastes.* New York, NY: Beaufort Books, Inc., 1981.

Robertson, Ben. *Red Hills and Cotton: An Upcountry Memory.* With a Biographical Sketch by Wright Bryan. Columbia, SC: University of South Carolina Press, 1960.

Romero, Sharon. *Gender and the Jubilee: Black Freedom and the Reconstruction of Citizenship in Civil War Missouri.* Athens, GA: University of Georgia Press, 2015.

Roth, Leland M. *American Architecture: A History.* Boulder, CO: Westview Press, 2001.

Royster, Charles. *The Destructive War: William Tecumseh Sherman, Stonewall Jackson, and the Americans.* New York, NY: Alfred A. Knopf, 1991.

Rubin, Anne S. *A Shattered Nation: The Rise and Fall of the Confederacy, 1861–1868.* Chapel Hill, NC: University of North Carolina Press, 2005.

Rusling, James F. *Men and Things I Saw in Civil War Days.* New York, NY: Eaton & Mains, 1899.

Russell, Sharman Apt. *Hunger: An Unnatural History.* New York, NY: Basic Books, 2005.

Rutkow, Eric. *American Canopy: Trees, Forests, and the Making of a Nation.* New York, NY: Scribner, 2012.

Sarna, Jonathan D. *When General Grant Expelled the Jews.* New York, NY: Schocken Books, 2012.

Schrijvers, Peter. *The Crash of Ruin: American Combat Soldiers in Europe during World War II.* New York, NY: New York University Press, 1998.

Schuck, Peter H. *Why Government Fails So Often and How It Can Do Better.* Princeton, NJ: Princeton University Press, 2014.

Shackley, Ted, with Richard A. Finney. *Spymaster: My Life in the CIA.* Dulles, VA: Potomac Books, Inc., 2005.

Shannon, Fred A. *The Organization and Administration of the Union Army, 1861–1865.* Vol. 1. Gloucester, MA: Peter Smith, 1965.

Sharpless, Rebecca. *Cooking in Other Women's Kitchens: Domestic Workers in the South, 1865–1960.* Chapel Hill, NC: University of North Carolina Press, 2010.

Sheehan-Dean, Aaron. *Why Confederates Fought: Family and Nation in Civil War Virginia.* Chapel Hill, NC: University of North Carolina Press, 2007.

Shields, David S. *Southern Provisions: The Creation and Revival of a Cuisine.* Chicago, IL: University of Chicago Press, 2015.

Siddali, Silvana R. *From Property to Person: Slavery and the Confiscation Acts, 1861–1862.* Baton Rouge, LA: Louisiana State University Press, 2005.

Silver, Timothy. *A New Face on the Countryside: Indians, Colonists, and Slaves in South Atlantic Forests, 1500–1800.* Cambridge: Cambridge University Press, 1990.

Simon, Robert I. *Bad Men Do What Good Men Dream: A Forensic Psychiatrist Illuminates the Darker Side of Human Behavior.* Washington, DC: American Psychiatric Press, Inc., 1996.

Simpson, J. A., and E. S. C. Weiner, eds. *Oxford English Dictionary.* 2nd edn. Oxford: Clarendon, 1989.

Sinisi, Kyle S. *Sacred Debts: State Civil War Claims and American Federalism, 1861–1880.* New York, NY: Fordham University, Press 2003.

Skelton, William B. *An American Profession of Arms: The Army Officer Corps, 1784–1861.* Lawrence, KS: University Press of Kansas, 1992.

Small, J. Kenneth. "The Giving of Hostages," *Politics and the Life Sciences* 16 (March 1997): 77–85.

Stern, Andrew H. M. *Southern Crucifix, Southern Cross: Catholic–Protestant Relations in the Old South.* Tuscaloosa, AL: University of Alabama Press, 2012.

Sternhell, Yael A. *Routes of War: The World of Movement in the Confederate South.* Cambridge, MA: Harvard University Press, 2012.

Stewart, Mart A. *"What Nature Suffers to Groe": Life, Labor, and Landscapes on the Georgia Coast, 1680–1920.* Athens, GA: University of Georgia Press, 1996.

Stilgoe, John R. *Landscape and Images.* Charlottesville, VA: University of Virginia Press, 2005.

Stoll, Steven. *Larding the Lean Earth: Soil and Society in Nineteenth-Century America.* New York, NY: Hill & Wang, 2002.

Storey, Margaret M. *Loyalty and Loss: Alabama's Unionists in the Civil War and Reconstruction.* Baton Rouge, LA: Louisiana State University Press, 2004.

Stout, Harry S. *Upon the Altar of the Nation: A Moral History of the Civil War.* New York, NY: Penguin Books, 2006.

Strasser, Susan. *Waste and Want: A Social History of Trash.* New York, NY: Metropolitan Books, 1999.

Sutherland, Daniel E. *A Savage Conflict: The Decisive Role of Guerillas in the American Civil War.* Chapel Hill, NC: University of North Carolina, 2009.

Seasons of War: The Ordeal of a Confederate Community, 1861–1865. Baton Rouge, LA: Louisiana State University Press, 1995.

Syrett, John. *The Civil War Confiscation Acts: Failing to Reconstruct the South.* New York, NY: Fordham University Press, 2005.

Tatum, Georgia Lee. *Disloyalty in the Confederacy.* Chapel Hill, NC: University of North Carolina Press, 1934.

Taylor, Joe Gray. *Eating, Drinking, and Visiting in the South: An Informal History.* Updated Edition with a New Introduction by John Egerton. Baton Rouge, LA: Louisiana State University Press, 2008.

Taylor, Lenette S. *The Supply for Tomorrow Must Not Fail: The Civil War of Captain Simon Perkins, Jr., a Union Quartermaster.* Kent, OH: Kent State University Press, 2004.

Thomas, Emory M. *The Confederate Nation, 1861–1865.* New York, NY: Harper & Row, 1979.

Tirman, John. *The Deaths of Others: The Fate of Civilians in America's Wars.* Oxford: Oxford University Press, 2011.

Torpey, John. *The Invention of the Passport: Surveillance, Citizenship, and the State.* Cambridge: Cambridge University Press, 2000.

Toussaint-Samat, Maguelonne. *History of Food.* Translated by Anthea Bell. Cambridge, MA: Blackwell Publishers, Inc., 1996.

Towne, Stephen E. *Surveillance and Spies in the Civil War: Exposing Confederate Conspiracies in America's Heartland.* Athens, OH: Ohio University Press, 2015.

Trefousse, Hans L. *Andrew Johnson: A Biography.* New York, NY: W. W. Norton & Company, 1997.

Tucker, Richard P. "The World Wars and the Globalization of Timber Cutting." In *Natural Enemy, Natural Ally*, edited by Richard P. Tucker and Edmund Russell, pp. 110–141. Corvallis, OR: Oregon State University Press, 2004.

Tucker, Richard P., and Edmund Russell. "Introduction." In *Natural Enemy, Natural Ally: Toward an Environmental History of Warfare*, edited by Richard P. Tucker and Edmund Russell, pp. 1–14. Corvallis, OR: Oregon State University Press, 2004.

  eds. *Natural Enemy, Natural Ally: Toward an Environmental History of Warfare*. Corvallis, OR: Oregon State University Press, 2004.

Uglow, Jenny. *In These Times: Living in Britain through Napoleon's War, 1793–1815*. New York, NY: Farrar, Straus, & Giroux, 2014.

Van Tuyll, Hupert P. *The Netherlands and World War I: Esionage, Diplomacy, and Survival*. Leiden: Brill Academic Publishers, 2001.

Varon, Elizabeth R. *Appomattox: Victory, Defeat, and Freedom at the End of the Civil War*. Oxford: Oxford University Press, 2014.

Venet, Wendy Hamand. *A Strong-Minded Woman: The Life of Mary A. Livermore*. Amherst, MA: University of Massachusetts Press, 2005.

Vlach, John Michael. *Back of the Big House: The Architecture of Plantation Slavery*. Chapel Hill, NC: University of North Carolina Press, 1993.

Walker, H. Jesse, and Randall A. Detro, eds. *Cultural Diffusion and Landscapes: Selections by Fred Kniffen*. Baton Rouge, LA: Department of Geography and Anthropology, 1990.

Ward, Harry M. *The War for Independence and the Transformation of American Society*. New York, NY: Routledge, 1999.

Watson, Samuel J. *Peacekeepers and Conquerors: The Army Officer Corps on the American Frontier, 1821–1846*. Lawrence, KS: University Press of Kansas, 2013.

Weigley, Russell F. *Quartermaster General of the Union Army: A Biography of M. C. Meigs*. New York, NY: Columbia University Press, 1959.

Weiner, Marli F. *Mistresses and Slaves: Plantation Women in South Carolina, 1830–80*. Urbana, IL: University of Illinois Press, 1998.

Weissbach, Lee Shai. *Jewish Life in Small-Town America: A History*. New Haven, CT: Yale University Press, 2005.

Wetherington, Mark V. *Plain Folk's Fight: The Civil War and Reconstruction in Piney Woods Georgia*. Chapel Hill, NC: University of North Carolina Press, 2005.

Whites, LeeAnn. *The Civil War as a Crisis in Gender: Augusta, Georgia, 1860–1890*. Athens, GA: University of Georgia Press, 1995.

  "Corresponding with the Enemy: Mobilizing the Relational Field of Battle in St. Louis." In *Occupied Women: Gender, Military Occupation, and the American Civil War*, edited by LeeAnn Whites and Alecia P. Long, pp. 103–116. Baton Rouge, LA: Louisiana State University Press, 2009.

Wiley, Bell Irvin. *The Life of Billy Yank: The Common Soldier of the Union*. Indianapolis, IN: Charter Books, 1962.

  The Life of Johnny Reb: The Common Soldier of the Confederacy. Indianapolis, IN: Bobbs-Merrill, 1943.

Williams, David, Teresa Crisp Williams, and David Carlson. *Plain Folk in a Rich Man's War: Class and Dissent in Confederate Georgia*. Gainesville, FL: University Press of Florida, 2002.

Williams, Michael. *Americans and Their Forests*. Cambridge: Cambridge University Press, 1989.

Williams, Susan. *Food in the United States, 1820s–1890*. Westport, CT: Greenwood Press, 2006.

Wilson, Mark R. *The Business of Civil War: Military Mobilization and the State, 1861–1865*. Baltimore, MD: Johns Hopkins University Press, 2006.

Witt, John Fabian. *Lincoln's Code: The Laws of War in American History*. New York, NY: Free Press, 2012.

Wolfe, Margaret Ripley. *Daughters of Canaan: A Saga of Southern Women*. Lexington, KY: University Press of Kentucky, 1995.

Wood, C. E. *Mud: A Military History*. Lincoln, NE: University of Nebraska Press, 2011.

Woodward, Ian. *Understanding Material Culture*. Los Angeles, CA: Sage, 2007.

Worcester, Donald. *A Passion for Nature: The Life of John Muir*. Oxford: Oxford University Press, 2008.

Wyatt-Brown, Bertram. *Southern Honor: Ethics and Behavior in the Old South*. Oxford: Oxford University Press, 1982.

Zimring, David Ross. *To Live and Die in Dixie: Native Northerners Who Fought for the Confederacy*. Knoxville, TN: University of Tennessee Press, 2014.

Secondary Sources Online

American Forests, Tree Facts. www.americanforests.org.

Bearss, Ed. "Fortress Rosecrans Research Report," 1960. www.nps.gov/stri/historyculture/foro.htm.

Driskell, Steven L., ed. History of the 25th Alabama Infantry Regiment, 1861–1865: A Narrative by Captain Wilson P. Howell, Company I. https://sites.google.com/site/25thAlabama/Home.

National Park Service, Charles City County, Berkeley. www.nps.gov/articles/Berkeley.htm.

National Park Service, The Civil War, Soldier Database. www.nps.gov/civilwar/search-soldiers.htm.

US Department of Agriculture, Natural Resources Conservation Service, Plant Guide. http://usdasearch.usda.gov/search.

US Department of Agriculture. www.usda.gov/media/blog. www.blogs.usda.gov/2013/01/28.

Index

7/17